God in Sound and Silence

God in Sound and Silence

Music as Theology

DANIELLE ANNE LYNCH

Foreword by David Brown

PICKWICK *Publications* · Eugene, Oregon

GOD IN SOUND AND SILENCE
Music as Theology

Copyright © 2018 Danielle Anne Lynch. All rights reserved. Except for brief quotations in critical publications or reviews, no part of this book may be reproduced in any manner without prior written permission from the publisher. Write: Permissions, Wipf and Stock Publishers, 199 W. 8th Ave., Suite 3, Eugene, OR 97401.

Pickwick Publications
An Imprint of Wipf and Stock Publishers
199 W. 8th Ave., Suite 3
Eugene, OR 97401

www.wipfandstock.com

PAPERBACK ISBN: 978-1-5326-4149-7
HARDCOVER ISBN: 978-1-5326-4150-3
EBOOK ISBN: 978-1-5326-4151-0

Cataloguing-in-Publication data:

Names: Lynch, Danielle Anne, author. | Brown, David, 1948 July 1–, foreword.

Title: God in sound and silence : music as theology / Danielle Anne Lynch ; foreword by David Brown.

Description: Eugene, OR : Pickwick Publications, 2018 | Includes bibliographical references and index.

Identifiers: ISBN 978-1-5326-4149-7 (paperback) | ISBN 978-1-5326-4150-3 (hardcover) | ISBN 978-1-5326-4151-0 (ebook)

Subjects: LCSH: Music—Religious aspects. | Theology.

Classification: ML3921 .L96 2018 (paperback) | ML3921 .L96 (ebook)

Manufactured in the U.S.A.   06/14/18

For Mike
with whom I make music

> "And the Word became human,
> and eternity entered time.
> I'm tasting the sound of your voice in mine."
> —Maeve Heaney, "Dancing in Our Minds"

Contents

Foreword by David Brown | ix
Preface | xiii
Acknowledgements | xv
Introduction | xvii

1 Approaches to Music in Modern Theology | 1

2 Embodied Encounter with God | 53

3 The Incarnate Form: The Classical Era | 97

4 The Transcendence of the Self: The Romantic Era | 131

5 The Self-Reflective Self: The Modern Era | 159

6 Conclusion | 187

   Afterword | 195

Bibliography | 197
Subject Index | 205
Name Index | 207

Foreword

David Brown

It was a pleasure to have been asked to write this preface to Danielle Lynch's *God in Sound and Silence*. The last few decades have witnessed a huge growth in the number of studies published on the relation between religion and the arts. This is no accident. Religion is concerned with breaking through the barriers that seemingly confine us to this material world, toward some sense of a transcendent reality existing beyond the normal confines of space and time. Although the arts do not usually have such a fundamental aim, there is nonetheless a common element to this degree. Artistic endeavour is usually concerned with taking us to a point beyond where we currently stand, with devices such as metaphor, analogy, and image used to transition the viewer or listener from one position to another—the new focus being in some ways like our existing perceptions, and in some ways not.

Of all the arts, it might seem as though music was best fitted to this shared move from one realm to another, inasmuch as music is often declared to be the least materialistic of all the arts. Thus, whereas a painter's autograph on a particular canvas would confirm the unique material identity of that work (including its use of specific paints and techniques), music does not quite work like that. There is something much more intangible in the air that we hear and to which we respond. Indeed, even the autographed musical score lacks precisely the same privilege that we would be prepared to accord to the canvas, in that the conductor and performers do not merely transmit or mediate the work; they also, in some sense, themselves produce a unique creation.

Yet, intriguingly, that apparent contrast is not where Lynch begins her analysis of how music and religion might relate. Instead, she contends that the immateriality of music is much exaggerated, and that it is precisely in its materiality that God will be found. In such stress on the materiality of music, it does seem that she is onto something quite important. Whereas half a century ago, concert performances were very formal affairs with little engagement with the audience, if nothing else, declining audiences have encouraged a different approach that returns us to earlier traditions that assumed, for example, willingness on the performers' part to reveal their emotional involvement, or else eye contact with the audience that acknowledges participation in a shared experience.

But Lynch's analysis takes us well beyond any such general observations as these. Lynch is well qualified in both theology and music, and so, perhaps not surprisingly, that perspective is reinforced by some profound reflections that draw upon recent work in both disciplines. Thus, drawing on analyses of popular culture and the history of classical music, she notes how much music's form and impact are dependent on particular contextual settings. Of course, we can continue to enjoy Baroque or Romantic music in our own very different setting, but the impact of the music will be considerably reduced unless we show some willingness to enter imaginatively into those different, earlier contexts. That is one reason why whole chapters are devoted to considering some of the main periods in the history of classical music, and the type of relation with listeners that was implied, including in our own much more pluralistic age.

But, as well as such overall assumptions about the cultural specificity of music and the accompanying detailed musical analysis that is then made possible, Lynch also draws on her deep knowledge of theology to supply us with a corresponding theological framework with which to approach such music. Here she identifies the key category as lying, not as readers might perhaps expect in the "sacred," but in a broader category which she labels as the "sacramental." In this, she applies an insight to music that is adopted by a number of Catholic theologians in the twentieth century, Karl Rahner being perhaps most obvious among them. Whereas the first millennium of Christianity had identified a very wide range of material objects as potentially capable of participating in transcendent reality, for various reasons, in the second millennium such terminology came to be more narrowly identified with specific sacraments. The return to the earlier wide usage allowed perception of the possibility that the material might, through its symbolic character, effectively already hint at or disclose the transcendent, and it is this notion that Lynch uses so powerfully in her treatment of music. At the risk of putting the issue in altogether too-crude terms, one might say, whereas an Aristotelian account of reality requires a sharp distinction between our world and transcendent reality with argument required for us to move from one to the other, this more participatory or Platonic conception permits us to see divine "signs," as Augustine might have expressed it, already there in the material order, waiting to explode into a fuller realisation of that alternative reality.

Even more profoundly, it also allows Lynch to challenge the view that God is only to be found in "sacred" music: music specifically devoted to the creation of religious sentiment, most obviously perhaps through the attachment of suitable words. Even without words, though, certain symbolic features within a specific piece of music might have exactly the same effect. If this is indeed so, then major questions are certainly posed about any attempt to ban non-sacred or "secular" music from churches, as though the "secular" is necessarily without religious impact. Although Lynch does not discuss these issues, one challenge would be to those who object to the "devil's best tunes" being usurped for Christian hymns. Another, perhaps more controversial topic would be the decision by Pope John Paul II to ban "secular" music concerts from the churches of Rome. Was the decision well-founded or not?

Any type of music whatsoever has, therefore, the potential in Lynch's view to enable an embodied encounter with God, and thus, so far from retreating to our spiritual core to provide the necessary means, it is the body in itself that offers this privilege. It does not do so by illustrating specific Christian doctrines, as some have suggested, but rather by providing a moment of revelation, and this it does most explicitly at points of liminality. This is one reason why the requiem form so interests Lynch, and in particular the way in which it has changed across the centuries, as social context has changed.

However, as the book's title already alerts us, such liminality can sometimes be seen at its most effective in sound's apparent opposite, in silence. That is no doubt one reason why the book's final chapter is devoted to that topic. Drawing on a wide range of music where silence plays a prominent or exclusive role, in composers both classical and popular, she argues that silence can not only conjure the liminality of death, as with Takemitsu's "Requiem for String Orchestra," but also (as in Cage's *4'33"*) human bodily limitation, and so an infinite beyond. This is in virtue of the fact that no human silence can be made absolute: precisely because human beings are embodied, we are always hearing new sounds even as others are suppressed, as experiments in anechoic chambers fully confirms.

God in Sound and Silence is a work of considerable erudition in which, even if readers do not always agree with Lynch, they will undoubtedly find their knowledge of the field greatly improved, not only in respect of some of the major figures (for example, Balthasar, Schleiermacher, and Tillich) but also of the multifarious other ways in which the relationship between music and religion has been approached in modern times. Her own style of argumentation is also always refreshingly clear and easy to follow. So, I have no hesitation whatsoever in warmly recommending this book. Danielle Lynch is making a substantial claim: music, because of its revelatory character, is nothing short of embodied theology. That she writes not only as an academic but also as both a practising musician (and composer) and faithful Christian add greatly to the book's depth and appeal.

Preface

My study of the relation between music and theology began as an undergraduate in the Music Department of Durham University, where my thesis explored the theological aspects of John Rutter's sacred music. As a musician, I am equally comfortable harmonizing Bach chorales as I am playing guitar in a rock band, and find inspiration and meaning in a wide range of music. The lyrics which begin each chapter, whilst hopefully encapsulating some key point of the chapter, are in some way a musical autobiography, in outlining my formative musical experiences as a teenager. Following my studies of music, I wanted to further explore how theological answers can be found in non-religious spaces. I pursued a Masters in Theology as a means of exploring such unanswered questions. This developed into a desire to undertake a PhD in the theology of music, which I worked on part-time as I became a teacher in Religious Studies in England, a job which entails encouraging students to ask and seek answers to big questions. This vocation brought me to Australia in 2015, where I work as Director of Mission in a Marist secondary boys' school in Cairns, a beautiful part of the world.

This work began out of a conviction that music is a theological means of knowing something meaningful yet indeterminate, and is a development of my doctoral work on a theology of music at Leeds University. I am wary of the ability of words to express the mystery of God. If theology is indeed faith seeking understanding, then that understanding must not be confined to linguistic understanding, but must incorporate all forms of knowing, including the sensuous and emotional, two means of knowing often evoked by music. Whilst I am an experienced liturgical musician, and well-versed in the Catholic traditions of liturgical music, this work is no attempt to explore the specifics of liturgical music. Rather, it is an attempt to broaden the usual understanding of what is considered to be sacred music; that is, music that connects the human to the divine.

Danielle Anne Lynch
Cairns, Australia, Feast of St Cecilia, 22 November 2017

Acknowledgments

I would like to express my appreciation for the support of theologians and musicians who have helped me to develop my thinking. In particular, I acknowledge my doctoral supervisor, Dr. Rachel Muers, whose encouragement and gentle critique was instrumental. Professor David Brown was a most gracious examiner, and his kind and critical feedback gave me much to think about. I am also grateful to members of the Society for the Study of Theology in the UK and the Australian Catholic Theological Association, to whom I have been able to present my work and with whom I have entered into critical discussion. I am especially grateful to Dr. Maeve Heaney, without whose encouragement I may never have published my work in an area that we both value, and whose academic and musical productivity is inspiring.

I thank my colleagues and friends with whom I have shared my work. I have been privileged to work in supportive schools, whose ethos and values have been a source of inspiration for me. I owe particular thanks to the Marist formation I've experienced in the last few years, which has taught me to reevaluate the meaning of simplicity and presence in all things, but especially music.

A special thanks also to my family for their unconditional encouragement and love, wherever I am in the world. Most of all, thanks to my husband Dr. Mike Lynch, whose love and support is invaluable to me.

> "Still a little bit of your song in my ear
> Still a little bit of your words I long to hear
> You step a little closer to me
> So close that I can't see what's going on."
>
> —Damien Rice, "Cannonball"

Introduction

Modern theologians have often studied the world of human imagination in the arts.[1] Whilst these theological accounts are often relevant to music as an art form, and sometimes explicitly discuss music, there are particular features of music that set it apart from other forms of art. These features—its temporality and embodied nature—are not exclusive to music, but together create a particular impact that is distinctive to music. I argue that, while music's meaning is by necessity indeterminate—linguistically, at least, since it does not speak in words—it is nevertheless significant. While music does not necessarily convey specific content, it can be used to convey something particular through the use of form, style, context, and musical technique. It also relies often on musical expectations to convey its meaning. Its lack of determinable meaning poses a challenge for theology, which is itself formed in words, and encourages a perspective of theological thought that accounts for the non-linguistic. Therefore, the relationship between the musical form and the embodied experiencer of the music is paramount to the following theological discussion.

There cannot be an all-encompassing theology of music, as music cannot be generalized, but must be analysed with regard to its particular context and in relation to particular musical experiences. Music is as temporally- and context-situated a way of "doing" theology as any other. Nevertheless, I hold that music is a means through which theological meaning can emerge. Theologies of culture have provided the tools for theology to approach all

1. Theologians from a variety of backgrounds have studied the arts generally, often in the form of theological aesthetics. Hans Urs von Balthasar's seven volume *The Glory of the Lord* is a key work which reignited interest in the arts and theology. Other general discussions of the arts more generally in modern theology can be found in Jeremy Begbie's *Voicing Creation's Praise: Towards a Theology of the Arts*; Richard Viladesau's *Theological Aesthetics: God in Imagination, Beauty and Art* and *Theology and the Arts: Encountering God through Art, Music, and Rhetoric*; Patrick Sherry's *Spirit and Beauty: An Introduction to Theological Aesthetics*; and more recently Frank Burch Brown's *The Oxford Handbook of Religion and the Arts*.

forms of music. In particular, theologies of popular culture show that music, and indeed theology, never exists in a cultural vacuum, but always in relation to the embodied individual, society, and the world. Analysis of the music itself must also feed into theological interpretation, and therefore I often turn to musicologists to give insight into analysis of specific musical works. In this exploration of music as theology, I will attempt to highlight the fundamental characteristics of music in relation to its cultural context, musical analysis, and existing theological thought. I have integrated three areas of scholarship in this book: theologies that explore music, theologies of culture, and secondary literature in musicological analysis. However, these merely serve to elucidate a shadow of the indeterminate meaning of music in words, they never can grasp the full extent of music as theology.

Music is as varied as any human creation, and certain features or styles may be better fits to certain strands of theological thought. That does not mean that theological thought should be limited to the best fit, but rather, music is enlightening beyond pre-existing conclusions, and helps open our eyes to new possibilities. Each genre and style of music therefore has a unique contribution to make to theological thought. However, there are underlying concepts which are relevant to much music, and can be used in specific analysis, and they will be identified at particular points throughout this work.

Outline of Book

In the first part of the book, the first two chapters, I will survey the groundwork that has already been done in theology in regard to music, in terms of approaches and concepts. In the first chapter, I will survey the work that has already been done on establishing the particularities of music in a variety of modern theological accounts. I identify two different approaches to music in theology. Firstly, I will explore the theologies which emphasize an approach to musical experience as a form of revelation. This perspective attempts to understand music in relation to human subjects. I will argue that the embodied experience of music is fundamentally important to any theological discussion, as music does not exist except in the musical experience: it only exists as a temporally-bounded form. Secondly, I will explore accounts of theologies which take music in its written form and attempt to understand given theological revelation through it. These theologies understand music as an object and tend to focus on the form of the music. Music understood in this sense can also help to elucidate given theology, but does not offer new theological perspectives.

I will draw aspects from both approaches to music, which I combine with theological analytical tools from theologies of popular culture, an area of contemporary theology that has contributed to theological discussions of music. Thought in this area has taken a positive attitude to human cultures and their ability to explore theological questions. Whilst this book focuses more on classical than popular music, the approach from theologies of popular culture is helpful in highlighting the importance of the context of the music, the social aspect, and in opening the possibility of God being found in all human creations, not only in the natural world, but in cultural artefacts. Most importantly, theologies of popular culture take a holistic approach to human life, showing that meaning is sought and found in all areas of life, not only in specifically religious contexts. I draw from theologies of popular culture an understanding of the importance of the embodied, social and contextual nature of music, and apply this to classical[2] music in a creative and original development of a theology of music.

In the second chapter, I take into consideration the particular issues that are relevant to a theology of music, and will be used in the second half of the book to construct an approach to music as theology. Firstly, music is often said to be "transcendent"[3] without determining what exactly is meant by the term, or how music achieves this transcendence. I will explore the definition of transcendence, and discuss in what way music could allow for transcendent experience. I will explore the concept of transcendence in music by means of "liminality"; the crossing of thresholds, in particular that between the subject and object of music, in other words, the human and the divine. I will then discuss the implications of this in the ways in which music can tell us anything about God, in relation to the key term "revelation." Music, in the context of revelation, helps us to understand better the relationship between humanity and God.

The music studied in this book is not all religious music. I will argue that "sacred music" as a category treats music as an object, and neglects its experiential dimension. As such, I suggest that music is considered as "sacramental" rather than "sacred." Revelation through music is therefore not confined to forms of music that are traditionally religious, for example, liturgical forms such as the Mass. Considering music as sacramental rather than sacred allows all music to play a role in revelation.

Having argued that experience of music is important in chapter one, I explore the ways in which it is experienced through the concept of

---

2. The term "classical" will be used to define the genre of music, whilst the capitalized "Classical" defines the particular era within the genre, 1750–1810.

3. One prominent theological example is found in Küng, *Mozart*.

embodiment in chapter two. Music, like dance or drama, requires the engagement and commitment of the body. Music is sometimes thought of as ethereal in nature; given that it does not occupy any physical space, it can appear that music communicates in a non-physical way. However, music is received by the physical human body, through the vibrations of sound waves created by physical musical instruments, and could not exist otherwise. Music therefore offers insights into the body's place in theology.

The second part of this book will demonstrate the key aims of the book through an approach to different musical eras. I will apply the approaches and concepts discussed in part one to particular examples of music. Following my understanding that different eras and genres bring something new to the table, a variety of music will be explored with regard to its individual context, and I will take the three most recent eras of Western classical music as examples. Musicologist Scott Burnham notes about music in general that the listener participates in the music, arguing against the traditional musical analysts' conception of musical work-listener relationship: "Listening to music is a two-way street, regardless of the efforts of various factions of musical academia to legislate one-way traffic, either from an absolute and self-sufficient musical work to the listener or from the relative situatedness of the listener to a decentralized musical work."[4] This understanding is fundamental to the analysis of all musical examples in this book: the contexts of the composer, the work and the listener all interact in the musical experience, contributing to its meaning. Above all, the meaning making happens in the embodied experience of the music.

Whilst all music is relevant to theological study, the musical form of the requiem is a common strand running through the three chapters, as it elucidates clearly the changing context and the issues presented to theology across the different musical eras. The requiem draws together many of the themes discussed in this book. In focusing on the question of mortality, it brings together two key concerns of the book, embodied human life and musical form. The requiem is a musical space in which theology can explore a universal feature of humanity—the reality of life and death—and is therefore liminal, concerned with the threshold between them. It does not deny or transcend death, but affirms it as a fundamental part of human existence. Composing a requiem is at once a personal undertaking, and yet the music produced is intended to be accessible to all: it holds in tension the individual and universal facets of death. In this way it helps humans to understand something about the nature of the embodied and finite reality of

---

4. Burnham, *Beethoven Hero*, 29.

being human: composers often compose only one requiem,[5] as humans die only one death. There is a personal aspect to writing music for a requiem, then, if you might only have one chance[6] to explore the certain event in every human life: death.

The relationship between musical form and embodiment in each of the three musical eras gives different nuances to understanding the music as theology. The Classical era, or the years 1750–1810, is the focus of chapter three. The context of the Enlightenment is the backdrop to the music written at this time. The musical examples analysed in this chapter were composed by the key composers of the era, Joseph Haydn and Wolfgang Amadeus Mozart. Musical form was an important compositional feature in the Classical era, and is a prominent feature of many musical analyses. I will explore these analyses of music as an abstract concept, as a written object, and highlight where such analysis might be deepened by a consideration of the musical experience in relation to the embodied experience. In highlighting the embodied form of music, the theological concepts of beauty, form and the incarnation come to the fore.

The Romantic era, 1800–1910, is the focus of chapter four, though the movement of Romanticism had begun before the turn of the nineteenth century in Germany, and this thought feeds into the shift in style of Romantic music. Developments in music shift the focus away from form, and the key theological concept that comes to the fore is transcendence. Romantic thought is concerned with the individual, and therefore the concept of the self is explored in theology and in musical composition. The natural world is also a concern of the Romantics: unlike in the Classical era, it is

---

5. The requiems studied in this book are the sole requiem by the respective composers, Mozart, Brahms, and Takemitsu. Other prominent examples of composers who have only written one requiem are, in chronological order, Ockeghem (who has written the earliest surviving example of a musical requiem), Cherubini, Berlioz, Verdi, Dvorak, Fauré, Duruflé, Britten, Stravinsky, Penderecki, Lloyd Webber, and Rutter, Jenkins. Contemporary composer John Rutter, when asked why he did not write another requiem following the death of his son, stated that composers only write one requiem (interview D. Lynch, 2008). He had already written a requiem, and therefore he wrote the *Mass of the Children*.

6. Though it is only convention that composers write only one requiem, they may flout this convention and write another. Classical composer—and brother of Joseph—Michael Haydn began a second requiem, though it was incomplete at his death. Romantic composer Robert Schumann also composed two works titled requiems (*Requiem fur Mignon* Op. 98b, 1849, and *Requiem* Op. 148, 1852), but the first is a small-scale single movement composition, whilst the latter is a full requiem. Like Mozart, Schumann's *Requiem* was one of his last compositions. Schumann also composed a work entitled *Sechs Gedichte und Requiem* in 1850 (Op. 90) in which Schumann added a requiem, in the form of an anonymous medieval poem, to the end of a cycle of songs based on his poems.

not presented as an external object, but is bound by the context of the self. Therefore, Romantic music speaks theologically about the place of the self in the whole of creation. The music of this era also relates the pastoral and the sublime together, two key concepts of Romantic thought. I will propose that the pastoral in Romantic music demonstrates God being made known through the created world.

The Modern era, from 1910 onwards, is the focus of the fifth chapter. The trend towards individualisation, commenced in the Romantic era, continued. Composers in this era intended their compositions to be more self-reflective, and so began to express their own thoughts on their work. As such, their reflections are often written down and become an important part of the context of the work. Therefore, this chapter will proceed in dialogue with composers' writings as well as theological understandings of the music.

In comparison to previous musical eras, the twentieth century of music was incredibly diverse. Composers began experimenting with many new ideas, and many new genres and styles emerged, including serialism, atonality, expressionism, jazz, and musique concrete, amongst other forms of experimentalism. One feature of some modern music is its self-conscious use of silence, a concept which has inspired much thought in theology, though not necessarily with reference to music. This is the feature of music that the fifth chapter will focus on, as time would not allow for discussion of such a diversity of features of modern music, though undoubtedly each of the other styles and genres would speak theologically.

Absolute silence, in the sense of the absolute lack of sound, will be seen to be impossible in the human body, as even in an anechoic chamber the body hears sounds it makes itself. However, composers continue to strive to achieve musical silence, the perceived stillness that reflects that absolute silence. When musical silence is achieved, it is a liminal experience which crosses the boundary of everyday noisy existence. Therefore, the use of musical silence allows the immanent experience to encounter the transcendent, whilst affirming the bodily nature of this human experience. Absolute silence is ultimately impossible, as the only way to achieve such a form of silence is to become disembodied, which defeats the theological aspiration to achieve silence. Musical silence, therefore, offers a glimpse beyond embodiment. The means by which this might be possible is explored.

Summary

This book will explore music as theology from the starting point of the embodied musical experience. It draws insights from theologies of popular culture which highlight the embodied, social and contextual nature of all musical experience. As music is not studied on the basis of any qualities it has, this book expands the remit of theologies of popular culture to include music that would not normally be considered to be popular, in this case, classical music. Drawing on theologies of popular culture in which the boundary between sacred and secular is removed; this book takes all types of music into consideration, arguing for a sacramental account of music, in which music is the conveyor of the otherwise invisible truth of God. Therefore, in this book there are musical examples which are traditional religious forms, and some which have no explicitly religious meaning.

The first two chapters provide the groundwork for the ensuing understanding of music as theology, as applied to the three most recent eras of classical music, but the reader who is more interested in the musical analysis than the theological framework might move straight to chapter three.

> "All my life I've been searching for something
> Something never comes never leads to nothing
> Nothing satisfies but I'm getting close
> Closer to the prize at the end of the rope."
>
> —Foo Fighters, "All My Life"

1

Approaches to Music in Modern Theology

Theologians have explored different ways of encountering music. Many of these approaches are intertwined with a theology of culture, which attempts to take seriously cultural artefacts and the meaning they have in people's lives. Music requires separate treatment from the other arts as it is unique and can bring something new to theology. Music is one way of "doing" theology, one which undoubtedly rests more in mystery than in language, but is perhaps all the more valuable for that reason.[1] Therefore, the approach taken here is one of music as theology, where the music does the work usually expected of the words.

This chapter surveys approaches that have been made to music in modern theology before drafting the groundwork of an understanding of music as theology. These approaches range from the experiential—focusing on the experience of music for the individual or a collective group—to the text-based—looking at the written form of music, including any text associated with it.

This chapter identifies two ways of reading music theologically: firstly, music as a theologically significant or revelatory experience, and secondly, music as expounding given theological truths. The first approach allows music to say something new and to challenge existing thought; and the

---

1. I alighted on the idea of "music as theology" separately from Maeve Louise Heaney—however, she has already outlined a convincing justification for consideration of music as a way of doing theology in *Music as Theology*. Heaney suggests that consideration of music as theology is "a missing piece in the theological method" (Heaney, "Mercy, Music," 43–62).

second approach considers music to be saying something that has already been said elsewhere, in theology, in scripture, or perhaps in other art forms. This is not a comprehensive account of the many approaches of theologies of music, but offers a comparison of two broadly different perspectives that are not mutually exclusive.

Approaches to music through contemporary theologies of popular culture is then explored in this chapter. These accounts offer the tools for a variety of different approaches to popular culture, of which popular music is an important part. Although the focus in these theological accounts of music is on popular music, they open new avenues for discussing music in all its forms. Most importantly, theologies of popular culture add new dimensions to discussions of music, in their stress on the social and embodied nature of musical experience, and thus go beyond the two approaches I just outlined. From this, I will construct a framework out of which I will work in later discussions of the theological significance of the music.

Music as Theologically Significant or Revelatory Experience

An account of music beginning with embodied human experience suggests that music, as a part of human experience of the world and of the greater reality we call God, has theological significance. This approach focuses on individual and collective human experience in theological knowledge: experience is an important part of understanding theological concepts, and in particular in understanding God; humans know God through embodied experience. Therefore, music is important to theology, in particular in the way that it might reveal something previously unknown or hidden.

Protestant theologian Friedrich Schleiermacher's thought is the starting point, as a key source of modern theological engagement with culture. The work of Rudolf Otto and Paul Tillich, who developed themes of Schleiermacher's engagement with the cultural world, will then be explored, before turning to the work of contemporary theologians concerned with music as experience, David Brown and Férdia Stone-Davis.

Central to this approach of a theological reading of the experience of music is an understanding of the embodied nature of human experience, and the relationship between objective knowledge and subjective experience, and this relationship will be drawn out in the discussion of this approach. The repercussions of this understanding of the relationship between subject and object in musical experience for an account of revelation will be discussed further in chapter 2.

Friedrich Schleiermacher

The discussion of theology's engagement with culture begins here with Friedrich Schleiermacher (1768–1834), as his theology marks a key turning point in the engagement of theology with culture:[2] he engages seriously with the culture of his time, and proposes that it has a place in Christian thought.[3] In his early work *On Religion: Speeches to its Cultural Despisers*, Schleiermacher argued that religion must take the whole of human experience into account. Religion is, for Schleiermacher, "the sensibility and taste for the infinite."[4] Religion is in human feeling, not traditions, doctrines and artefacts, and such feeling is not confined to the realm of organized religion.[5]

For Schleiermacher, religion is thus a lived experience, not an abstract concept. As Gerrish notes, Schleiermacher "concerned himself with facts and phenomena—with real, live religion, not simply with 'God' as a philosophical construct."[6] In other words, Schleiermacher was concerned with what could be known about God through experience. However, this experience also requires an objective basis. David E. Klemm writes that Schleiermacher's understanding of Christianity acknowledges that the "absolute is necessary to the system, that nothing is known or knowable without the absolute, yet that a knowing of the absolute is impossible."[7] Although all human experiences are important, religion has an objective basis in the absolute.

Religion in this view has two forms: positive religion, or historical revelation and religious traditions; and natural religion, or finding truth of God

---

2. Further discussion of Schleiermacher's theology can be found in Marina, *Cambridge Companion*; Clements, *Friedrich Schleiermacher*; Barth, *Theology of Schleiermacher*; Wallhauser, *Schleiermacher*; and Sykes, *Friedrich Schleiermacher*.

3. This is the assumption on which his work *On Religion* is based. This work will provide the background to dialogue with Schleiermacher in this book, but his *Christmas Eve Celebration* also engages with culture, and deals with music in particular, and will be the focus of discussion in chapter 4. *Christmas Eve Celebration* is a work of fiction exploring the meaning of Christmas through the thoughts of a group of friends who have gathered together to celebrate. The characters Eduard and Karoline have much to say about music, and it is set against a backdrop of the child Sophie playing the piano. The music is supposed to reflect the speeches made by each character, encapsulating the feelings evoked by the stories told. Music saves the day when the men begin their theological arguments, and thereafter it becomes a part of the discussion and is given high praise, even by the ever-critical Ernst.

4. Schleiermacher, *On Religion*, 23.

5. Ibid., 22.

6. Gerrish, *Prince of the Church*, 7.

7. Marina, *Cambridge Companion*, 263.

everywhere in the world.⁸ Each form on its own is problematic: positive religion is found to be too particular (Schleiermacher believes that religion will always be pluralistic and will have many forms); natural religion is too universal, and has no unique character.⁹ Schleiermacher thus proposes a philosophical theology which takes both into account, and which admits a need for both.¹⁰ This requires a reflective and critical approach to religion, in both its forms. Schleiermacher writes: "Once there is religion, it must necessarily also be social. That not only lies in human nature but also is pre-eminently in the nature of religion."¹¹ In other words, religious experience must have a social, as well as an individual, aspect.

Alongside feelings, there is intuition, which is another aspect of religion. Schleiermacher writes, "religion's essence is neither thinking nor acting but intuition and feeling."¹² Intuition and feeling are not the same thing, and neither does the German word that Schleiermacher uses for feeling, *Gefühl*, mean precisely the same as the English translation. Manfred Frank explains that there is a distinction between intuition and feeling: "Intuitions represent the world, while sensations are states in the subject. Feelings shape the qualitative or phenomenal character of sense impressions."¹³ Intuition is oriented toward external objects, such as the infinite or the universe, while feeling or *Gefühl* is usually centered on the individual.

Robert Merrihew Adams notes that in the first edition of *On Religion*, Schleiermacher holds intuition as the "senior partner," but that by the second edition, feeling has taken on more importance than intuition.¹⁴ Because of this shift in importance, religious experience has become more focused on the individual self: "Defining the essence of religion as a matter of feeling rather than intuition is thus in line with the view that the primary religious consciousness is a sort of self-consciousness."¹⁵ However, he also notes that Schleiermacher retains a basis for the experience that is external to the individual, and this is shown in the intentionality of all religious feeling: it is feeling of absolute dependence, and in order for that to be the case, there must be something other than the individual for them to be dependent on.¹⁶

---

8. Schleiermacher, *On Religion*, 98.
9. Ibid., 98.
10. Ibid., 111.
11. Ibid., 73.
12. Ibid., 22.
13. Marina, *Cambridge Companion*, 28.
14. Ibid., 36.
15. Ibid., 37.
16. Ibid., 37.

For Schleiermacher, it is justified in the feeling of absolute dependence, or God-consciousness, which is a pre-reflective response to God. Thus, self-consciousness brings about God-consciousness.[17] Self-consciousness and the feeling of absolute dependence are important in justifying the approach to music as a religious experience.

According to Schleiermacher, there is a strong link between humans and the world. Humanity represents one form of the universe: "Humanity itself is to the universe as individual persons are to humanity; it is only an individual form of the universe."[18] One part represents the whole, even if it only reveals one aspect. Humans represent a link between the world and God, "a middle term between the individual and the One, a resting place on the way to the infinite" and religion is the means of expressing that link.[19] As such, there is a sense of unity between the universe and humanity, which is expressed in human creativity, in culture and religion.

Schleiermacher's theology takes account of individuality in the religious experience.[20] In his discussion of two opposing impulses of the soul, he suggests that people are on a spectrum between individuality and surrendering to the whole.[21] There are some people in the world who are "benevolent genies . . . [They] quietly create and disseminate a nobler happiness . . . [and] prove themselves to be ambassadors of God and mediators between limited man and infinite humanity."[22] In other words, there are particular individuals whose actions mediate the presence of God. For Schleiermacher, mediators of the divine are in the middle of the spectrum between individuality and the whole. They mediate between the forms of positive and natural religion. Thus, mediating the divine affirms its objective reality, but allows for subjective experience of it. Those who have a religious experience may then seek to communicate this experience to others through cultural products, such as the arts.

Schleiermacher proposes that music is a better way to communicate religious feeling than through words, following Schleiermacher's thought that music cannot be grasped by definite speech, but is an interchange of

---

17. Schleiermacher, *Christian Faith*, 133–34.
18. Schleiermacher, *On Religion*, 44.
19. Ibid., 44.
20. Though Baiser notes that Schleiermacher's understanding of the ethic of individuality as self-realisation is not an understanding of the individual in isolation, rather the individual's self-realisation is developed through interaction with others (Marina, *Cambridge Companion*, 61).
21. Schleiermacher, *On Religion*, 5.
22. Ibid., 7.

sounds and feelings.[23] If religion is feeling, then sounds can evoke and interact that feeling. Moreover, music is at one level an almost universal or absolute form of communication, whilst remaining an individual embodied human experience. Music is a means by which those who have something to say which has a meaning beyond words can communicate that, thereby potentially mediating the presence of God to those that experience the music.

For Schleiermacher, the unity of the whole is felt in individual inner revelation. The individual aspect of positive religion must always be present, even in transcendent experience, but it must be understood in the context of natural religion: "Wherever you suspect a sublime unity, a relationship that reflects greatness, there must necessarily be circumstances in the particular, in addition to the general tendency toward order and harmony, which cannot be completely understood in terms of the individual."[24] Human experience will always be bound by the fact of being human, of standing in a particular time and place, and of feeling or intuiting in a particular way, always in relation to the absolute.

Schleiermacher's emphasis on the importance of intuiting the divine in a religious experience makes music a prime medium for such an event. In the second speech, Schleiermacher likens music to religion: music is, like religion "one great whole; it is a special, a self-contained revelation of the world."[25] Music, like religion, can reveal something of the universe. What music reveals, "definite speech can no longer comprehend," as "sounds of thought and feeling support one another and alternate until everything is saturated and full of the holy and infinite."[26] Music can offer genuine revelation of the truth of the universe, but, according to Schleiermacher, this cannot necessarily be expressed in words.[27] The experience of the sacred and the infinite is the form of revelation of the unity of the universe. Music's freedom from words is of importance for Schleiermacher, in that it speaks directly to the feelings—in other words, to embodied human experience—and is not mediated: music can bring an encounter with God through its experiential impact on the human.

---

23. Ibid., 75.
24. Ibid., 35.
25. Schleiermacher quoted in Blackwell, *Sacred in Music*, 77.
26. Schleiermacher, *On Religion*, 75.

27. For Schleiermacher, music is most closely related to religious feeling because they are both meaningful and ineffable. This conclusion is explored in *Christmas Eve Celebration*, which Karl Barth summarizes, saying, "Exactly because of its lack of concepts, music is the true and legitimate bearer of the message of Christmas" (*Theology and Church*, 157).

The experience of God that is universal is a form of "original revelation" for Schleiermacher. This is different from the historical revelation through Christ, but is not separate from it.[28] Original revelation can add to historical revelation, can pose challenges to it, but ultimately must be assessed alongside it. God, for Schleiermacher, sustains everything in the world. Gerrish believes "it would surely be true to his intention if we concluded that every natural event is for him an act of God in the sense that it is grounded in the eternal activity of God."[29] If this is so, then it is not only possible, but perhaps even likely, that humans would experience the divine in nature (whether they recognize it as such or not). Everything, thus, is united in God, and "to be religious is to sense the unity of all finite things, including oneself, with the infinite, so that the most basic definition of God is 'the highest unity.'"[30] The particular embodied experience of the individual is always in relation to the divine.

Revelation, for Schleiermacher, is an original and new intuition of the universe.[31] On this account, revelation is personal to an individual, and something which is already known by some can be revelatory to others. Schleiermacher holds that the more religious a person is, the more they would see miracles.[32] This suggests that the more open one is to religious experience, the more likely it is to occur. Perhaps the same is true of music: the more open one is to encountering the divine through music, the more possible it becomes. Individual revelation impacts on the overall form of religion. This revelation can affect the forms and traditions of the religion; they can be changed through revelation, as religion is an ongoing process of revelation. Revelation in Schleiermacher's view is a personal event which can occur through experience of cultural products such as music, more so through music than any other form given its close relation to religion.

In summary, Schleiermacher's theology opened the way for cultural products to be assessed in terms of their theological value. This has much influenced theologies of culture, and more recently, theologies of popular culture. Schleiermacher acknowledged that culture has an impact on the outward representation of religion. Different cultures will produce different religious products, but that ought to be embraced as different aspects of religious experience rather than subsumed under one established form of religion.

28. Gerrish, *Prince of the Church*, 46.
29. Ibid., 60.
30. Ibid., 55.
31. Schleiermacher, *On Religion*, 49.
32. Ibid., 49.

Schleiermacher's thought on religion, religious experience, God, and revelation, shape his understanding of music in theological terms. Religion, he maintains, is feeling and intuition. Music speaks directly to feeling without the necessity for words, and therefore is able to speak directly to religion. As it is not linguistically bound, it has the potential to say what cannot otherwise be said.

Schleiermacher's work suggests that an account of music in which experience is taken seriously is important in order for music to be genuinely revelatory of something beyond itself. He highlights the importance of the experience of the individual, and in particular their feelings and intuitions, in both religion and music. There is not a particular form of music that mediates God, but rather, different music may inspire the religious feeling or intuition in certain individuals. His thought is also important in accounting for the subjectivity of individual experience, again important for a theology of music.

Rudolf Otto

Rudolf Otto (1869–1937) was a Lutheran theologian from Germany. His key work, *The Idea of the Holy*, was published in 1917 and is undoubtedly influenced by Schleiermacher's thought on religious experience. It investigates the particular form that religious experience may take.[33] He uses music to illustrate his understanding of the holy at certain key points. There is a close connection between his understanding of music and his understanding of revelation.

Otto critiques Schleiermacher, and aims to correct what he believes to be a failing of his thought, that his idea of holiness does not, to Otto at least, refer to something beyond itself.[34] Otto criticized Schleiermacher's notion of "feeling of dependence" as a secondary effect of *mysterium tremendum*, that experience of awefulness, majesty, and urgency in the wholly other.[35] For Otto, there must be an objective foundation to the experience, which transforms Schleiermacher's "feeling of dependence" into experience of the numinous.[36] "Numinous" is a term Otto coins from the Latin "numen," meaning "divine presence," to describe an experience of the divine.[37]

---

33. See Barton, *Holiness*, for detailed discussion of Otto's understanding and development of Schleiermacher's thought.

34. Otto, *Idea of the Holy*, 10.

35. Ibid., 20.

36. Ibid., 11.

37. Ibid., 7.

Otto also criticizes Schleiermacher's universalisation of experiencing the holy, which Otto calls "divination," believing Schleiermacher assumes it to be present in every human. Experience of the holy for Otto is something which must be cultivated, not a natural ability. He holds that it is a potential capacity of all humans, and, in this sense, is universal, but may not actually be found in every human.[38] Otto uses the analogy of music to elucidate this, noting that only with musical training can one receive an "impression" of the music.[39] This is contentious, as many people untrained in music do have highly engaged experiences of music[40] in which they have an "impression" given by the music.

For Otto, the sacred or holy is an *a priori* concept, which every human is capable of experiencing, but not every human does experience. Such experiences, according to Otto, "do not, as experience teaches us, occur spontaneously, but rather are "awakened" through the instrumentality of other more highly endowed natures."[41] According to Otto, it seems that there are certain pre-conditions to experience of the numinous. In Otto's view, the more one is educated in both music and religious experience, the better able one is to discern a musical religious experience. Whilst it is reasonable to suggest that the better one's musical training is, the more one will understand the music, Otto's perspective that the subject must have some prior understanding of the object—whether that is God or music—before the subject can have an impression of it, would exclude spontaneous intuition without prior knowledge or training. This would limit the potential impact of music, as the feelings of the subject in the pre-reflective moment would be most revelatory when the subject was already well trained. This contradicts Schleiermacher's view that music speaks directly to the feelings: musical experience is not limited to a musical elite.[42]

The idea of religion depending on feeling, from Schleiermacher, is present in Otto's understanding of religious experience, of experience of the

---

38. Ibid., 149.

39. Ibid., 160.

40. See, for example, Lynch's discussion of the impact of music in clubbing (Lynch, *Understanding Theology*, 162–83).

41. Ibid., 177.

42. Schleiermacher does, however, formulate the idea of the religious virtuoso in *On Religion*. This could be interpreted as making religious experience exclusive to the religious elite. However, it is not unreasonable to suggest that, if one is open to religious experience, one might be more likely to encounter it, and if one is open to music, one is more likely to have an engaging musical experience. I would suggest that it is not that any special training is required for an experience of the sacred through music, but that one is open to the possibility of such an experience.

holy.[43] Like Schleiermacher, he holds that this may be experienced within or outside of the church. What is required for an experience of the numinous is *mysterium tremendum et fascinans*. The Latin phrase *mysterium tremendum et fascinans* literally means "mystery that is tremendous and fascinating."[44] For Otto, there are simultaneous contradictory feelings of terror and fascination that occur in the numinous experience: it is meaningful and incomprehensible, overwhelming and intriguing. Experience of the numinous can thus be deeply affecting, and yet ultimately ungraspable. Otto's understanding of numinous experience—experience of the divine presence—suggests that any music, regardless of genre, that evokes those feelings of *mysterium tremendum et fascinans*, is able to provide an experience of the numinous. Otto does not mention music as a facilitator of numinous experience, but does draw on musical experience as an analogy for his account of the holy.

Otto's conception of experience of the numinous is as an "overplus of meaning," which is caused by something objective which is external to the experience.[45] For Otto, this numinous experience is found in a specific "moment . . . which remains inexpressible."[46] A discussion of a "moment" of time in which experience of the numinous occurs seems particularly pertinent to music, the art form that is in time, which can grasp a person and direct their time to such a moment. Temporality is fundamental to the embodied experience of music.

Otto and Schleiermacher agree that there is an encounter between the human and the divine Other in religious experience. For Otto, there is an objective basis in the sacred, which the subjective self meets. The influence of Schleiermacher is seen here, and Otto uses his language to elucidate his idea: "In Schleiermacher's language the 'presentiment' goes out to meet the 'revelation' to which it belongs."[47] In other words, to experience the sacred means to "cognize or recognize in [it] a peculiar significance and to humble oneself before it . . . [it is] an element of cognition, comprehension, and valuation in one's own inner consciousness, that goes out to meet the outward presented fact."[48] A numinous experience is dependent upon humans

---

43. Otto's use of the words "holy" and "sacred" are interchangeable. The sacred is a key concept in this book, and as this term will be used throughout the book, it is used here in discussing Otto's work.

44. Otto describes this phrase at great length in *The Idea of the Holy*, 12–40. He compares *tremendum* to scriptural ideas of awe and majesty, and compares it to Schleiermacher's feeling of dependence.

45. Otto, *Idea of the Holy*, 11.

46. Ibid., 5.

47. Ibid., 160.

48. Ibid., 160.

recognising themselves as in relation to the divine, with the powerful response that ensues.

Music is a useful analogy of experience of the numinous for Otto, though he stresses that the musical and sacred experience should not be confounded. Music is—like the numinous—non-rational, and its content is "wholly other" from the ordinary emotions.[49] Otto notes the way that music directs emotions without those experiencing it necessarily being aware of why it does so, or what the "object or ground" of the feeling is.[50] However, Otto makes an unnecessary distinction between feeling aroused by the music and ordinary feeling. In some way, for Otto, feelings aroused by music are replica feelings, not the same as feelings in other aspects of life. In this way, Otto is claiming that music is set apart from the world in a way that makes it a good analogy to the sacred, but neglects the fact that music exists as part of the created world, and does not have access to a range of substitute feelings as distinct from other aspects of the reality of embodied human existence.

Otto considers music to be an ethereal art, which has a non-physical form, and which does not connect fully with worldly human experience. That music is given this remove from the human world supports his analogy that music, like the holy, is "wholly other." However, all experience of music is embodied.

Though music is so closely related to the numinous for Otto, at least in terms of analogical experience, even music has no positive way to express the holy. Otto believes that music does not arouse true emotions and therefore criticizes programme music[51] for its attempt to arouse familiar feelings in its narrative.[52] He believes that programme music therefore "misinterprets and perverts the idea of music by its implication that the inner content of music is not—as in fact it is—something unique and mysterious, but just the incidental experiences—joy and grief, expansions and repression—familiar to the human heart."[53] In other words, for Otto programme music misses the true aim of music, which is beyond words, by attempting to communicate narratives and emotions which are linguistically expressible. However, it is

---

49. Ibid., 49.

50. Ibid., 48.

51. Programme music is "Instrumental music which tells a story, illustrates literary ideas, or evokes pictorial scenes," as defined in Michael Kennedy and Joyce Bourne Kennedy's *The Concise Oxford Dictionary of Music*, which also notes that the term was coined by Romantic composer Franz Liszt.

52. Otto, *Idea of the Holy*, 48.

53. Ibid., 48.

unlikely that one would distinguish between sadness brought about by a musical experience and sadness caused by other events.

Otto's focus is on traditional classical religious music, though some of the composers he holds up in high regard for their religious music were also writing programme music. Felix Mendelssohn (1809–1847), whose setting of Psalm 2 (op. 78) Otto celebrates,[54] also wrote the *Hebrides Overture*, which is highly programmatic. Thus, Otto places emphasis on the intention of the composer, and relies the composer's intention to communicate something religious in order for it to produce a religious experience. However, according to Otto's own account of the numinous experience, it would appear to be unnecessary to treat sacred and secular music differently: to use Otto's criteria, if the music produces an experience of *mysterium tremendum et fascinans*, whether or not it has explicit religious content, then it has effected a numinous experience.[55]

According to Otto, the closest music comes to the numinous is through silence.[56] He gives the example of Johann Sebastian Bach's (1685–1750) B Minor Mass (BVW 232) where, at the most holy and numinous point, that of the transubstantiation, the music can only descend into silence long enough to "hear the silence."[57] Otto interprets this in the biblical sense of "keeping silence."[58] In choosing examples of Bach and Mendelssohn, Otto upholds the notion of hierarchy in music, specifically choosing two composers who are usually elevated in any hierarchy of classical music, religious or otherwise.

In summary, Otto has a limited understanding of music's potential to allow an encounter with the divine. The genre of the music, as well as the prior conditions of those experiencing it, are limiting factors. This is in contrast to Schleiermacher's understanding of music as closely associated to feeling, and experience which allows an intuition that is pre-reflective. However, Otto's criteria for numinous experience—that it is an experience of *mysterium tremendum et fascinans*—can be applied to any form of music that has this effect.

---

54. Ibid., 70.

55. This numinous experience is an experience of the divine, and as such impacts on thoughts of revelation. This will be explored more fully under the concepts of revelation and the sacred in the following chapter.

56. The metaphor of silent music is used to describe other religious experiences, as (for example) in Catholic theologian William Johnson's work on meditation, entitled *Silent Music: The Science of Meditation*.

57. Otto, *Idea of the Holy*, 70.

58. Ibid., 68.

Perhaps the reason Otto finds musical experience such a fitting analogy for numinous experience is because embodied musical experience is particularly effective at allowing encounter with the divine other, and therefore the embodied experience of music can be a numinous experience. Whilst this may be the case, the way in which humans encounter the divine in music need not necessarily be through the overwhelming experience of *mysterium tremendum et fascinans*: there is also the possibility of a gentler type of encounter with God.

Paul Tillich

The German theologian and philosopher Paul Tillich (1886–1965) was a proponent of theological engagement with culture. His thought, in particular in his *Theology of Culture*, has had a lasting impact on theologians studying culture and in particular those engaging with popular culture today.[59] He formed a theology of culture which allowed for the sacred to be found outside of the church.[60] Tillich's work continues to value individual religious experience, but his understanding shifts from the religious person being acted upon by the culture of the time, to the religious person actively searching for meaning in the "ultimate concern."[61] For Tillich, God is one's ultimate concern, and the search for this ultimate concern need not occur only within religion but in all areas of life.

In his *Theology of Culture* Tillich advocates engagement between the religious and the secular.[62] Tillich writes, "The form of religion is culture."[63] In other words: "The Church and the culture are within, not alongside, each other. And the Kingdom of God includes both while transcending both."[64] For Tillich, culture and religion are inextricably connected. Everything in culture can express ultimate concern, and "ultimate concern is manifest

---

59. As will be shown in the following sections, theologians such as Gordon Lynch and Kelton Cobb draw heavily on Tillich's theology of culture in their understanding of theologies of popular culture.

60. Tillich had close contact with Otto when he was appointed in Marburg. John Heywood Thomas explores their friendship and shared theology in *Tillich*, 9; and Eric C. Rust describes how Tillich develops Schleiermacher's and Otto's ideas on the cognitive aspects of religious feeling in *Religion, Revelation and Reason*, 37.

61. Tillich writes, "Religion, in the largest and most basic sense of the word, is ultimate concern" (*Theology of Culture*, 8).

62. Ibid., 42.

63. Ibid., 47.

64. Ibid., 51.

in all creative functions of the human spirit."⁶⁵ Culture is the sum of the creative functions of humans. Tillich aims for a "consecration" of the entire world following the theology of Martin Buber, "in the double sense of seeing the divine in everything."⁶⁶ Therefore music would not have to be explicitly religious in order to be of value to Tillich's theology.

However, his theology stops short of truly allowing the binary understanding of the sacred and the secular to be overcome, because of his wariness of religion endorsing all forms of culture, no doubt influenced by the cultural context in which he lived. Russell Re Manning notes that Tillich always upholds the division of the sacred and the secular, and is cautious about religion endorsing culture, particularly because of the era in which he was writing, following the Second World War.⁶⁷ Following this catastrophic shift in culture, it is evident that not all forms of culture should be endorsed, and that sometimes theologians may need to stand against culture instead of supporting it, as indeed Tillich did with his move away from Nazi Germany to United States in 1933.

Tillich holds that religious and philosophical attributes coincide in truth, and that all truth is God. That truth precedes division into subject and object.⁶⁸ Existential philosophers also influence Tillich in their search for a "creative realm of being which is prior to and beyond the distinction between objectivity and subjectivity."⁶⁹ For Tillich, the two realms of reality, the inner and exterior reality, come together in the arts. In his words, "in poetry, in visual art, and in music, levels of reality are opened up which can be opened up in no other way."⁷⁰ Whilst theologians today might have a more holistic rather than binary understanding of the reality of being human, the creative realm is a place in which the distinction between object of truth (God) and subject (the human) is overcome, and therefore allows for human encounter with a pre-existing truth, God. In a similar way, for Schleiermacher, through pre-reflective religious feeling the barrier between human subject and divine object was overcome.

In summary, Tillich justifies the use of culture in theological ways because of this understanding of the arts as a facilitator for accessing a truth that precedes the distinction between human subject and divine object, but also in his definition of religion, which, in its largest sense, is "ultimate

65. Ibid., 8.
66. Ibid., 194.
67. Re Manning, *Theology at the End*.
68. Tillich, *Theology of Culture*, 14.
69. Ibid., 107.
70. Ibid., 57.

concern," or the search for encounter with the divine. Tillich's concept of religion as ultimate concern expands the idea of religion to include that which is important and necessary to people, but would otherwise be called secular. Tillich's theology of culture allows for the encounter with God in all forms of music which express and reveal a human consideration of the ultimate concern.

David Brown

David Brown (1948–) is an Anglican theologian who has engaged extensively with cultural resources. Brown has explored the created world in his theology, in particular with his trilogy *God and Enchantment of Place*, *God and Grace of Body* and *God and Mystery in Words*. In this trilogy Brown reflects on the situatedness of humans in the world, and the sources of revelation that are available, of which music is one form. Brown's theology is experiential: it holds that God can be found in all aspects of human experience. Music is relevant to this in that music permeates the whole person. Brown argues that this is why God can be found in a variety of music, because all music speaks to the whole person, the body, imagination and emotion.[71] In musical terms, this applies to all types of music, through all periods.

Brown dedicates the second half of *God and Grace of Body* to music, as he holds that the musical experience is, after all, a bodily experience, but not the less important or sacramental because of that. This highlights the importance for Brown of the embodied nature of musical experience. Brown turns his attention to different types of music, from the classical (mainly nineteenth and twentieth century) to the modern popular. In his view, not all of the music he discusses is of equal value, but it is all open to the same possibilities and is all of *some* value, whatever genre it comes from.[72] Brown's focus on music primarily from the nineteenth and twentieth centuries is, for him, justified for two reasons: it has shaped the composition of music today, as well as shaping the way in which humans today encounter music; and the growth of programmatic music allowed for greater chance of religious experience through music that is solely instrumental.[73]

---

71. Brown, *God and Grace of Body*, 294.

72. This is highlighted above in relation to the quality of the music. For Brown, music's sacramental nature lies not in any particular qualities of the music, but in the particular way in which it is experienced through the body (ibid., 219).

73. Ibid., 247.

Brown suggests that there is not a divide in religious experience between the sacred and the secular, or revealed and natural religion.[74] As well as exploring natural theology through music, Brown also notes where the Romantics moved forward from the pastoral to the exploration of darker aspects of human experience, for example with Ludwig van Beethoven (1770–1827) and Franz Schubert (1797–1828) exploring their suffering through their music, which will be discussed further in chapter 4.[75] Thus music allows humans to explore and understand more of their own predicament, as well as providing a bridge to understanding the object of sacramental experience, God. Whilst music might allow for encounter with God, or of another important theological issue, such as suffering, musical knowledge must be integrated with prior theological understanding. Brown holds that "experience only ever reveals God partially, aspects of the divine, as it were. So it remains the task of the intellect to bring them into some kind of compatible resolution."[76] Therefore encounter with God through music would only reveal a particular aspect of God, that must be integrated into the greater theological picture.

Brown acknowledges that some music has specific religious intent which gives it meaning, but does not give this music a privileged position. His account of music also is open to the natural theology he perceives in the compositions of Bach and Beethoven. Brown explores how Bach lays the ground for composers to take up natural theology in the nineteenth and twentieth centuries. This suggests that although the nineteenth and twentieth centuries have been instrumental in shaping our current relationship to music, and were the times in which natural theology came to be prevalent, some of the traits of natural theology are seen much earlier in music and have been in development for hundreds of years.[77]

Brown proposes a sacramental account of music, allowing humans to grasp that which cannot be seen: he does not divide music into sacred and secular, but allows that all music can become a pointer toward God, not only sacred music. Brown makes an analogy between musical experience and the

---

74. Ibid., 422.

75. Ibid., 256–67.

76. Ibid., 294.

77. The much older idea of the harmony of the universe could be interpreted as natural theology. Carol Harrison notes that this idea is present in Augustine's thought: "The basic but revolutionary insight is that God is music: he is supreme measure, number, relation, harmony, unity and equality" (Begbie, *Resounding Truth*, 31). Earlier understandings of music's reflection of nature can also be found in the stress on number in ancient Greek thought. See Flora R. Levine's *Greek Reflections on the Nature of Music* for further discussion.

sacrament of the Eucharist noting that the musical experience is one which can be re-enacted in order to make God's presence known again.[78] Anamnesis, a word meaning remembrance and being linked to remembrance of the Passion of Jesus, plays an important role in Brown's understanding of the Eucharist and of sacramental musical experience.

For Brown, as for many other theologians discussed here, secular music has as much to say to theology as religious music. Brown's interest in culture is based on the belief that God is relevant to every part of the human life, and he aims to overcome the separation into the sacred and the secular. He argues that "If God really is our creator, then the urge to deepen contact with him is likely to permeate human creativity in whatever form it is found."[79] This is also evident in the ongoing disagreement as to which forms of culture and creativity can facilitate access to the experience of God.[80] Brown allows that all music may have a sacramental role to play, even though it may be of differing quality.[81]

The discussion of musical experience can focus solely on the hypothetical listener, but Brown's thought, like Otto's, also includes discussion of the composer's intentions.[82] In contrast to Otto, Brown holds that programme music is a feasible means of producing religious experience, perhaps because he is guided by the composer's intentions, but primarily because it is a form of bodily musical experience as all other music is, and can thus reveal something of God.[83]

Brown's theology allows for the possibility of new forms of revelation through music that might contradict older forms of revelation, most notably, the biblical account.[84] He therefore allows for genuine and new revelation through music because "certain features of music help an already present God to be perceived."[85] The music is thus the vehicle rather than the

---

78. Brown, *God and Grace of Body*, 247.

79. Ibid., 222.

80. Ibid., 222–23.

81. Ibid.

82. As in, for example, his discussion of how Johann Sebastian Bach (1685–1750) leads listeners in different directions with the text "It is finished" at the end of his *St John Passion*, first toward despair and then triumph (ibid., 229).

83. It gives another perspective of God, or of the issue the music sets out to tackle, for example suffering. Brown holds that "experience only ever reveals God partially, aspects of the divine, as it were. So it remains the task of the intellect to bring them into some kind of compatible resolution." Therefore, programme music offers one particular aspect that must be integrated into prior knowledge (ibid., 294).

84. Ibid., 245.

85. Ibid., 237.

provider of knowledge, it is the means through which God reveals God's self. As a sacramental form, music makes something of the invisible God perceptible, and, on the understanding of revelation drawn outlined in chapter 2, reveals something of God.

In summary, Brown proposes that all music can have theological value. For Brown, music is a sacramental bodily encounter which reveals something of the otherwise hidden God, and in this way music can be a source of revelation. It is as valid a form of revelation as other available sources of revelation, and may challenge existing revelation. However, it must always be integrated into existing theological understanding, as it can only ever provide one aspect of revelation.

Férdia Stone-Davis

Contemporary theologian Férdia Stone-Davis's thought on musical beauty has resonances of Schleiermacher's understanding of pre-reflective feeling and intuition in the religious experience. Her recent book *Musical Beauty: Negotiating the Boundary between Subject and Object* understands the experience of musical beauty in a similar way to the pre-reflective nature of feeling and intuition in Schleiermacher's thought relating to the importance of the experience of music.[86] She has proposed a theology of music based largely on the experience of musical beauty. In her account of music, Stone-Davis takes a stance between Boethius and Kant, which takes into account the subjective and objective properties attributed to music and the relationship of the subject and object.

Stone-Davis highlights that, for Boethius, God is the source of everything.[87] As such, musical meaning is objective, coming from God. Moreover, beauty—as a transcendental—is therefore a conduit of absolute knowledge from the ultimate objective source, the transcendent God. However, music is not simply a transfer of meaning from the objective source of the transcendent. It has a dual role, firstly in being a means of understanding the world in having meaning, and secondly in being a part of that which is to be known. Music, then, is both epistemological and ontological.[88] The bodily experience of music is therefore important in this, and thus, from Boethius, Stone-Davis takes the importance of physicality of music.[89]

86. Stone-Davis, *Musical Beauty*.
87. Ibid., 62.
88. Ibid., 121.

89. She notes, however, that for Boethius, the intellect is given precedence over the senses, and thus the meaning of the physical music is located in "a prior, underlying, non-material ground," or God (ibid., 77).

Stone-Davis notes that in contrast to Boethius, Kant holds that there is neither absolute source nor guarantor of knowledge.[90] Knowledge is thus subjective, the basis of knowledge is in the one who knows, not an external source. Unlike Boethius, Kant understands beauty epistemologically but not ontologically. Beauty is a means of knowing (which is, in itself, subjective), rather than something to be known in and of itself. There are two types of beauty: free and adherent. Stone-Davis notes that, for Kant, free beauty, like music, has no content of its own and adherent beauty is conditioned by presupposed concepts.[91] The meaning of free beauty thus derives solely from its descriptive capacity. Beauty is only recognized inter-subjectively, for Kant, because of the common nature of humans, which may give it the appearance of being in some way objective.

As regards beauty, Kant finds the physicality of music problematic, and it leads to a tension in his classification of music. On the one hand, if music is mere sensation, it is therefore conceptless. On the other, as a physical experience, it therefore contributes to epistemological knowledge. Stone-Davis is critical of this account, noting that if music is mere sensation, then music cannot mediate beauty since, for Kant, the beautiful is about the free play of the imagination and understanding, grounded primarily in concepts. On the other hand, this conceptlessness and freeness places it alongside fine art, which Kant allows can communicate beauty.[92] Stone-Davis believes Kant is thus unsure whether music can mediate beauty or not. For Stone-Davis, this uncertainty is "insoluble."[93]

Musical beauty, for Stone-Davis is not conceptless, and is an experience of the subject, grounded in an object. She highlights the limitations of Kant's discussion of music, in that Kant takes a very general idea of music, and does not make any distinction between different types of music. This is particularly problematic because of his supposition that music is conceptless, when in fact some music can convey concepts: Stone-Davis here takes an example of Scruton finding Bach's Chaconne in D minor (the fifth movement of *Partita for Violin No. 2*, BWV 1004, completed in 1720) with the solo violin "bearing the burden of the world's greatest sadness."[94] The concept of sadness is manifestly linked to the music in the evidence of many musical experiences.

90. Stone-Davis agrees with Donald Crawford's reading of Kant's notion of "common sense" which underpins the aesthetic judgement, and is both the feeling itself and the principle we all have in common that underlies the feeling (ibid., 94).

91. Ibid., 79–89.

92. Ibid., 132.

93. Ibid., 145.

94. Ibid., 152.

Happiness and sadness in their many forms are two concepts that are often linked to music, though these two broad concepts merely scratch the surface of the vast array of concepts evoked by music. Indeed, much musical analysis is based on the application of concepts in interpreting the meaning.[95] In this way, music may be seen to be associated with concepts and therefore can be involved in the free play of the imagination and understanding. The concepts may also have much to do with the experience of beauty, as in the aforementioned example Stone-Davis gives of the conveyance of sadness in the Chaconne.

Stone-Davis proposes another way of understanding the relationship between the subject and the object that retains the integrity of both. Musical experience and the meaning derived from it is neither wholly subjective, entirely derived from the subject, nor is it imposed on the subject from an external objective source.[96] She accepts neither Boethius nor Kant's understanding of the relationship between the subject and the object. From Kant, she draws the idea that music communicates knowledge to the subject, though this knowledge may be indeterminate, and from Boethius she draws the source of this knowledge, the object. In her view, in the interaction between the subject and object, the boundary between the two is blurred or suspended in some way. The encounter between the subject and the object is "mutual and indeterminate": "The subject becomes receptive to the object and the object likewise to the subject."[97] There is thus an exchange that occurs between the subject and the object in the musical experience.

Stone-Davis recognizes a "pre-reflective moment" in the experience of music, in which the boundary between the subject and the object is suspended: "the boundary between subject and object is postponed and the intimate connection between the two is disclosed."[98] The subject, for Stone-Davis, is the one who experiences the music, and the object is beauty. This avoids the conclusion that musical experience is purely subjective, but also allows scope for difference in individual experiences of beauty.

Stone-Davis's pre-reflective moment is reminiscent of Schleiermacher's concept of intuition, although she does not refer directly to his work.[99] For her, the musical experience is understood in the moments before reflective thought. It is based on a feeling or an intuition as the listening subject

95. For example, when Charles Rosen discusses Mountains and Song Cycles in chapter 3 of *The Romantic Generation*.

96. Stone-Davis, *Musical Beauty*, 190.

97. Ibid., 178.

98. Ibid., 190.

99. Richard Crouter notes that Schleiermacher understands religion as "immediate pre-reflexive feeling and intuition" in the introduction to his translation of *On Religion*, xi.

merges with the beautiful musical object. However, the object of this pre-reflective merging may not only be musical beauty. Stone-Davis's thought can be developed by drawing on the object of Schleiermacher's pre-reflective feeling of absolute dependence, God. If the object of the pre-reflective overcoming of subject-object boundaries was God, not just musical beauty, then the music is also revelatory. In other words, there is a pre-reflective encounter of the human subject with the divine object in musical experience. Music therefore reveals something, in this pre-reflective moment, about the relationship between object and subject, in other words, between God and humans. Indeed, music need not be beautiful in order to allow a pre-reflective suspension of the distinction between human and divine.

Music, then, is another way of acquiring knowledge about God, perhaps even a particularly good way of acquiring it, as music is particularly good at suspending this boundary between object and subject. Stone-Davis believes music is able to do this because of its ability to draw one into the experience, in capturing them and encouraging an ecstatic mode of attention. Stone-Davis's account of the pre-reflective moment which suspends the boundary between subject and object can be developed theologically by drawing on Schleiermacher's theology, thus interpreting the subject and object in musical experience as humans and God rather than humans and beauty. Embodied human experience of music enables this suspension of the boundary, but the result of considering the object to be God mean that the experience is also revelatory.

Summary

This section explored theological accounts of music that focus on the experience of music, rather than on music in its written form. These accounts hold that all music has a place in theological thought, though it is not all of equal value. I have suggested that music is more than an analogy for encounter with the divine: music allows encounter with God.

Schleiermacher's thought provided a shift in understanding in terms of theological engagement with culture, suggesting that music is closely associated with feeling, and therefore is closely related to religion, in allowing experience of the objective source behind the feeling of absolute dependence, God. Stone-Davis's thought develops Schleiermacher's, in that musical beauty suspends the boundary between the subject and object, for her, humans and beauty, and interpreted the object as God, following Schleiermacher. This reflects Tillich's thought that since truth precedes the division of subject and object; music can thus reveal something truthful of reality. This opens the potential for revelation through musical experience.

Beyond Otto, I proposed that an experience of the numinous, or, in other words, an experience of the divine, is closely related to musical experience and in some cases is the very same. Musical experience of *mysterium tremendum et fascinans* is one means by which the encounter with the divine might occur, but not the only one. In this account music overcomes the boundary between the subject and object, at least temporarily. The threshold is suspended between the human subject, the one who experiences the music, and the object, or God.

With the approach of the theologians above in mind, I suggest that music allows for genuine revelation that may not be expressible in words, the traditional form of theology. This musical experience may be pre-reflective and therefore not require specialist musical training. It is not through any particular quality of the music that this happens, but the embodied nature of all music, and the defining feature of this nature is its physicality and the way in which it impacts on the embodied human.

Music as Expounding Given Theological Truths

In this section I will explore several ways that music has been used by theologians as a way of expressing, understanding, or investigating theological truths, though this approach is not exclusive of the first approach outlined above. This goes some way toward assisting with theological understanding, but is ultimately constricted by pre-existing thought. Presenting theological givens through music allows theological reflection to take place, and new possibilities and conclusions can be aired, but are ultimately secondary to existing knowledge. In this way, music can also be used to ask theological questions and to illustrate given theological answers. This approach is particularly characteristic of the thought of Hans Urs von Balthasar, Karl Barth and Jeremy Begbie.

Hans Urs von Balthasar

Catholic theologian Hans Urs von Balthasar (1905–1988) has done much to reignite interest in theological aesthetics.[100] He holds that the

---

100. In Catholic theology, Richard Viladesau has continued research in theological aesthetics. His research interests are in theology and aesthetics, and his key works in this area are *Theology and the Arts*, *Art and Rhetoric*, and *Theological Aesthetics*. His more recent research has focused on the history of aesthetics and the arts in theology, in *The Beauty of the Cross*, *The Triumph of the Cross*, and *The Pathos of the Cross*.

transcendentals—beauty, goodness and truth—are a means of knowing God, and therefore laments their loss in the modern world.[101] Unsurprisingly, then, he has an interest in music, and has good musical knowledge, having trained as a pianist and being a keen listener of Classical music.[102] Music plays a key role not only in his theological aesthetics, but also in exploring his theological thought.

Music can be used in theology as an explanatory tool: it can help to elucidate theological arguments. Balthasar uses music as an elaborate analogy in his book *Truth is Symphonic*.[103] It is an analogy as there is true likeness between the music and the theological truth. This account of music reflecting the rest of the created world and theological understanding is based on an understanding of creation as united. The analogy is possible because the likeness is already written into creation by God.[104] Balthasar expects music to reflect theological truths because they are built into the structure of creation, and music is a part of that creation.

For Balthasar, the musical symphony is a useful tool to help one understand Christian pluralism.[105] Balthasar uses the symphony to explore creation, God's actions in the world, and Christian understanding of these. For Balthasar, the "sym-phony"—which means the simultaneous many sounds—is a tool of understanding. The parts of creation are the many sounds, and the different timbres of instruments each have their own unique role to play in the overall composition.[106]

God makes these different instruments in creation. This accounts for diversity in humanity and across all of creation, as the instruments in an orchestra are hugely diverse. The world is thus like a symphony in being pluralist, as there are many competing ideas to the truth, even within Christianity, and allows there to be opposing positions, held in tension but not necessarily contradicting one another. That there can be a perceived contradiction paradoxically held musically in tension is also used as an analogy

---

101. Balthasar, *Glory of the Lord*.

102. Balthasar is quoted as saying "My youth was defined by music. My piano teacher was an old lady who had been a pupil of Clara Schumann. She introduced me to Romanticism. As a student in Vienna I delighted in the last of the Romantics—Wagner, Strauss, and especially Mahler. That all came to an end once I had Mozart in my ears. To this day he has never left those ears. In later life Bach and Schubert remained precious to me, but it was Mozart who was the immovable Pole Star, round which the other two circled (the Great and Little Bears)" (Schindlerm, *Hans Urs von Balthasar*, 36).

103. Balthasar, *Truth is Symphonic*.

104. Ibid., 9.

105. Ibid., 9.

106. Ibid., 8–9.

to understand Christ's human and divine natures. Balthasar writes, "Then came the Son, the "heir of all things," for whose sake the whole orchestra had been put together. As it performs God's symphony under the Son's direction, the meaning of its variety becomes clear."[107] Balthasar expresses an understanding of the Trinity: the composer is the Father, the Son is the conductor, and the actual music that is played is the Holy Spirit. Balthasar uses the image of the conductor to express his views that it is Jesus that is in control of the direction of creation. Jesus is thus at the heart of Balthasar's thought on creation: it is for Jesus' sake that creation exists, and it is in following Jesus that it has purpose.

Through understanding of the musical symphony, Balthasar's theology becomes more tangible. He writes "As for the audience, none is envisaged other than the players themselves: by performing the divine symphony . . . they discover why they have been assembled together. Initially, they stand or sit next to one another as strangers, in mutual contradiction, as it were. Suddenly, as the music begins, they realize how they are integrated. Not in unison, but what is far more beautiful—in sym-phony."[108] There are many layers to Balthasar's thought here. He acknowledges that often humans suffer from a lack of understanding of purpose: the players are not sure why they are assembled together, and they play for themselves rather than for an audience, showing the importance of self-transformation. Balthasar suggests a unity of creation through his musical analogy.

In summary, Balthasar is able to use musical analogies here to express his theological account of the unity of creation and the trinity more clearly, and to help others with the understanding of his theology. Music represents the different purposes of creation, through its multi-faceted nature, and shows that one unified form can include much diversity. This is a useful tool for the reader, allowing them to make links between their understanding of the world of music and the theological viewpoints offered by Balthasar.

Karl Barth

Swiss Reformed theologian Karl Barth (1886–1968) is a strong proponent of the view that no culture can give access to God.[109] God is ultimately unknowable, and there is a qualitative difference between humans and God:

---

107. Ibid., 8.

108. Ibid., 9.

109. Here I discuss Barth, as his work is a major influence on, and dialogue partner for, many of the twentieth-century theologians whose work I engage with at more length. Given the limits of this book, there is not enough space to discuss the extensive debates around Barth's work.

God is "wholly other."[110] However, although Barth holds there to be an unbridgeable distance between humans and God, he gives a privileged place to Mozart's music. Barth has written recreationally about Mozart's music,[111] but he has also explored Mozart's music alongside creation in his later theology in *Church Dogmatics*.[112] He does not talk about music in general, only ever specifically the music of Mozart.

For Barth, Mozart's music expresses the goodness of creation. Jeremy Begbie notes that "for Barth, Mozart's music embodies and gives voice to the authentic praise of a finite, limited creation."[113] Barth holds that Mozart's music teaches us about creation: "Mozart causes us to hear that . . . creation praises its Master and is therefore perfect."[114] This music is, for Barth, the perfect response to God's creation. Mozart's music accesses a truth about creation that is otherwise hidden.

In Mozart, Barth hears both the positives and the "shadowside" of creation. For Barth, Mozart "heard the negative only in and with the positive."[115] In other words, it is a true reflection of the nature of Creation, in all its aspects. Mozart's music therefore praises creation in its totality, with all of the positives and negatives: "he heard the harmony of creation to which the shadow also belongs but in which the shadow is not darkness, deficiency is not defeat, sadness cannot become despair, trouble cannot degenerate into tragedy, and infinite melancholy is not ultimately forced to claim undisputed sway."[116] Therefore Mozart embraced and praised creation in its finitude, its shadowside included. Like Balthasar, then, music reflects something fundamental to creation in being an aspect of that creation that represents the whole.

In summary, for Barth, God is ultimately unknowable as there is a qualitative difference between God and humanity. Therefore, no human creations or human culture can reveal any knowledge about God. However, one particular composer's music is able to teach us about the nature of creation. In Mozart's music Barth not only finds an expression of creation in its goodness and shadowside, but also an appropriate response to creation.

---

110. Barth, *Epistle to the Romans*, 49.
111. Barth, *Wolfgang Amadeus Mozart*.
112. Barth, *Church Dogmatics III*:3, 298–99.
113. Ibid., 95.
114. Ibid., 299.
115. Ibid., 298.
116. Ibid., 298.

Jeremy Begbie

Contemporary Anglican theologian Jeremy Begbie (1957–) often uses music as analogy to explicate theological truths in *Theology, Music and Time*.[117] The influence of Barth's understanding of culture is evident in Begbie's cautiousness about allowing music to say anything new to theology. For Begbie, music cannot challenge existing theological understanding. Music can only bring fresh understanding to theology by re-presenting theological truths, re-imagining them in the light of the musical culture of the time. In this way music can teach us what theology is already trying to teach us, perhaps by making it more accessible by presenting it in a different format from theology, a format which may be more familiar to us.

For Begbie, music never brings anything new to theology in its own right. When music does advance theology, it does so by reflecting what theology already knows: music benefits theology when "central doctrinal loci are explored, interpreted, re-conceived and articulated."[118] In this way a fresh viewpoint through music assists theology to re-examine itself and make changes for the better. Begbie goes on to say "It is important to stress that when music advances theology in this way, it does so first and foremost by *enacting* theological wisdom."[119] Music may dramatize and represent theology, but it never comes up with new theological ideas that are not already given, in Begbie's view.

At the end of the twentieth century, at the time of Begbie's most expansive writing on music and theology, *Theology, Music and Time*, there had been a further undermining of traditional musical structures and techniques by some composers, but largely a return to tonality and some traditional structures, whereas in the 1960s when Balthasar was writing his theological aesthetics, there was much experimentation with sound.[120] As in Balthasar's thought, so too for Begbie music can be used as an analogy to help us to understand theological thoughts. He explores this in relation to the Christian understanding of the humanity and divinity of Jesus Christ, and again in relation to the concept of the Trinity. This he does by using the aural world, where musical space is opened up. Using John Hull's understanding that there is such a thing as a musical space, Begbie clarifies further, saying "sounds and spatial framework (and temporal framework . . .)

---

117. Begbie, *Theology, Music and Time*.

118. Ibid., 5.

119. Ibid., 5.

120. For a history of the modern era in music, see Cook and Pople, *Cambridge History*; and for the particular compositional techniques moving back toward tonality, see Leeuw, *Music of the Twentieth Century*.

are completely intertwined."[121] Music has space, and yet it has not: a sound of one note takes up no less physical space than a chord of three notes: they occupy "the same aural space."[122] In this way we can understand the divinity and humanity of Christ, as being different truths but taking up the same space.

In this way, for Begbie, music reinforces understanding of existing theological truths. For Begbie, music teaches us that being transient is not a negative quality of human existence. Rather, music is always transient, it must be transient or else it could not exist, and this is an innate quality of it. Without transience, music could not be experienced. In this way it reflects creation which is also limited and transient. Therefore, music "challenges the assumption that because something takes time to be what it is, it is thereby of deficient value or goodness compared to that which is not subject to created time."[123] Value is thus given to the transient. It acknowledges that there may be a delay in something reaching its potential, and that the journey toward this is also important. In a similar way, "it need not be seen as a vice of creation that it can only reach its fulfilment, its perfection, through time."[124] Music takes time to reach its potential, and once it has achieved this, it dissipates, but the experience is no less valuable for this. Music therefore helps us to understand the nature of created time, and how best to understand its transient nature. It allows us to re-evaluate the meaning of the passage of time, and to value those things that take time.

For Begbie, music can help us to understand that death is a part of life, and that transience need not be feared: "Christian hope speaks of a life through death which is fuller than this life, a life given by God, this life transformed into the life of the 'age to come.'"[125] In this way, music can help us to understand another aspect of the created world: death. Like music, life takes time to reach its potential, and eventually is lost. Begbie is influenced by Rowan Williams, former Archbishop of Canterbury, in his writing "What we learn, in music as in the contemplative faith of which music is a part and also a symbol, is what it is to work *with* the [temporal] grain of things, to work in the stream of God's wisdom."[126] As Williams highlights, then, music is part of the Christian faith, but is also able to shed light on it from the outside. According to Williams's thought, music thus allows an opportunity

---

121. Begbie, *Theology, Music and Time*, 25.
122. Ibid., 25.
123. Ibid., 86.
124. Ibid., 86.
125. Ibid., 92.
126. Ibid., 97.

to join in the temporal nature of God's wisdom. In experiencing and participating in music, we participate in the reality of temporal life and of knowing God.

For Begbie, this participation in time is an essential part of human experience. He is critical of John Tavener's (1944–2013) attempts to express eternity through the removal of a sense of time in his music, for example in *The Protecting Veil*: "There seems more than a hint in Tavener of the idea that the more deeply we relate to God, the more we will need to abstract ourselves from time, develop an immunity to time's opportunities and threats."[127] For Begbie, understanding time is accepting its limits and boundaries, and living in them musically, not escaping from them into an illusion of timelessness. Understanding God is about understanding God in time.

Begbie holds that music reflects Christian beliefs about time; it correlates with biblical passages that Begbie goes on to explore. Beyond this, music reflects the underlying themes of scripture: "In both music and scriptural renderings of promises and fulfilments, we are dealing with interweaving trajectories, overlapping short-term promises, interruptions and so on."[128] Music, in correlating in this way, helps scripture to be understood better. One is often led into particular expectations by music, which may be fulfilled, delayed, or abandoned. In a similar way, Begbie sees this worked out in scripture. Music cannot challenge scriptural revelation, however, as Begbie only has examples of music that fit his analogies with scripture, condemning those which offer a perspective which conflicts with his theology. That is not to say music cannot offer a re-imagining of theological concepts, but only as they expound existing given theological truths. Begbie suggests that improvisation "provides a powerful enactment of the truth that our freedom is enabled to flourish only by engaging with and negotiating constraints."[129] Again, music is helping us to understand our being in the world in relation to concepts theology often grapples with: freedom and limitations.

One final example encapsulates Begbie's use of music as an analogy for Christian theology: "Eucharistic repetition both stabilises and destabilises . . . in metrical music, repetition can both stabilise and destabilise. It can both close the wave and provoke a desire for further fulfilment, and it can do both concurrently."[130] Considering music as successive waves, part of a larger wave, which may, in turn, be part of an even larger wave helps

127. Ibid., 145.
128. Ibid., 110.
129. Ibid., 199.
130. Ibid., 166.

us to understand the Eucharist in terms of relating "not only directly in an over-arching wave to the death and resurrection of Christ, but also, via its 'bottom-level' waves to every previous Eucharist."[131] Musical repetition, in its waves which both consolidate and create new tensions, helps us to understand Eucharistic repetition relating to both a one-off event and the trajectory of salvation. However, for Begbie, in contrast to Brown's understanding of this, music does not participate in this sacramentally.

In summary, characteristics of music—temporality, repetition, etc.— teach us about the fundamental reality of the created world. Begbie uses music to expound given theological truths. There is little possibility of changing or developing established theological truths through music, because "good" music reflects them. Indeed, the theological truths provide a means by which one can judge the music to be of value: if the music is worth discussing, it reflects these theological truths. Theology is used as a measure of music.

Moreover, in reflecting theological truths, as in Balthasar's theology, music can be used as analogy to help us understand them. Music is able to assist us in looking closely at a particular aspect of creation, such as time or death, and to enlighten us about it both by reflecting revealed truths of, for example, scripture, or by reflecting its true nature, as in the transient nature of life. Thus far, music has presented these theological concerns in ways that may allow a deeper understanding of the already given revelation. Unlike Balthasar, however, Begbie is more critical of attempts to engage with theology through music, and of attempts to develop theological concepts such as time, as in Tavener's musical portrayal of eternity.[132] Begbie is therefore cautious of composers that attempt to subvert or transgress usual musical expectations, as well as theological ones.

Summary

The approaches in this section have used music to expound given theological truths. In this sense, music is a useful tool in exploring and explaining existing theology, but it is not a meaning-making tool, nor does it offer new answers to theological questions. Rather, it is a means by which to explore and understand better pre-existing theological insights. Where interpretation of the music differs from the accepted theology, it is condemned.

This approach treats music as an object to be studied and compared to existing theological thought, rather than exploring its meaning through

---

131. Ibid., 169–70.
132. Though much of Tavener's music was written after Balthasar's death in 1988.

experience of the music. It is therefore considered at a remove from human experience, which misses out on much gained from consideration of music as a part of embodied human experience. It may also lead to a focus on any words associated with the music, rather than music itself, as existing revelatory forms are largely based in language. In this way, too much emphasis may be given to the composer's intentions, rather than the meaning created in the embodied experience of music.

However, whilst it is important to understand and reflect on the experiential nature of music, this approach has shown that is still much to be learnt from using music to demonstrate theological thought and to explicate pre-existing theological truths. In particular, these theologians agree that music reveals something of the nature of creation. Following the thought of Balthasar, Barth, and Begbie, music is enlightening about the fundamental reality of the world in which humans live. Begbie's theology has shown that music is particularly useful in examining the nature of particular aspects of creation, for example transience and death, two concepts which will be explored throughout this book.

This second approach, then, might encourage us to hold to our existing accounts of theological truth, and to close off potential openings for new knowledge or revelation. Musical creations are condemned when they do not reflect God's creation. Music can also be used in contrast to existing theology, and this may pose challenges, but these are challenges that help to make theology relevant to meaningful experiences. Too much emphasis on music as expounding existing theological truths misses potential new insights provided by music, and in embodied experience of music, which may challenge accepted versions of truth. Therefore, following solely this approach might lead to missing potentially challenging new forms of revelation.

Theologies of Popular Culture

The following accounts from theologies of popular culture are perhaps more accepting of new theological knowledge being revealed in all human creations. The ways in which theologians have investigated popular culture have aspects of both the approaches outlined above, but go beyond these approaches in ways that are more creative. Contemporary theologies of popular culture add new dimensions to a theology of music, in that they take into account the worldly circumstances in which humans live and the cultural context in which thought arises and develops. Theologies of popular culture also highlight the nature of human beings living in human bodies, but also in social communities, which more frequently recognize the virtual as well as the physical communities in which we live. These accounts contend that there is a capacity in popular culture to convey particular truths about material and social embodiment.

Whilst theologies of popular culture provide useful insights into some aspects of music, some issues also arise. The variety of approaches offered by different contributors to the field is evidence of the difficulty in defining popular culture and the diversity of interpretations that are possible. The definition each theologian holds of popular culture may be a determining factor in the development of their thought. However, it is not my intention to defend any one definition of popular culture, but to use insights from these accounts to approaching a broader range of music.

Popular music has many associations with text as well as sound. It often has lyrics, as well as song titles, and album notes. The meaning of the lyrics cannot be divorced from the music accompanying them, as they undoubtedly contribute to the meaning of the music as a whole. Theologies which study popular music are useful in developing an approach to music which contains text, as theologians develop methods for accounting for lyrics in popular music. Thus, the meaning-making process in music that contains lyrics is a balancing of the experience of the music and the lyrics, alongside interpretations of the experience of the music influenced by previous musical experience.

In this section three main approaches to popular culture in general will be discussed, before exploring theologians who have engaged theologically with popular music. Firstly, T.J. Gorringe's *Furthering Humanity: A Theology of Culture* supports the idea that God can be found in the material world. Gorringe argues that culture plays an important role in human development. Secondly, Gordon Lynch emphasizes the social aspect of theological meaning-making in popular culture. Thirdly, Kelton Cobb takes a concept-based approach in *The Blackwell Guide to Theology and Popular Culture* and approaches various media of popular culture through theological themes. Further contemporary accounts of popular music will then be outlined, which raise theological questions and, in this way, aim to develop theological understanding. Michael Iafrate uses a whole genre of popular music—punk—to challenge theological assumptions, and Myles Werntz and Gina Messina-Dysert use two particular bands, Pearl Jam and Dave Matthews Band respectively, to raise theological questions on a particular issue. Finally, Jeffrey Keuss's thought will provide insights into the relationship between music and language in popular music.

Timothy Gorringe

Timothy Gorringe (1946–) is an Anglican theologian, influenced strongly by Barth and liberation theology, who encourages thinking of the created world as a valuable resource for theological understanding. He has engaged theologically with architecture, art, and the senses.[133] Gorringe draws on Schleiermacher and Tillich as well as Barth in his book *Furthering Humanity: A Theology of Culture*. This work advocates theologically engaging with artefacts of human creation as well as God's creation, arguing that both the natural and man-made creations are important. Gorringe endorses the study of all things in culture, arguing that culture is primarily about meaning and is concerned with the spiritual, ethical, and intellectual significance of the material world.[134] This is also what concerns theology, and thus culture is a theological concern. For Gorringe all things have been created by God, and therefore are relevant to theology.[135]

Gorringe's theology emphasizes that, through creation, all things come from God, and therefore theology should be concerned with everything that is created, not just with the world of religion, or that which is culturally determined to be sacred. Culture is marked by creativity, but it is also marked by sin, idolatry and grace. It is both a part of God's creation, and a "life-giving response to the God of life."[136] In this latter role, culture is part of what Gorringe calls the "long revolution," a concept he takes from Raymond Williams' idea of societal improvements, and Herder's "furthering humanity," the notion that the essence of life is a process of becoming.[137] Cultural creativity is a God-given means of progressing humanity. Culture is an integral part of the development of humanity.

The tension in the idea that culture is both part of God's creation and a human creation marred by human errors is a tension Gorringe believes is reflected in the incarnation, in Jesus being of two natures united. It affirms

---

133. Gorringe's work most relevant to this study is *Furthering Humanity*. His other relevant works include *Earthly Visions*, *The Common Good and the Global Emergency*, *A Theology of the Built Environment*, and *The Education of Desire*. Also of interest in terms of using an analogy from the arts—in this case from the realm of drama—to explain God's work in the world, in a way similar to Balthasar's *Truth is Symphonic*, is Gorringe's *God's Theatre*.

134. Gorringe, *Furthering Humanity*, 3.

135. He writes, "Theologically understood, culture is the name of that whole process in the course of which God does what it takes, in Paul Lehman's phrase, to make and to keep human beings human. Culture, in this sense is, under God, 'the human task'" (ibid., 4).

136. Ibid., 102.

137. Ibid., 17.

both the universal and the particular. Products of culture are both a part of God's creation, but also are made by humans, and thus are united as reflected in the incarnation. For Gorringe, there is an underlying unity in culture, which makes his theology of culture a theology of diversity in unity in which difference is valued.[138]

Gorringe's theology is eschatological and bears the influence of liberation theology. In its eschatology, it is concerned with the process of furthering humanity, a process of direction and meaning, or, as Gorringe says, "the hope that sustains us in the midst of hopelessness."[139] Cultural creativity may liberate us from unjust conditions of our society, giving hope where there may seem to be none. It is a reminder of artistic—and in particular musical—responses to political injustice. Punk will be explored below in relation to political critique, but it is not the only music to have made comment on injustice or to work toward a fairer society.[140] Russian[141] governments in particular have attempted to censor political criticism in its music, since the days of the USSR censoring Shostakovich and other classical composers by forcing them to submit their works to the state-controlled Union of Soviet Composers. This has led to creative responses, for example from Pussy Riot, a contemporary popular punk band, three of whose members were imprisoned in 2012 for protesting by song in Moscow's cathedral.

Gorringe is also influenced by Barth, whose eschatology, as noted by Stefan Skrimshire, eternalizes the present "now."[142] God is present and active in the process and progress of culture. For Gorringe, the Spirit is at work through culture, and the "life-affirming aspects of culture" are the results of God acting in culture.[143] The meaning of cultural creativity is thus not only human-made, but also God-given.

Gorringe considers the place of the poor in culture, noting that all cultures have some injustice; they are not all inherently positive.[144] Whereas the church has often aligned itself with so-called "high" culture, or, "great" painting, music and architecture, Gorringe argues that it should, in fact, be

---

138. Ibid., 102.

139. Ibid., 102.

140. So-called "charity singles" may fall into this category, in that they are attempting to move toward justice; for example, the recent Band Aid 30 song "Do They Know It's Christmas" (2014) raising funds for tackling Ebola. This may been seen as one means of "furthering humanity" through music.

141. For a fuller account of the history of Russian music, taking into account the political climate, see Maes's *A History of Russian Music*.

142. Scott and Northcott, *Systematic Theology and Climate Change*, 167.

143. Gorringe, *Furthering Humanity*, 102.

144. Ibid., 45.

looking to the poor as the authentic theological source for understanding Christian truth and practice. To be true to the scriptural commitment to the poor, Gorringe argues that the church ought to cherish popular culture.[145] This reflects the approach to music from experience, which holds that all music is of theological value, despite its musical merit or lack thereof.

Gorringe draws on Barth in his negative view of apophatic theology, which, he writes, "make[s] God a pauper."[146] In other words, to deny that anything may be said about God is to the detriment of human existence and progression. He follows Barth's dialectic that God is both revealed and hidden, and that is what makes the silence or negation important. Gorringe holds that apophatic theology does not define the hiddenness of God radically enough. Where there is silence, this is not the absence of the ability to speak about God, but rather is the presence of the "Wholly Other" in the text.[147] Gorringe follows Barth in his understanding of revelation. The stress on the importance of the silence suggests that there may be something in the silence that reflects the radical hiddenness of God. Gorringe's perspective here is based on his reading of scripture, in that "all the different forms of struggle for and against silence can be found in the gospels." This, he argues, gives rise to the "twofold practice of prophecy and discipleship."[148] Silence is thus both affirming and unsettling, but is an important part of how we have known God from biblical times.[149] Silence may reveal God, in God's absolute hiddenness.

Gorringe highlights the issue of connecting truth to culture as "culture is *process*. Cultures never stand still."[150] The way in which truth is expressed in both religion and culture changes over time. However, Gorringe believes that we must have faith that the Holy Spirit will continue to guide us in discerning truth, and that "if there is a God, and if God has been revealed, there must be a meaning which is not only universal, but in some sense transcendent to all human culture, and able to critique it. If it cannot do that, it is not clear that we have a revelation."[151] In other words, there must be a transcendent truth that is beyond culture, that is expressed through cultural creativity, in order for there to be revelation in culture. For

---

145. Ibid., 47.

146. Ibid., 124.

147. Ibid., 120.

148. Ibid., 120.

149. Gorringe, in his discussion of silence, also allows for the pauses in creation in which God can become known, which will be useful in discussions of silence in the following chapter on Modern Music (ibid., 120–24).

150. Ibid., 179.

151. Ibid., 210.

Gorringe, the transcendent truth must lie beyond all particular cultures, though they may provide access to it.

In summary, Gorringe has argued that all human cultures are valuable, as human creations are a part of creation, which comes in its entirety from God. However, there is a tension in human creativity as it is both God-given and flawed by human nature, and this tension reflects the tension of the incarnation. Understanding this tension can help to understand the incarnation better, and therefore to know God. In particular, popular culture is important, as it reflects the authentic search for meaning in the lives of the majority of people. Gorringe argues that these popular forms of culture should be the basis of theology's engagement with human creations, rather than aspiring for high culture, which is too often exclusive. Gorringe's theology is also a reminder of the potential in music for inciting change, particularly in cases of injustice.

Gordon Lynch

Gordon Lynch (1968–) is a theologian whose work has been instrumental in igniting interest in popular culture in theology.[152] He holds that popular culture is theologically important because it is a part of the process of making meaning in the contemporary world. Lynch defines theology as "the process of seeking normative answers to questions of truth, goodness, evil, suffering, redemption, and beauty in the context of particular social and cultural situations."[153] This is reminiscent of Tillich's "ultimate concern," as these questions are the basis of every person's exploration of what is of utmost importance.[154] This may be interpreted as an anthropological generalisation, assuming that across all cultures all humans have the same set of theological questions. However, it is possible to leave the list open, to allow for different social and cultural contexts: all human theological undertakings are context- and time-bound.

Whilst Lynch lists a set of questions in his definition of theology, he does not explicitly indicate that this is a comprehensive list of theological questions. Lynch makes no assumption about the truth content of answers to theological questions brought by culture. He does not assume a source

---

152. Gordon Lynch's key works on theology and culture are *Understanding Theology and Popular Culture*, *The New Spirituality*, *On the Sacred*, *The Sacred in the Modern World*, and his edited collections *Between Sacred and Profane* and *Religion, Media and Culture*, edited with Jolyon Mitchell and Anna Strhan.

153. Lynch, *Understanding Theology and Popular Culture*, 36.

154. Tillich, *Dynamics of Faith*, 1–2.

for the answers to these questions beyond the medium itself, unlike the theological accounts above in which the theological encounter in music has an objective basis in God. Theological propositions found in popular culture, for Lynch, are human-constructed answers found through the various media.

Lynch rejects definitions of popular culture that often define it in relation to *something else*: opposing high culture, displacing folk culture, or resisting mass culture. Lynch suggests a wider definition of popular culture, based on a common thread in these definitions, but following Barry Reay's suggestion that popular culture "refers to widely held and commonly expressed thoughts and actions."[155] Lynch's definition of popular culture then is "the shared environment, practices, and resources of everyday life."[156] In other words, there is theological value in the everyday. Lynch does, however, bias this toward the symbolic and human-constructed artefacts, with the result that the natural environment is not considered by Lynch as part of this popular culture. Nor does he consider the ways in which popular culture may replicate or utilize the natural environment.

The idea that popular culture consists of shared resources in "the everyday lives of the wider population" is useful as it precludes judgement on particular forms of culture. It thus leaves aside prejudices toward certain forms of media. It is important in this definition that it allows for all resources of what Lynch calls "everyday life" in an attempt to avoid some of the complications of other words such as "ordinary." Using this definition, popular culture can be that which is otherwise considered to be "high culture." For example, Beethoven's setting of Friedrich Schiller's "*An die Freude*" in the fourth movement of *Symphony 9* (1824) is present in everyday life, through the films *A Clockwork Orange* (1971) which also uses Edward Elgar's (1857–1934) *Pomp and Circumstance* marches, and *Die Hard* (1988), whose sequel *Die Hard 2* (1990) uses Jean Sibelius's (1865–1957) *Finlandia*. The use of classical music in popular films is but one example of where classical music becomes part of everyday life and, therefore, has a place in theologies of popular culture.

Lynch's definition also considers popular culture to be a way of life, not a collection of cultural products, as these resources may be valuable in and of themselves, but only have a meaning in relation to the interaction of people with them. This understanding is helpful, then, in that the music will not be analysed in isolation or abstraction, but in action, as it were, in human lives. Music is analysed as an experience, rather than an

---

155. Reay, *Popular Cultures in England*, 1.
156. Lynch, *Understanding Theology and Popular Culture*, 15.

object. This definition does not limit the resources of popular culture, but allows a more open inventory of whatever is a part of the everyday lives of many people.[157] Lynch claims the study of everyday life is important for theology because it "has an important *explanatory* significance in helping us to understand more about the nature of human existence or the nature of human society."[158] Theology is not judging the quality of the music as *music*, which is the role of the musicologist, but its value in its capacity to answer theological questions.

Lynch's approach to culture is broad, in that popular culture is allowed a platform to contribute to any theological question provided it is understood alongside other theological, religious and philosophical contributions. Lynch follows Don Browning's writing on practical theology, to outline three stages of what he calls a *revised correlational approach*.[159] Firstly, *descriptive theology* is required to understand the "horizon" of the particular example of popular culture, and to explore its meaning and significance by asking what it offers to a particular question. The second stage is in *historical theology*, or, understanding the religious or philosophical tradition to understand the "horizon" of questions and perspectives established by these traditions. Finally, *systematic theology* is required to bring together the two previous horizons into a fuller understanding. Lynch suggests some questions which should be asked at this point, which include whether popular culture offers a truthful account, and if the experiences of popular culture are adequate or constructive experiences of beauty, pleasure or transcendence.[160]

This approach requires an exchange between popular culture and existing theological thought. This conversational model is a useful tool for reflecting theologically on music throughout the ages, as it takes into account its historical and cultural context and the existing theological perspectives, whilst contributing an additional horizon, or understanding, which allows for further insight into the question. This approach is followed in this book by bringing existing theological thought into conversation with musical analysis and composers' writings.

Two other advantages of this approach, as Lynch notes, are that it takes account of the writer's own experience, context and religious context in understanding the writer's relation to the horizon of the example of

---

157. David Brown expresses a similar insight when he notes that all of the music he explores is not of equal value, but that it may still be useful to theology (*God and Grace of Body*, 220).

158. Lynch, *Understanding Theology and Popular Culture*, 18.

159. Browning, *Fundamental Practical Theology*.

160. Lynch, *Understanding Theology and Popular Culture*, 106–7.

popular culture, and it recognizes that truth and goodness are not the sole possession of a single religious or philosophical tradition.[161] This reflects the thought of other theologians writing on popular culture, notably Deacy and Ortiz who write in *Theology and Film* that "no theological activity can ever be conducted in a cultural vacuum."[162] In other words, the context of the work and the cultural situation of the audience or theologian play a role in determining its theological meaning. Lynch writes, "religious experience is not something that takes place prior to cultural practices and expressions, but . . . religious experience is constructed precisely through engagement with particular cultural practices and resources."[163] Religious experience does not exist apart from cultural experience. Indeed, no individual can ever be separated from their cultural context. Sometimes more than one cultural context must be taken into account, as when contemporary theology encounters music from different eras and places.

This counters Otto's notion of the religious experience as "an internalized, privatized encounter with the sacred or the numinous which may only later take the externalised forms of the social and cultural practices of institutional religion."[164] In fact, to put this in terms of music, each individual may bring to their musical experience a wealth of religious or theological beliefs, understandings and thoughts, as well as a range of musical experiences that have established musical expectations. Each person's existing beliefs and expectations have been formed in a particular social and cultural religious or musical environment, which contributes to the way in which they experience and interpret the music. Culture affects the individual's experience of music, and the music in turn affects how the individual responds to music in the future.

For Lynch there are three functions that religions may serve: social, existential/hermeneutical and transcendent functions.[165] In other words, the functions of religion are: to give people a sense of community; a set of resources and beliefs to give meaning and purpose; and a medium through which to experience God, the numinous, or the transcendent. This last function links with the first approach outlined above, in that music is understood as a revelatory experience. Lynch notes the difficulty with defining religion as serving these functions, as not everything we call religion serves all three functions at once and there is undoubtedly a cultural bias in forming such a

---

161. Ibid., 106.
162. Deacy and Ortiz, *Theology and Film*, 66.
163. Lynch, *Between Sacred and Profane*, 137.
164. Ibid., 137.
165. Lynch, *Understanding Theology and Popular Culture*, 28.

list of functions.¹⁶⁶ However, it remains interesting that music may be seen to perform some of these functions, at least for some people some of the time, but it is questionable whether they are theologically relevant as well as sociologically interesting. What is important is not whether music performs similar functions to religion in popular culture, but whether is tackles theological concerns, and is thus a theological meaning-making tool.

Lynch argues that there may be some mileage in discussing the way popular culture functions as religion, but he has three criteria he believes it must meet in order to do so: it must provide an experience of community with shared beliefs; it must provide a set of resources to live with a sense of identity, meaning and purpose; and it must provide a medium through which people are able to experience "God," the numinous, or the transcendent.¹⁶⁷ Lynch sees the role of religion as having a communal aspect, a meaning-making aspect, and an experiential transcendent aspect. Culture becomes a vehicle of transcendence, in this third function in allowing an embodied encounter with the mystery of God.

In summary, Lynch defines theology as a process of seeking answers to important or ultimate questions. The everyday is theologically significant, and exploration of it can answer theological questions. This allows for a diverse range of questions to be part of the meaning-making process in one's life, and for a range of cultural media to suggest answers. However, this understanding need not be restricted to popular music, but may be applied deliberately to music that is not normally considered to be popular, classical music. Lynch highlights that cultural resources—in this case musical resources—are a medium for theological investigation and reflection.¹⁶⁸

Kelton Cobb

Contemporary American theologian Kelton Cobb has also engaged with popular culture, though in a different way to Lynch. He has analysed popular culture through a set of key concepts, unlike Lynch who studies popular culture through a range of approaches—author-focussed, text-based, ethnographic. Cobb chooses a theological theme for each of the chapters in the second half of *The Blackwell Guide to Theology of Popular Culture*: images of God; sin and salvation; human nature; and life everlasting. Cobb, like Lynch, is much influenced by Tillich's *Theology of Culture* and he holds

---

166. Ibid., 29.
167. Ibid., 28.
168. Lynch, *Understanding Theology and Popular Culture*, 36–40.

that a study of theology and popular culture must "check in" with Tillich.[169] Despite Tillich's prejudice against popular culture, Cobb holds that the ideas and concepts of Tillich's theology are a useful point of access in discussing all forms of cultural resources, and many of his key concepts are drawn from Tillich's work.

Cobb's definition of popular culture differs from Lynch's understanding of it as the practices and resources of everyday life. Instead, he defines popular culture against "high culture," reinforcing a binary understanding of culture. This approach is evident in his approach to the Disney cartoon *Fantasia*, in which "popular culture," the cartoon form, meets "high culture," in the form of classical music.[170] The key example of this is the use of Paul Dukas's (1865–1935) "The Sorcerer's Apprentice" (1897) alongside a Mickey Mouse cartoon. For Cobb, Disney encapsulates the consumerism prevalent in popular culture, but for many it is a way of understanding their own lives in a world that sometimes bears resemblance to Disney, but often does not.

There are two assumptions on which Cobb's exploration of theology and popular culture is based: firstly that there is a loss of faith in the ability of modernity to provide lives with meaning; and secondly the disillusionment with promises of material consumption.[171] The first pessimistic assumption sets up a negative tone for approaching popular culture, and focussing on cultural resources as material objects leads to Cobb treating the media of popular culture as abstract objects rather than interactive items. Cobb's analysis of the meaning of the texts focuses on the media of popular culture as objects, rather than as interactive entities, both shaped by and shaping the individual and society. There is a level of remove between the person experiencing popular culture and the item itself: because of this, Cobb is free to interpret the texts as they stand as texts. The emphasis is thus on the word—spoken, written or sung—which is limiting in discussing music. He gives precedence to the visual and the literary. Cobb notes that "it has been suggested by some that the *idea of culture* has replaced religion as the preferred abstraction into which we have stashed our most sacred truths, the vessel into which we now place our fetishes to be guarded and revered."[172] In other words, the concept of culture is abstract, not interactive, and it is the place in which we expect to find meaning.

169. Cobb, *Blackwell Guide*, 98.

170. Ibid., 33.

171. Cobb sees this reflected in Paul Ricoeur's notion of the present as a "period of mourning for the gods who have died" which necessitates a search for meaning elsewhere, in popular culture (ibid., 24).

172. Ibid., 44.

This makes it difficult to relate Cobb's approach to music, which always has a subjective and indeterminate element: music only exists in the embodied human experience. It would be difficult to relate Cobb's two assumptions to music without a text. Cobb does discuss popular music; however, he has made much textual analysis of popular songs, often with little musical analysis. Cobb's discussion of music overlooks any analysis of the music itself, and experience of it, and focus on the lyrics, as he does in his discussion of the music of Bruce Springsteen.[173] This is evidence of his giving precedence to the linguistic. The lyrics are of importance in their own right, as the music is, but it is in the unique combination of these with music that the deepest theological meaning is to be found. Neglect of the musical analysis overlooks particular nuances that it can give to the text.

Cobb follows French philosopher Paul Ricoeur's notion that we are in mourning for the gods who have died. For Cobb, the present is "an intermediate time in which the ancient gods of morality have died of obsolescence and exhaustion."[174] Cobb's pessimistic outlook on theology suggests that existing theological truths are outdated or redundant. There are, of course, many different claims to truth in popular culture, and Cobb follows Ricoeur in proposing that these texts may be helpful. Ricoeur suggests that what is necessary in the present time of mourning is "a long recuperative wandering, a detour through the texts of our culture."[175] On such a journey, "we might discern a new way of being-in-the-world in response to a new understanding of divinity."[176] Ricoeur thus proposes taking seriously the cultural media that we produce, as it will help us to understand better our position in the world and our way of responding to God. As Gorringe and Lynch both suggest, Cobb agrees here that humans can use popular culture to better understand and to improve the way of "being-in-the-world."

Cobb suggests that resources in popular culture can help us to understand better themes or concepts which theology is concerned with. There is no discussion of Cobb's prior theological understanding, which the examples from popular culture elucidate. Cobb takes examples from popular culture on a theme, such as "spirits of escape" or "angels." For instance, in his chapter on sin, Cobb uses the example of Gothic music's[177] references to

173. Ibid., 182.
174. Ibid., 24.
175. Ibid., 24.
176. Ibid., 24.

177. Gothic music has a similar stance to Gothic literature: it deals with the macabre, the unexpected, and suffering. For Cobb, it first appeared "through the melancholic music of groups like Echo and the Bunnymen, Joy Division, The Cure, Nick Cave, and the Psychedelic Furs" (ibid., 221).

"God and devils, heaven and hell, blood, death, judgement" to tie it into his chapter, noting, "it was as if religious symbols were organs being removed from dying bodies by surgeons with limited knowledge of anatomy, who were nonetheless enthralled by the evocative, still throbbing life force they held in their hands."[178] In other words, Cobb looks for religious or theological concepts in popular culture, and explores how they are used and what meaning they convey in that context.

In another instance, Cobb takes a theological theme –that there is a theological explanation for what is wrong with the world—and attempts to draw an analogy with popular culture: "Like theology, popular culture has its lost paradise myths to help it account for the shortcomings of human life and to address the question: What went wrong?"[179] Popular culture is here involved in a meaning-making process, which Lynch has also been seen to suggest above. Cobb, however, does not suggest that exploration of these concepts could provide further theological knowledge. The religious themes that Cobb finds in popular culture may elucidate religious or theological understanding of the concepts, but Cobb often notes where they merely reflect already given theological understanding. For Cobb, it is in reflecting pre-existing theology that popular culture is theological, not in helping the development of theological understanding. There is no account of popular culture helping to discern theological truth.

In summary, Cobb's approach to popular culture is based on two pessimistic assumptions: that today's theologians no longer have faith that they will find answers in theology; and that society is disillusioned with material consumption. Cobb's work explores the way in which religious and theological themes appear in secular resources of popular culture, without suggesting that popular culture may provide answers to our theological questions. His focus on the materiality of popular culture has encouraged an engagement with cultural resources as objects, rather than as interactive entities or embodied human experiences. This contrasts with Lynch's approach, in which popular media are interpreted in relation, as people engage with them in everyday life.

It is not necessary for culture to have replaced religion for it to have truth in it. Religion and culture are not mutually exclusive, but in fact closely intertwined. Culture, or music, which is the focus of this book—is not assumed to replace religion. Rather, a holistic approach to human life is taken, understanding all aspects of human life to be potential sources of theological truth.

178. Ibid., 221.
179. Ibid., 227.

Michael Iafrate

Catholic theologian and musician Michael Iafrate uses music to re-evaluate given revelation. Iafrate notes that music can be a tool to help us reconsider, re-evaluate and develop theological thought and indeed our understanding of theology itself, its scope and authority. His theology differs from earlier accounts in attempting to gain insights from a whole genre of music, in this case, punk music, rather than music in general or specific pieces of music.[180] Like the other theologians in this approach, Iafrate is not challenging theological truths through his thought on punk music, but the way in which theology is done. He challenges the self-assured attitude of theology and, in particular, the Catholic Church's "pretension" of "system-building."[181] In this way, a genre of music can help theologians to reflect on their thought processes and assumptions.

In his essay on "staying punk" in theology, Iafrate notes that theology may benefit from some the viewpoints of punk, in particular, from its humble approach to truth. He writes, "a punk take on theology must insist that everyone has a theological voice, not only theological experts or magisterial defenders of ecclesial traditions, and that the voices of those on the margins, those often deemed "indecent," are voices to which we must attend and which we must indeed amplify."[182] The musical perspective of punk, then, allows theologians to stand back from their theology and consider its value, its shortcomings, and its potential. This may also be due to the non-musical aspects of punk, as it is well-known as the genre of political criticism. For example, in the aftermath of the 9/11 terrorist attacks in the United States, much of the political critique came out of the popular pop-punk musical genre. So by its long-standing association with critical commentary, punk is an ideal medium through which to consider different or subversive approaches to theological truth.[183]

---

180. Punk, as defined by Roger Sabin, "was/is a subculture best characterised as being part youth rebellion, part artistic statement. It had its high point from 1976 to 1979, and was most visible in Britain and America. It had its primary manifestation in music—and specifically in the disaffected rock and roll of bands like the Sex Pistols and the Clash. Philosophically, it had no 'set agenda' like the hippy movement that preceded it, but nevertheless stood for identifiable attitudes, among them: an emphasis on negationism (rather than nihilism); a consciousness of class-based politics (with a stress on 'workingclass credibility'); and a belief in spontaneity and 'doing it yourself'" (Sabin, *Punk Rock*, 2–3).

181. Beaudoin, *Secular Music and Sacred Theology*, 55–56.

182. Ibid., 53.

183. As, for example, in the criticism of George Bush's government; also in Green Day's *American Idiot* album.

Moreover, for Iafrate, "in being more humble about theology's importance, a punk approach to theology should be significantly more occasional and less concerned with being all-encompassing or systematic."[184] In other words, theology should be ready to relate to different scenarios as they arise. It recognises that the search for a universal truth in theology is always context-bound, and that those recognised truths of the past in which theologians felt assured may not stand the test of time. This recognises that revelation can only ever be partially understood, and develops over time. In this way, theology is not restricted solely to pre-existing doctrine which may not be relevant to the people's lives. Moreover, theology can look to the margins and to new voices to express their understanding of the truth of their reality.

In summary, the genre of punk music challenges the certainty of theological assumptions and doctrines through its close association with critique and empowerment of disadvantaged voices. In this way, this form of music can challenge theological assumptions and claims. Theology, in Iafrate's view, should be relevant and readily applicable to people's lives, as music often is. Punk music as a genre, for Iafrate, teaches us to have a different perspective on theology and on its claims to truth. In listening to punk, theology ought to become much more humble.

Myles Werntz

Protestant theologian Myles Werntz, co-editor of two volumes of the American pacifist John Howard Yoder's work,[185] draws on Yoder in exploring an example of when music raises theological questions without necessarily proposing answers.[186] He takes the American rock band Pearl Jam as a case study. His discussion of Pearl Jam's first album *Ten* (1991) notes that it raises theological questions about trauma, and goes on to "explore how Christian theology might endeavor to answer this question."[187] He allows music to raise the question, but gives theology the first response in offering an answer. Only then does he compare the answer offered by the music itself to the question it has raised. This is a variation of the conversational model proposed by Lynch, but gives theology precedence over music.

Werntz concludes that that Pearl Jam's music does not go far enough to meeting existing Christian theology's answers in the theology of John

---

184. Beaudoin, *Secular Music and Sacred Theology*, 56.
185. Yoder, *Non-Violence* and *Revolutionary Christianity*.
186. Beaudoin, *Secular Music and Sacred Theology*, 108–25.
187. Ibid., 108.

Howard Yoder, and therefore falls short and must be compensated by theology. Werntz writes, "As a Protestant theologian listening to Pearl Jam, this is where I must part ways with Vedder and company: grateful for the companionship and surprised by the overlap between a Christian confession and the structure of *Ten*, but recognizing that there remains material differences between how I understand violence to be overcome and the resources which *Ten* in and of itself provides."[188] Werntz does not necessarily expect comprehensive theological answers to questions raised in popular music, but acknowledges it may go some way toward proposing thoughtful responses.

It is not surprising that an album does not offer a full answer to a difficult theological question that remains a hotly debated topic in theology. However, for Werntz, the answers provided by the album are seemingly only accepted so far as they agree with his existing understanding of Christian theology's answers. He does allow the music to highlight weaknesses in the theological account: "Pearl Jam's journey exposes a particular weakness in Yoder's account . . . the need to tell stories about trauma, for this is, in part, *how* the trauma is overcome."[189] In some ways, then, in telling these stories, the music is allowed to be a corrective to theology. However, the music itself always remains secondary to pre-existing truth claims in his theology.

For Werntz, the music has more to offer by way of raising the question than by suggesting the answer. This is valuable in itself, because theology may be neglectful of issues that are raised in culture through music. Werntz notes that music may not provide answers to the questions it raises, although it may be a tool to explore them. However, Werntz does not recognize that in offering a different perspective to theology, music can challenge theology to re-evaluate its existing answers.

Gina Messina-Dysert

American feminist theologian Gina Messina-Dysert also uses music to raise particular theological questions, but is more open to the possibility that music may suggest possible answers. Her discussion of the theological meaning of suffering draws on the music of another American rock band playing in the early 1990s at the same time as Pearl Jam, Dave Matthews Band, and in particular their song "Grey Street."[190] This song goes some way toward proposing a theological answer to the question of evil and suffering. Messina-Dysert notes the inclusive nature of popular music and warns

---

188. Ibid., 123.
189. Ibid., 124.
190. From Dave Matthews Band's 2002 album *Busted Stuff* (RCA).

that limiting theology to doctrine excludes some who are struggling to find theological meaning.

Messina-Dysert believes a song can go beyond doctrinal theology for many. This takes an existing theological stance on theodicy, but considers how it might be applied to a real example through song. Of the song "Grey Street" she writes: "Because of the song's unrestricted exploration and articulation of suffering, it can act as a theological resource for women in abusive relationships."[191] The song therefore explores a particular example through which the doctrine of theodicy can be explored, without giving an existing answer, but being open to the answer being determined by the music and lyrics.

For Messina-Dysert, the song addresses questions of theodicy from a standpoint of real-life experience, without theological limitations, allowing for "momentary salvation" when suffering temporarily ceases and the victims experience "transcendence" when they "become their own liberators" through song.[192] The song thus becomes a cathartic experience, through which a person can deal with their own personal experience in comparison with another's experience told through the music, and through which theodicy can be reimagined in their own particular context. This retains an existing theological truth in the concept of theodicy, but applies it to particular contexts and individual circumstances, allowing some room for movement in its understanding.

Messina-Dysert notes the importance of the supportive framing narrative in the text of the song for those asking questions to do with suffering,[193] and she recognizes the emotional impact of the comforting feelings evoked by the song, but again attributes this to the lyrics. Messina-Dysert refers to Anthony Pinn's "nitty gritty hermeneutics," which deals with the style of music—for example rap or the blues,[194] but she does not apply it to the style of rock employed by Dave Matthews Band. Further to this, musical analysis suggests that the key of B minor and the prevalence of the B minor chord at the start—the most emphatic part—of almost every line of the song reflects the ongoing suffering.[195] It may also be the case that listening to a song that

---

191. Beaudoin, *Secular Music and Sacred Theology*, 75–89.

192. Ibid., 87–88.

193. Ibid., 86.

194. Beaudoin, *Secular Music and Sacred Theology*, 82.

195. The association of the minor key with suffering or sadness is long-standing. *The Harvard Dictionary of Music* states that the "most enduring of . . . associations, with roots in the 16th century, is that of major keys with happiness or brightness and minor keys with sadness or darkness" (Randel, *Harvard Dictionary of Music*, 443).

evokes sad feelings through a minor key is another one of the ways in which the listener stops feeling isolated, alongside the narrative.

In summary, Messina-Dysert has highlighted the ways that music can directly engage with theological questions. She has considered the impact the lyrics have on the feelings of those experiencing the music, and has therefore shown how text can be treated as an experience as well as an abstract form. This example uses the lyrics to develop a theological response to suffering, but could be developed further by considering the contribution the music makes in relation to the lyrics. In most popular music, there are words that have a great impact on the meaning of the song. There is a danger of analysing the text without paying much attention to the music. This is easily done: theology itself is word-based, and theologians are trained to interpret texts. The text often has bearing on the meaning of the music, yet it is important to remember the impact of the music, even when analysing the text, as too great a focus on the lyrics neglects the contribution of the music. This example has highlighted that it is more difficult for specific theological questions to be answered when the music does not have a text.

Jeffrey Keuss

Presbyterian theologian Jeffrey F. Keuss has encouraged engagement between theology and popular music in *Your Neighbor's Hymnal: What Popular Music Teaches Us about Faith, Hope, and Love*.[196] Keuss also offers a theological account of the relation between lyrics and music in popular music. He claims that "language that is at once particular and solid, yet transcendentally rises and falls when entwined with music, can truly subvert, challenge, strain against restriction, and ultimately embody both the presence and absence of the Sacred in all the power and the glory, all the beauty and terror, all the shouting and silence of the truly poetic."[197] In other words, language has particular meanings that can be given new and challenging nuances when combined with music. It stretches beyond itself transcendentally. This means that music is able to communicate something of God's revelation, in its simultaneous revealing and concealing, through both sound and silence.

For Keuss, it is the music that has the ability to turn a meaningful text into the "truly poetic." The music must have an effect on the meaning of the text: there would be little point in putting the words to music in the first place if the words were as effective on their own as poetry. So, granted that

196. Keuss, *Your Neighbor's Hymnal*.
197. Beaudoin, *Secular Music and Sacred Theology*, 152.

most people find that music contributes something to the lyrics and would rather listen to a song than the lyrics read out as poetry, the music must add something to the lyrics, a layer of meaning that takes the words beyond what they could mean on their own. The second part of Keuss' statement, that music can embody the Sacred—in other words, God—is not as easy to explain. Every theology of music in some way attempts to account for the mechanisms by which music can embody the sacred.

Summary

Theologies of popular culture encourage engagement with human creations as a means of developing theological knowledge and thought. Theology can seek answers to ultimate questions, indeed can seek the questions themselves, through engagement with the resources of the culture and the ways in which they are used to make meaning in the lives of many. The search for theological truth is not restricted to an area of life that can be labelled as religious. The theologies of popular culture agree that theological meaning can be found in the human creations that are prevalent in the created world.

The lyrics of popular music can pose a particular challenge to a theology of music. It is possible to focus solely on the lyrics, but this would neglect a layer of meaning nuanced by the particular musical way those lyrics are expressed. A focus on the linguistic aspect of popular music would also neglect an understanding of the embodied experience of the music, which again adds a dimension of meaning. Lyrics are useful in determining theological meaning, and they often guide music toward theological questions, as seen in the two particular examples relating to two more negative aspects of theological discussion: trauma and suffering. However, musical analysis also helps determine the meaning of a song, and the lyrics and music must be analysed together in order to discover the nuances of meaning found in the music and experience thereof.

Particular theological concepts are important in approaching popular music. I will explore the key concepts in this book in chapter 2, focusing on three key areas: how God is understood, through the concepts of *transcendence*, *revelation*, and *the sacred*; how humans understand themselves, in terms of *embodiment*. The prior understanding of each of the concepts, as well as a preliminary glimpse at the insights possible through approaching them through music, will be discussed in greater detail in the next chapter. This is not intended to be a comprehensive list of concepts that are relevant to a theology of music, but they underpin this theological approach to music.

Music, as a thoughtful medium of a developing culture, is a means of furthering humanity. It is a means of deepening knowledge of the created world and of God. Moreover, it is a tool which liberates theology from preformed conclusions, and allows it to look afresh on theological issues from the many and varied perspectives of those that make up society, especially those on the margins.

Conclusion

Music, as a human creation and as a part of human culture, is part of the way humans make and discover meaning in the world. Music is an important and unique part of the meaning-making tools of culture. Therefore, music is theology, in raising and exploring ultimate questions and allowing encounter with the divine. There is both a human aspect of creativity in culture, and God is at work in the progress of culture. In the progress of humanity through culture, the potential for deepening understanding of God is opened up.

Therefore I hold a positive stance on music as a part of human culture, hopeful of its theological potential. It is not possible to negate the influence of culture: humans cannot live in a cultural vacuum. It is an important part of human life and impacts on how people live. Theologies of popular culture remind us that it is not possible negate the influence of culture, whenever or wherever one lives. As Deacy and Ortiz remind us, there is no cultural vacuum in which theology can be studied. Not only must culture be accounted for in establishing potential biases, but, more importantly, it is a contributing factor to knowledge.

Music is a physical experience; it could not exist without the body. Therefore, theology must account for the experience of music rather than treat it as an abstract object in its written form. As a created form, music tells us about another created form, the world of God's creation. Moreover, in suspending the boundary between the human subject and divine object, music tells us something about God.

The distinction between music that is intentionally religious and music that is not, is not a determining factor in the theological value of the music, nor in music's potential for allowing encounter with the mystery of God. Music allows an already present God to be perceived. It does this by suspending the boundary between the human subject, and the object of the experience, God. If, as assumed here, all music is sacramental, it is not relevant to theology on the basis of particular qualities that it has, and therefore there is no need to make a distinction between popular and non-popular music.

All music may have theological value, regardless of its popularity or quality. Therefore, the divide between sacred and secular will not be reinforced in this book. It is not the quality of the music that is important, but the nature of music in general. Therefore, theology should not concern itself with evaluating musical quality, but the impact it has on the embodied human person and their relation to God. This negates any attempt at constructing a musical hierarchy.

A variety of approaches to music in modern theology have been explored in this chapter. The first treats the musical experience as theologically significant or revelatory and the second examines how music can be used to expound given theology. These approaches may be coherently enlightening alongside each other, although too much focus on the latter approach risks treating music as an abstract object, either in its written form or as a general concept. Music is always more than this, as it is always both embodied and particular. In a similar way, using theology as the measure by which to judge music limits the potential of music to convey revelation as it treats music as an object to be measured against an abstract form. On the other hand, too much focus on the subjective nature of interaction with music risks losing an objective basis for truth in revelation. Therefore, I suggest an approach to music which accounts for both the objectivity basis for truth and subjectivity of the musical experience in a consideration of music as theology.

Stone-Davis holds that experience of musical beauty suspends the boundary between the subject—the human—and the object—beauty. This can be developed through Schleiermacher's understanding that there must be an objective ground of religious feeling—God—in contending that musical beauty could in fact suspend the boundary between the human subject and divine object. Music unites the subject and object in a special way: it brings them together in a way that momentarily suspends the boundary between the two. It is pre-reflective and allows the subject—humans—to acquire knowledge of God, the object. Music opens up a level of reality that precedes the division into subject and object.

Music has been seen to be a useful analogy for many theological concepts, and is therefore helpful in elucidating theological arguments. For Balthasar, the analogy of the symphony helps to understand the nature of creation, which is ultimately united in one harmonic whole, but has many individual parts which each have their own role to play. God is acknowledged as the composer of the symphony, as the creator, and therefore gives purpose to each part. Another analogical use of the symphony is in understanding the nature of Jesus' divinity and humanity, a theologically challenging concept. Barth also understands creation through musical analogy, specifically through Mozart's music. Mozart, for Barth, not only helps us to understand the nature of creation, but also how to respond to it. Begbie uses music to expound his theology, but music cannot challenge theology in his thought. It does develop our understanding of concepts, however, as is evident in his exploration of the concept of time. Music, through being an affective, temporal experience, allows theologians to re-evaluate temporality theologically.

Music has a far greater theological reach than its use as an analogy, as it can be used to address particular theological questions and concerns. The indeterminate nature of meaning in music makes it a particularly helpful way for thinking about the mystery in revelation and for expressing what cannot be expressed in words about God. Theology can also re-evaluate its existing understanding through music. A whole genre of music, punk, was seen to be of use in challenging accepting theological norms in Iafrate's account. Werntz and Messina-Dysert also used particular songs to address the theological concerns of trauma and suffering. The concerns of theology are thus addressed in all areas of human life.

Theologies of popular culture have here been shown to assist a theology of music by noting the importance of the created, personal and social dimensions of music. It has also helped broaden the remit of theology to include wider meaning-making processes, and to avoid self-assured claims for truth. In doing so, it has gone some way toward deconstructing the musical hierarchy, with symphonies and operas at the top, and at the bottom, programme music, musicals and lowest of all, popular music. It is possible to base a theology of popular music on the content of the lyrics, but in doing so, potential meanings are missed which are given by the particular nuances of the music.

Music, therefore, is a sacramental medium of human culture, experienced only in embodied temporality, which allows encounter with the divine. In the discussion of music that follows, there is an emphasis on the embodied, social and contextual. Music is analysed in relation to the human subject, with particular regard to the individual's cultural and social context. In this, music is treated as an embodied experience rather than as an object.

> "I know you're in this room
> I'm sure I heard you sigh
> Floating in between
> Where our worlds collide."
>
> —Muse, "Thoughts of a Dying Atheist"

2

Embodied Encounter with God

The first chapter outlines a theology of music through an exploration of theologies that deal with culture, and in particular music, in relation to three different approaches: firstly, viewing music as a means of religious or revelatory experience, giving new knowledge; secondly, using music as an explanatory or elucidatory tool in theology to help understanding of pre-existing beliefs and ideas; thirdly, through an engagement with culture as a human creation which communicates something of God, as part of God's creation. Against this backdrop, it is necessary to explore the particular concepts through which music is theology, or, through which music allows an encounter with God.

This account of music as theology begins with embodied human existence: what it means to be human in the world, as a participant in the musical experience. This leads to discussion of the means by which embodied existence can be in encounter with God, through understanding sacramentality, transcendence, liminality, and revelation, concepts which are central to an understanding of music as theology, as they are fundamental to the way in which humans know God.

Music and Embodiment

The way in which the embodied experience of music relates to the musical form is key to understanding music as theology. The body is an essential part of human life. Humans know everything through their bodies, and therefore knowledge of God is communicated through the human body.

Moreover, God's form of communication with humans, God's self-revelation, is in human form in the incarnation. However, knowledge is often considered an abstract collection of what is known, rather than in relation to the knowing human subject. In any study of music, it is possible to discuss music in the abstract, as a score or a work, and neglect the physical experience of performing or listening to it. Any text that accompanies the music can be given precedence when discussing the meaning of the music. This overlooks the fact that music is an experience of the human body, as indeed all revelation is in embodied form.

The focus on music as explicating theological truths tends to be done at a remove from the body: it is a conceptual process that happens in thought, not body. Many musicians recognize the importance of music as a bodily experience, so it is important not to neglect this aspect of music in theological consideration.[1] Canadian feminist theologian Heidi Epstein notes that theologies of music rarely emphasize that the human body itself is a musical instrument.[2] Moreover, any experience of music is a bodily experience. All revelation is in and through embodied human life, and so it is important to recognize the particularities of the embodied experience of music in understanding music as a form of revelation.

Understanding the relationship between human embodiment and musical form is not a recent theological undertaking, however: in order to understand the relationship between music and theology in terms of embodiment, it is important to go further back into theology than ventured thus far. Saint Augustine of Hippo, writing in the late fourth and early fifth centuries, has given an influential account of the theological implications of the embodied nature of music. Augustine's thought on music continues to influence theologies of music today, such as that of Catherine Pickstock. Many of the theologians encountered in chapter 1 have outlined an account of the embodied experience of music, as in Férdia Stone-Davis's understanding of the physical experience of musical beauty. Music as a form of bodily communication with God will then be discussed with reference to the work of David Brown, as well as Clive Marsh and Vaughan S. Roberts, who have also explored the bodily nature of musical experience in theological terms,

---

1. For example, see Corness's "Musical Experience," in which he argues that humans' embodied existence ensures the body's engagement in musical experience. Sociologist of music Tia de Nora has written an account of embodied musical meaning in *Music in Everyday Life*, especially chapter 4, "Music and the Body," 75–108. Other accounts of the embodied nature of music can be found in Butler, *Bodies That Matter*; Cox, "Embodying Music"; Miell et al., *Musical Communication*, 215–37; Leman, *Embodied Music*; and Leppert, *Sight of Sound*.

2. Epstein, *Melting the Venusberg*, 122.

and have shown how important it is for a theology of music to take account of the embodied experience.

Physicality of Music

Augustine has written about his personal experience of music in *Confessions*, but has also grappled with an academic account of music in *De Musica*. In *De Musica*, Augustine is influenced by the Greek philosophers, notably Pythagoras and Plato, to impose a theory of number on to music.[3] His *Confessions*, however, give more explanation of the theological implications of music, and will be the focus of this brief introduction to his thought before turning to Pickstock's interpretation of *De Musica*.

Augustine is torn in his personal stance on music; on the one hand, he appreciates the beauty of music, and notes that it is capable of leading some to God, but on the other hand, music distracts him from God or turns itself into an idol.[4] This is evident in his writing about music in his *Confessions*.[5] Augustine was captivated by music, so much so that he was extremely wary of its potential for distraction: he noted the danger of music with a text distracting from worship, in becoming moved by the music and not the words. During worship, the sin in listening to music in worship is in being moved more by the music than by the text.[6] He was very much aware of the power of music and its bodily nature.[7]

The fact that much of the music Augustine would have encountered, particularly in the context of worship, is vocal, may account for Augustine's understanding of the embodied encounter with music, as singing is a physical action directly produced by the body.[8] Epstein notes that music becomes

---

3. The influence of Pythagorean numerology extended beyond music into other aspects of Augustine's life, such as his interpretation of the Bible (Kahn, *Pythagoras and the Pythagoreans*, 153–54).

4. In his discussion of Aquinas and music, Sander van Maas proposes that, for Augustine, music is both indispensable—because it warns the soul better than words—and dangerous—because it turns itself into an idol (Geest et al., *Aquinas as Authority*, 319).

5. In Book X of *Confessions*, Augustine praises the beauty of music and admits that he fluctuates between the peril of pleasure and approved wholesomeness.

6. Augustine, *Confessions X*, 207–52.

7. Augustine was deeply influenced by the Platonic divide between body and soul, and was thus cautious of allowing the body pleasure at the expense of the soul. The influence of Plato's dualism on Augustine's conception of the division of body and soul is explored in Pate's *From Plato to Jesus*, 236–38, and O'Daly's *Augustine's Philosophy of Mind*, 189–99.

8. The music Augustine discusses is likely to have been only vocal, as the early church

problematic for Augustine when it becomes embodied.[9] Augustine is wary of the body, when the body is in fact the primary instrument of the time. The physicality of music is problematic for Augustine, as it is all-consuming. There is no consideration in his thought that this bodily absorption in the musical experience may itself be an encounter with the divine.

For Augustine, music can, particularly for "weaker minds," be a vehicle to God, such that "by the delights of the ears the weaker minds may rise to the feeling of devotion."[10] In other words, through music, the text has a greater effect, giving those who are not moved by the music further motivation to be moved to feelings of devotion. Notably, however, for Augustine the text remains of utmost importance, not the music. Music is acceptable in supporting and endorsing a text, though, in itself, its powers should be regarded with a degree of suspicion, lest it distracts from the true focus of the text, God. Therefore, in Augustine's account, music has its uses in worship, but should be employed with a degree of restraint.[11]

In summary, Augustine recognized the bodily nature of music. He enjoyed music in worship, but feared it would distract him from any associated text, and the purpose of that text, inspiring devotion to God. As the music of his discussion was largely vocal and not instrumental, it required a text. His thought does not account for instrumental music, which was not as common at the time, particularly in the context of worship which is the focus of his discussion, partly because of suspicions about Pagan associations, and partly because of the lack of quality instruments. Augustine recognises the all-consuming nature of some bodily experiences of music that it total absorption in the music. However, he understands this as a possible distraction from God, rather than understanding the potential of this embodied moment to be an encounter with God, rather than a movement away from God.

---

was suspicious of instrumental music, having been used in pagan rituals. Instruments have also developed greatly since Augustine's time in both variety and practicality. Where music was employed in worship, it would have been monophonic singing. For a detailed account of the music Augustine would have been familiar with, including a chapter which gives a reading of Augustine's thought on music, see Stapert's *New Song*.

9. Epstein, *Melting the Venusberg*, 20.
10. Augustine, *Confessions*, xi.33.
11. Ibid., x.

A Higher Music

Catherine Pickstock[12] recommends a return to Augustinian conceptions of music, as that which holds objectivity and subjectivity in tension, and can go some way to healing the rift between arts and sciences, and, on a more universal level, between time and space. For Pickstock, music is both bodily and spiritual; it affects both the physical and the non-physical. She holds that music plays an active role in the way an individual comes to know God: "To believe the evidence of our ears is . . . to deny nihilism. Moreover, it is to believe in transcendence. More, it is to believe in the healing of time, and, therefore, sacramentally to receive the incarnation of God in his time, his passion and resurrection."[13] In other words, music is a sacramental reception of the incarnation. If this is the case, then music is undoubtedly theology.

Pickstock's account of music working sacramentally, allows some truth about God to become known. However, she follows Augustine's wariness of the physicality of music, and abstracts music from the realm of bodily experience. In her discussion of music, Pickstock shifts from a focus on physical music, to an abstract (and non-existent) metaphorical form of music, the highest form of music which is "heard" in the Eucharist. It is then but a small step to replace music in the discussion with the sacrament of the Eucharist. Therefore Pickstock turns music into a conceptual metaphor rather than a physical bodily experience. The highest form of music for Pickstock is thus no longer music. Or, as Epstein puts is, Pickstock finds a better music "outside music's body."[14] For Pickstock, the best form of music is not music at all, but a thought process that uses experience of music to conceptualise theological claims.

Augustine's thoughts on music have implications for an account of creation. Augustine held an account of creation that was *ex nihilo*.[15] In terms of music, this is applied in that musical sound comes into being, as if from nothing, and disappears again into non-being, though not necessarily non-existence. For Pickstock, it is the relationship between silence and sound which resembles the Christian understanding of this nothingness as

---
12. Catherine Pickstock is one of the key contributors to the Radical Orthodoxy school of thought that appeared in the 1990s which rejects modern secularism and seeks to revive traditional doctrine. Her work on music draws heavily on Augustine's thought, and is found in "Music: Soul, City and Cosmos after Augustine" in Milbank et al., *Radical Orthodoxy*.

13. Milbank et al., *Radical Orthodoxy*, 269.

14. Epstein, *Melting the Venusberg*, 97.

15. Augustine, *Confessions*, xi.11–30, xii.7–9.

performing an ontological role, whence creation proceeds.[16] For Augustine, silence has cosmological properties, a concept which Pickstock would like to see revitalised, particularly in its ability to reflect and explore the Christian notion of creation. Pickstock holds with Augustine that, because this universe was created out of nothing, because "human beings are situated within a universe which springs from nothing," there is potential for human creativity that allows new creations.[17] In other words, human creations are indeed authentic creations. They must, however, acknowledge the nothingness at their source.

Pickstock holds that there is an objective proportion to the beauty of music, but that appreciation of this is subjective.[18] For her, "Meaning, therefore, is seen to be the *world's* meaning, and yet, at the same time, our *own* meaning."[19] These are claims for a universal meaning of music as well as an individual meaning. In Pickstock's account, then, there is an objective basis to musical beauty, which she relates, like Augustine, to proportion, which itself is closely related to form. She also notes that there is subjectivity in the appreciation of this objective form.

Pickstock notes that Augustine allows for a degree of subjective judgement by the fact that we stand within the universe that is measured, and our judgement is therefore inherently limited. She notes that heavenly bodies constitute, for Augustine, the supreme harmony and the measure of that supreme harmony.[20] Music relates to the universe in that it, too, "is at once a thing measured and the measure itself."[21] By contrast, rather than music being the measure and the thing to be measured, for Balthasar the Christ-form takes on this role, which is the ultimate measure of revelation in being God's definitive self-revelation, and is also the form against which all other worldly forms can be measured. In revealing anything of their form, in their proximity to it, worldly forms are ultimately revealing the Christ-form. As such, Pickstock notes then, to "measure music means no more than to sound our right note which no other can sound and which then forms part of the cosmic poem which is its own best measure."[22] This implies that it is only by producing music which in coherent with the whole of creation that one

---

16. Milbank et al., *Radical Orthodoxy*, 247.
17. Ibid., 248.
18. Ibid., 268–69.
19. Ibid., 268–69.
20. Ibid., 258.
21. Ibid., 255.
22. Ibid., 258.

is able to measure music. The meaning of music is only found in a holistic approach to the whole of the created universe, of which humanity is a part.

Augustine's understanding of music as embodied has been seen to influence Pickstock's contemporary theology. Pickstock's account, whilst highlighting the importance of the bodily nature of musical experience, through conceptualising a "higher" or better form of music than that which is physical, in fact reinforces the divide between music in the abstract, and physically experienced music. It neglects Augustine's feeling that music penetrates the body[23] and seeks a form of music that is no longer enfleshed but exists only conceptually and in abstraction in the Eucharist.

Dimensions of Embodiment

Two recent theological accounts express the importance of embodiment in music, but relate it differently to the musical form: Marsh and Roberts, and Stone-Davis. Marsh and Roberts point to different aspects of bodily experience and, like Pickstock, attempt to transcend the physicality of music, and conceive of a social, symbolic and metaphorical body affected by music. Their movement from the individual body, to the social body, and beyond, is a movement toward the abstract and non-physical, rather than an affirmation of the bodily experience of music. For Stone-Davis, however, every musical experience is grounded in the bodily. The body may encounter a non-physical object—for Stone-Davis, the objective form of beauty—in music, but music always remains a bodily experience.

Marsh and Roberts note the importance of human bodily experience to meaning-making in popular music.[24] Their account includes different bodily dimensions, drawing on social outlook of theologies of popular culture. For them, it is important to acknowledge that "Human experience and thought is acquired in and through our embodied form."[25] In other words, human knowledge is acquired through our bodies. Marsh and Roberts develop the notion of embodiment beyond the physical body of one individual, to account for different physical and non-physical dimensions of embodiment.

---

23. Epstein reads this in sexual terms: she holds that music is a temptation, like women, to Augustine. For her, keeping music in its place is analogous to keeping women in their place: subservient—to a text in music—and virtuously pure—or free from dissonance (Epstein, *Melting the Venusberg*, 57).

24. Marsh and Roberts, *Personal Jesus*, xiii.

25. Ibid., 60.

For Marsh and Roberts, the incarnation is the basis of a sacramental account of music: "To adopt a sacramental approach to the material world and to human culture means, then, to take the example of God's incarnation as celebrated in the theology and practice of sacraments and apply it to the rest of life."[26] To take the incarnation as fundamental to theology, and apply it to reality as humans live it, leads to a sacramental account of all things, music included. God has already given the ultimate example of the importance of the body, which is reaffirmed in the sacraments: therefore, sacramental bodily experiences that continue to acknowledge the importance of the body to all humans in bringing the human body into encounter with the divine.

However, Marsh and Roberts go on to undermine the importance of the physicality of the sacramental experience in their development of their claim to various aspects of bodily experience. The body is not one-dimensional for Marsh and Roberts: "Not only is the body a complex biological organism; it is also a multifaceted social and symbolic phenomenon."[27] It has "four dimensions: (1) the *physical* body; (2) the *social* body; (3) the *symbolic* body; and (4) the *metaphorical* body."[28] The first two categories indicate that music is an individual or personal bodily experience, but it can also be a collective embodied experience. However, their last two categories attempt to transcend usual understandings of embodied musical experience, taking it up into abstract concepts: "the symbolic body describes songs where the body is an analogy or to describe something else in terms of similarity, while the metaphorical body describes something else in terms of dissimilarity."[29] The musical experience starts with the body, but moves beyond it. This is similar to Pickstock's account of the highest form of music, which is no longer physical music. The direction of these four bodily concepts, alongside Marsh and Roberts's understanding of transcendence, that the "*physicality of transcendence . . .* [is a] way music can transport people out of themselves,"[30] suggests an outward movement from the personal individual embodied experience, through collective embodied experience, transcending these to abstract forms of the body. In this way Marsh and Roberts also disconnect musical experience from the bodily.

This division is further reinforced with the concept of "affective space"—a conceptual space. The experience of evaluating the sacred can be

26. Ibid., 33.
27. Ibid., 74.
28. Ibid., 59–60.
29. Ibid., 67.
30. Ibid., 82.

understood to be working in an "affective space," an intangible space given over to one's "inner life." This includes one's conception of the sacred. Marsh and Roberts believe there to be an "affective space" in which music works: they qualify this, stating that this means "any practice or activity that entails significant emotional engagement, through which a person can be shown to be doing more than just enjoying the moment."[31] The affective space is the space in which the "doing more" takes place.

Whilst Marsh and Roberts recognize the importance of the body, their understanding of musical workings is largely conceptual: spiritual development through music occurs in the non-physical realm of affective space rather than in the body. Music begins as a physical experience, but transcends that into a social, symbolic and metaphorical experience, which is where theological meaning is primarily found.

Physical Experience of Music

An account of the embodied form of music which affirms the bodily and does not strive to go beyond it is found in Stone-Davis's thought. For her, the physicality of music is a quality that is inseparable from the music itself: when she speaks about music, it is the physical, bodily experience of music, not music in an abstract written form. It is because of its physical character that music has the ability to suspend the barrier between the subject and object, that was discussed in relation to beauty: "the physical character of musical experience discloses a first-order mode of being, one that involves a suspension of the distinction between subject and object (promoting instead their mutuality) or, rather, a retrieval of the pre-reflective moment before this distinction asserts itself."[32] This account of the musical experience is similar to Schleiermacher's understanding of intuition and religious feeling, which he holds to be stirred easily by music.

The ability to become absorbed in the physical experience of the music momentarily suspends the division between the person and the music, it involves what for Stone-Davis is a mode of attention that makes one temporarily unaware that the music is external to oneself, and, in this way, suspends the divide between subject and object: "music creates a certain mode of attention that is pre-reflective."[33] Like Schleiermacher, this is a subconscious effect rather than achieved by conscious thought. For Stone-Davis, this is something that is particular to music, or that music is particularly

---

31. Ibid., 16.
32. Stone-Davis, *Musical Beauty*, 158–59.
33. Ibid., 162.

effective at achieving. Music affects the feelings for Schleiermacher, whilst it affects the bodily mode of attention for Stone-Davis.

It is when the music engages the someone, rather than when they make a conscious decision to listen to the music, that the boundary between human subject and object is suspended. "Music's physicality arrests and sustains our attention. It encourages a focus on that which is other than ourselves and thereby promotes an interweaving of subject and object, an attunement between the two (in fact an already existing mutuality)."[34] In other words, it is precisely because it is a physical experience that music can create a pre-reflective moment, which may be a moment of "doing" theology. By focusing on the "other," or God, and in doing so attuning the person and God, music allows an encounter between human and divine which reveals that pre-existing mutuality.

This relationship is characterised by its indeterminate nature. It is this which makes it difficult to describe in words. Stone-Davis argues that this is not making a claim for music going beyond human experience, or for transcending the physical. She writes, "This model does not call for a transcendence of the physical for music is inherently indeterminate and cannot articulate any one particular avenue of meaning.[35]" Instead the physical body of the human encounters God, through the pre-reflective suspension of the boundary between subject and object, in the physical experience of the music. Music's intrinsic indeterminacy might be a helpful feature in allowing an experience of God which is not bound by the traditional linguistic forms.

Music is a physical experience. If the musical form is related to embodiment through ever more abstract concepts, of the social body to the metaphorical body, music is removed from its physical experience and is no longer understood in terms of the impact it has on the embodied person. When embodiment relates to musical form through the concept of the individual self, the power of music is evident in the way in which the physical body interacts with the musical form. Through engagement with the music, or absorption in it, the individual is drawn into a liminal pre-reflective experience in which the boundary between the human subject and the divine object is suspended. This experience is inherently indeterminate and may not be expressible in words, which is both a gift and challenge to theology.

---

34. Ibid., 189.
35. Ibid., 159.

God's Incarnation

The recognition of the importance of the bodily experience of music is ultimately founded on incarnational theology, grounded in Christology: the self-revelation of God is in human form. None of the experiences discussed in this book could happen if it were not for the fact that humans are bodily, physical beings. Revelation is thus in and through embodied human life, and music is an important embodied form of revelation.

Christian theologians cannot explore the meaning of human embodiment without considering Jesus as a human, God in human form. Jesus' incarnation plays an important role in theological understanding of embodiment. God's self-revelation in a human body encourages a positive account of the human body. Brown also writes "God's pre-eminent form of communication is seen to lie in a particular human body and it is its interaction with other human bodies (including one's own) that constitutes humanity's way to salvation."[36] In other words, God communicates primarily through one specific body, Jesus, to other human bodies. Jesus' body is not less physical than other human bodies, as it is Christian belief that the paradox of the incarnation lies in Jesus' being both fully human and fully God.

Brown argues that some contemporary sacramental theologies do too much to exclude God: he writes that this approach seems "to make the divine presence altogether too extraneous to our world, as though it has always to be searched for, rather than being already there, deeply embedded in our world in virtue of the fact that God is the creator of all that is."[37] In Brown's sacramental account, God is present in the music of everyday life. Music, as a sacramental form, makes God knowable.

Brown understands all human communication to occur through the body: if we are to communicate with God in any way, it is through our bodies.[38] Further, Brown suggests that we must consider what "space" is left for God, concluding, "One way of making that space would be to say that bodies can at least sometimes point beyond themselves, that they are open to the possibility of transcendence."[39] If bodies point beyond themselves, in striving to communicate with God, it must be through the bodily experience that humans encounter God. Music as a bodily experience points beyond

---

36. Brown, *God and Grace of Body*, 12.
37. Ibid., 12.
38. Ibid., 11.
39. Ibid., 12.

itself, and is thus an effective tool in this regard, being a liminal form, which allows for the possibility of transcendence.

Although Brown acknowledges the importance of embodiment in the music experience, he too believes there is a musical dimension that is beyond the bodily. Brown writes, "there is always the ethereal and the material working together, the apparently disembodied sound supported by total commitment in bodily movements and reactions."[40] The terms "apparently disembodied" are interesting here, as music itself can never be disembodied. It is possible, though, that the physical experience of music may evoke such a sense of disembodiment.

The body is the starting point of human attempts at communicating with God, as well as God's definitive form of communication with humans in Jesus' incarnation. Brown notes that the "Gospel's insistence upon the Empty Tomb indicates the perceived indispensability of a body to the Risen Christ."[41] The body is integral to Jesus, as it is to all humans. It is the means through which God is known to humans. As Brown noted, human creativity, of which music is a significant form, is the primary means by which humans attempt to encounter God. God as creator is made known in all created things in the world. Therefore, in understanding the created things of the world, there is connection between humans and God.

For Brown, music is a bodily experience. All human communication is through the body, including all aspects of the relationship with God. God has established a bodily form of human communication through the incarnation of Jesus, and the human body is in this way shown to be an integral part of knowing God. Not only is God's revelation in the form of the human body, but it is through the body that humans reach out to God, in human creativity. Music falls into this category.

Summary

The body is God's primary means of communicating with humans, as shown through God's own self-revelation through incarnation. Humans encounter God in their bodily experience: the body is the means through which humans acquire theological knowledge. Without a body, there is no musical experience. However, the way in which the body relates to musical form differs generally across musical styles and eras. Moreover, whilst all musical experience is situated in the body, it is in the relation of a particular body to a particular musical form that the nature of the musical experience is

---

40. Ibid., 219.
41. Ibid., 17.

determined. Embodiment is an important concept, then, in discussing musical experience, and a proper account of the embodied experience prevents an analysis of music solely in abstraction. The way in which the body relates to the musical form is through its physicality: bodily music arrests our attention, which is fundamental to experiencing the liminal pre-reflective suspension of the boundary between humans and God. The possibility of encounter between humans and God is found in the physical experience of music.

Sacramentality

An account of humans knowing God through the created world stems from a conviction of the sacramentality of all things in the world. In terms of music, sacramentality does not only apply to so-called "sacred music," or music with a religious intent, intended to be used in religious context, which often makes use of existing religious forms, and therefore expounds given theology. The concept of "sacred music" reinforces the unnecessary divide between sacred and secular treats, and encourages theological understanding of music as an object rather than an experience. An account of the sacramentality of music makes the concept of the sacred obsolete, as all of creation will be seen to be connected to God in a sacramental way, including human creations.

The Sacred

The sacred is that which is connected with God, and "sacred music" is a term that may be used to describe explicitly religious music. Sacred music intentionally seeks to connect with God. This music often uses the traditional religious forms of the religious institutions. In other words, sacred music uses pre-existing sacred forms, such as the mass, the requiem, or religious scriptures in Bible passages, prayers, and psalms.

Theologians may be tempted to look only to sacred music to discover music which conveys theological meaning. For example, Jeremy Begbie's *Theology, Music and Time*, primarily takes into consideration sacred music, or music through which the composer's intention was to reflect their religious belief. Such theological understanding of music is also evident in the approach of two edited collections on theology and music: Martin V. Clarke's *Music and Theology in Nineteenth-Century Britain*, which is an example of such a theological approach: hymns, oratorios, and modern parables are discussed, but no mention is made of music that is not explicitly Christian, and *Music and Theology: Essays in Honour of Robin A. Leaver* edited by Daniel Zager, which has a broader range of sacred music, from hymns and chorales to church cantatas, but only contains religious music.

Theologies of popular culture tend to move beyond a binary opposition of sacred and secular. Lynch's theology of popular culture allows all forms of music to answer theological questions. However, for Lynch there is not necessarily an objective grounding to these answers: they are truthful only as they are culturally relevant. Lynch's sacred, then, is a social construct which does not have a basis in revelation. The sacred is that which people believe to be a timeless reality, and therefore exerts a claim over people's lives.[42] For Lynch, the context within which the sacred is not only experienced, but also constructed and adapted, is of great importance to the meaning of the sacred object. For Lynch the profane is an evil which threatens the sacred, but is not everything that is not sacred. There is a third dimension, which is the "mundane," or, the logics, practices and spaces of everyday life.[43]

Whilst the notion that there is no objective truth in that which exerts a claim over people's lives is potentially problematic to theologians, Lynch's understanding of the importance of mundane parts of culture is significant to an understanding of music as theology. Lynch holds that "if we think in terms of religion and the sacred through lived cultural resources and practices, this will help to dissolve the unhelpful distinction of religion *and* popular culture."[44] If a distinction is made between religion and cultural resources, "it fails to recognize the role of the mundane in the construction of the sacred."[45] The value of such an understanding of the sacred is that the experience of a timeless reality, which might be named God, evidently might occur through cultural resources without recourse to the usual forms of religion. Moreover, particularly important in a world of cultural and religious pluralism, it "allows for the possibility of different competing and complementary sacred objects to function at the same time within a given cultural system."[46] In other words, two piece of music may be perceived to be contradictory, and yet they may both allow experience of that timeless reality.[47] Indeed, music is particularly good at holding contradiction and paradox in unresolved yet meaningful tension.

---

42. Lynch, *On the Sacred*, 26.
43. Lynch, *Sacred in the Modern World*, 28.
44. Lynch, *Between Sacred and Profane*, 163.
45. Ibid., 136.
46. Ibid., 139.
47. This may be allowed under accounts of revelation such as Brown's, discussed

Lynch highlights the importance of acknowledging the social aspect of sacred forms, and that the cultural resources, through which people experience a timeless reality named by theologians as God, are changeable, not universal, and are influenced by the cultural context in which it was created. This means that there is no set form of so-called "sacred" music, but all music might be considered to be sacramental. For Lynch, there is no objective basis for the sacred: it is a changeable construct of society, which is problematic for theologians making claim to an encounter with God through experience of cultural creations. However, understanding revelation as a temporal process which is by necessity incomplete and aspectival would allow for the timeless reality perceived in music to be understood as encounter with God.

From this account of popular culture, we can learn that what people understand to be sacred is context- and culture-bound: one's understanding of what is sacred, and therefore what can allow encounter with God, is influenced by the society in which one lives. Lynch's account of sacred recognises the role of the mundane in such encounters, which allows encounter with that timeless reality that is God to occur without recourse to the usual religious forms. Indeed, any musical form might allow for encounter with such a truth that exerts a claim over one's life.

Therefore, an account of how all music may allow people to connect with God is better understood through the notion of the sacramental, rather than the sacred. The range and diversity of music allows for a plurality of forms to offer encounter with a timeless reality theologians name God. These forms may complement or contradict one another, but in order to allow humans to connect with God, these forms must ultimately have one objective source—God.

The distinction between sacred and secular music encourages the treatment of music as an object in the abstract, as a musical form, rather than as an embodied experience. Music which does not adopt a traditional religious form and yet allows encounter with a timeless reality may take any mundane form. This music, then, is sacramental, in allowing encounter with God, which then exerts a claim over one's life. This does not preclude sacred music from being sacramental, but allows the possibility of revelation through all forms of music.

---

above, which hold that music can only ever reveal one aspect of God, and different forms of revelation may therefore provide difference accounts.

The Sacramental

The sacramental is that which reveals the otherwise hidden: a sacrament is an outward sign of an invisible grace. The Catholic Church has seven sacraments ordained by Jesus Christ, which convey God's grace through given forms.[48] The term sacramental better accounts for human experience of music as revelatory. Music is sacramental by allowing an otherwise impossible encounter with God through God's grace. There is no division of music into sacred and secular, as all music can be sacramental.

Tillich had a positive understanding of the sacramental: "Objects which are vehicles of the divine Spirit become sacramental materials and elements in a sacramental act."[49] Any object, for Tillich, can become a vehicle of the divine Spirit. Several recent theologies of music, written from within a variety of Christian perspectives, consider the sacramental quality of music, notably those of Albert L. Blackwell, David Brown, and Tom Beaudoin.[50] They move away from understanding music in terms of sacred forms, to allow for all genres and types of music to play a sacramental role. This represents an underlying change: these theologians no longer treat music as an object to be analysed, but explore the sacramental experience of music. For Tillich music can be the vehicle of the ultimate concern without claiming ultimacy for itself.[51] As the music is the vehicle, rather than the sacred object, the same music can lead in different directions for different people. Catholic theologian Tom Beaudoin writes "these symbols and experiences can still manage to convey that which is really of God even though they are not themselves sacraments: God can be encountered through the most common of experiences."[52] In other words, the music is sacramental because it allows an encounter with God.

---

48. Chapman, *Catechism of the Catholic Church*, §1210.

49. Tillich, *Systematic Theology III*, 120.

50. Albert L. Blackwell, a Protestant theologian brought up in the Baptist tradition, has proposed a sacramental theology of music in his book, *The Sacred in Music*. Anglican theologian David Brown proposes a sacramental account of music in his work *God and Grace of Body*, though the background to this theology of revelation is found in *Tradition and Imagination* and *Discipleship and Imagination*. Catholic theologian Tom Beaudoin also takes a sacramental approach to music. His early work *Virtual Faith* began exploring the sacramental uses of music within this generation. Beaudoin's theology is evident in *Secular Music and Sacred Theology*, wherein the sacramental theology of music encompasses a wide and eclectic range of styles and genres. Christian Scharen's chapter explores a particular sacramental approach to a theology of music.

51. Tillich, *Systematic Theology I*, 13.

52. Marsh and Roberts, *Personal Jesus*, 34.

Brown's theology follows this sacramental form. He writes that "certain features of music help an already present God to be perceived."[53] In other words, music is sacramental as it allows an otherwise impossible encounter with God to occur. For Brown, "music can help break down the barriers between the invisible world of the divine and our own."[54] Music, as a feature of the world, suspends the boundary between human and divine. Music is an enactment, not just a score. For Brown, music "is so designed that, as with the eucharist, the original experience can be re-enacted as God's presence in our midst once more made known."[55] Music is, for Brown, a physical act of experiencing God, which can be re-enacted, as can all things sacramental. This raises the potential for further investigation into the role of memory in the sacramental experience.

Marsh and Roberts highlight the understanding of music as sacramental in contemporary theology and draw on Brown and Beaudoin, as well as philosopher James K. A. Smith, whose work crosses into theology and cultural criticism.[56] For Marsh and Roberts "a sacramental theology provides the basis for any aspect of popular culture's becoming a channel of the self-revelation for God, or of the grace of God."[57] For them, the experience of listening to popular music becomes a vehicle of making God known to an individual. Marsh and Roberts note that in Brown's theology "To adopt a sacramental approach to the material world and to human culture means, then, to take the example of God's incarnation as celebrated in the theology and practice of the sacraments and apply it to the rest of life."[58] In other words, drawing on Brown, the incarnation is the exemplar form of the sacramental. It is significant that the incarnation is God in embodied form, and that all human relations with God are through bodies.

Summary

The concept of sacred in music, or "sacred music," limits the potential for theological engagement with music. The concept of sacred music objectifies music, and leads to treating it in the abstract as a conveyor of given theological truths, already expressed in the existing religious form. Instead I have drawn on Brown's sacramental account of music, as well as Blackwell

53. Brown, *God and Grace of Body*, 237.
54. Ibid., 237.
55. Ibid., 247.
56. Marsh and Roberts, *Personal Jesus*, 32–37.
57. Ibid., 37.
58. Ibid., 33.

and Beaudoin, which insist that there must be an objective source of truth in order for music to connect to God. In functioning sacramentally, music reveals the invisible God: music allows an encounter with the divine through God's grace in revelation. In other words, music makes the already revealed God knowable. To take the exemplary form of God's revelation, the incarnation, and the sacrament which is drawn from this theology, the Eucharist, and apply it to the rest of human life, allows an understanding of culture as sacramental. This prevents a compartmentalisation of life into that which is religious or secular, and otherwise. It takes a holistic approach to human existence and revelation. The connection with God through sacramental experience of music is the ongoing process of revelation at work in and through human musical creations.

Knowing God: Revelation

Revelation is given by God, but is known in a variety of different ways by humans. It is thus always has an objective source, but is also a subjective experience. The account of the balance between objectivity and subjectivity varies in theological accounts, and this has implications for whether music can be allowed as revelation. Two general understandings can be conceived as either as revelation from above, as it comes from God and is revealed to humans, or as revelation from below, coming from the human search for the divine through human experience. These two approaches to revelation are not mutually exclusive. Different accounts of revelation also vary in the understanding of revelation as a complete or ongoing process. Some place more emphasis on the existing body of revelation, whether that is in scripture, tradition or in the person of Jesus Christ, whilst others emphasize the ongoing nature of revelation. This also has implications for an understanding of music's revelatory potential.

The understanding of revelation with an emphasis on the subjective, as a human process of searching for and developing understanding of God, fits the first approach from the chapter 1 of understanding musical experience as revelatory of knowledge of God. The understanding of revelation with an emphasis on the objective uses music to explain given revelation: there is an existing objective truth which is already fully revealed and expounded by music.

Top-Down Revelation

Balthasar understands that God is revealed once and for all in the incarnation of Jesus, the objective form of revelation. In revelation through the incarnation, God perfects creation through a form that surpasses all of creation: "By not crushing and surpassing the form of the world with his revelation, but, rather, by taking it up and perfecting it, God honours his creature, honours himself in it as its Creator."[59] Creation is perfected in one form, the Christ-form.

Worldly objects can only be revelatory insofar as they replicate or re-present this form of God's revelation, the Christ-form. This form reveals God's beauty, and therefore, for Balthasar, beauty is a means of revelation. Beauty is a transcendental and is therefore inextricably linked with the good and the true.[60] Revelation only occurs because of the grace of God, because God chose to reveal God in the incarnation. All revelation is therefore through Christ, the *Gestalt*, or form, of God on earth.

For Balthasar, revelation is objective, given by God in the form of Jesus Christ, and the only differential is human ability to discern it. All revelation must conform to the archetype of revelation, the Christ-form, or else it is not revelation, and as such one has a duty to share it with the church for the benefit of others. Balthasar writes "regardless of how personal the individual has felt his experience to be, he must nevertheless deprive himself of it for the sake of the Church; he must pass it on even if this should at times seem to him a sort of profanation."[61] Revelation is not for the individual, but for the church, and must conform to given revelation. Thus, if revelation must conform to the archetype, revelation outside of the church can rarely, if ever, challenge the church's understanding of God. On Balthasar's understanding, music must therefore replicate the Christ-form in order to be revelatory.

For Balthasar, there is no one form of Christian truth to which the Christian can have access. As we have seen, Balthasar uses the musical analogy of the symphony to describe his understanding of truth. He writes that "Sym-phony by no means implies a sickly sweet harmony lacking all tension. Great music is always dramatic: there is a continual process of intensification, followed by a release of tension at a higher level."[62] Like a symphony, despite the differences and tensions within Christianity, there is a higher unity, represented by the symphony itself. There is an objective

---

59. Balthasar, *Glory of the Lord*, 303.
60. Ibid., 9.
61. Ibid., 414.
62. Balthasar, *Truth is Symphonic*, 15.

truth beyond the disharmony. This approach to music allows it to explicate given truths. In this case, Balthasar is developing understanding about the created world through the analogy of music.

Not only is the Christ-form the ultimate form of revelation for Balthasar, but it is also the archetype of the human relation with God. "The Christological form as such is, absolutely, the form of the encounter between God and man [sic]."[63] Christ's experience of God is, for Balthasar, the archetype of human experience of relationship to God; "Christ is the archetypal relationship of man [sic] to God, a relationship measured only by itself, and he is this as a true historical man."[64] Even Balthasar allows for some differentiation in revelation, however, writing "In his revelation, God performs a symphony, and it is impossible to say which is richer: the seamless genius of his composition or the polyphonous orchestra of Creation that he has prepared to play it."[65] God's revelation, through being played on the different "instruments" of creation, sounds differently and is not therefore an unchanging revelation to human perception. Only the manner of performance changes: it remains a united whole: "The unity of the composition comes from God."[66] Revelation is already created by God, then, and always united in itself, but expressed differently through creation. Creation, or the created world, has a role to play in revelation. However, there remains one ultimate form of revelation, the Christ-form, in whose incarnation God is revealed once and for all.

Balthasar allows human subjectivity a place in his understanding of revelation, though it remains focused on given revelation, but as we have seen, Barth's account goes much further in widening the gap between God's reality and human experience. Barth's early account of revelation is given by God; the initiative has been taken by God. There is, in Barth's early work, a strong condemnation of culture, in that it fails to tell humans anything about God.[67] God transcends everything that is worldly, and thus is inaccessible except through God's own reaching out through given forms of revelation. Here, Barth is following the thought of Kierkegaard. In his later work, however, Barth engages more with culture, in particular through Mozart's music, and suggests that it may reflect the fundamental truths of

---

63. Balthasar, *Glory of the Lord*, 303.
64. Ibid., 305.
65. Balthasar, *Truth is Symphonic*, 8.
66. Ibid., 9.
67. Jessica DeCou, however, draws on Barth in her theology of popular culture in *Playful, Glad, and Free*, which focuses on television.

God's creation.[68] However, human efforts at cultural creations remain distant from the reality of God.

Bottom-Up Revelation

Some accounts of revelation place more emphasis on the human search for and understanding of God, emphasising the subjectivity of the self in encountering the objective revelation of God. For Schleiermacher, revelation is where an individual receives new knowledge, and is not immediately subsumed by the church's archetype of revelation. Schleiermacher's account of revelation in the *Speeches* may be understood from a "bottom-up" perspective: for him, revelation is when something new is revealed to an individual human: "What is revelation? Every original and new intuition of the universe is one."[69] Each person's human experience is thus important in this form of revelation.

Tillich's understanding of revelation is drawn from Schleiermacher's account. It is related to his understanding of the sacred in that, as we saw, he believes resources do not have to be "holy" or religious to be sacred. He holds that everything that he calls "secular" is potentially sacred, and that there is movement between the two categories.[70] The world of culture, he holds, can tell us something of reality, and can therefore be revelatory.

Tillich highlights two possible ways in which culture can reveal something of the truth of reality, through a scientific and an artistic approach. These approaches form two basic functions of culture: the cognitive function and the aesthetic function. Whilst they are not restricted to particular realms of creativity, the cognitive function is likely to be found in the realm of scientific creativity, and the aesthetic function is more likely to be found in artistic creativity. For Tillich, truth is a meeting of the subject and object. As Tillich notes, "the knowledge of revelation can be received only in the situation of revelation, and it can be communicated—in contrast to ordinary knowledge—only to those who participate in this situation."[71] The aesthetic allows this encounter to take place, and therefore it can be revelatory.

Tillich maintains, however, that answers to these questions of ultimate concern come mostly from religious tradition, and not from culture. As Lynch understands it, however, Tillich opens up the possibility of culture

---

68. Barth, *Church Dogmatics III*:3, 298–99.
69. Schleiermacher, *On Religion*, 49.
70. Tillich, *Systematic Theology I*, 218.
71. Ibid., 129.

"shaping our understanding of existence."[72] In other words, Tillich brings the idea that truth can be found in the meeting of subject and object, and allows the potential for culture to contribute to this.

In Tillich's view, the aesthetic function—a piece of music—is a mirror which reflects encountered reality, and is therefore a fragment of a universe of meaning: it is part of the greater reality. It is not without ambiguities, though, as although the aesthetic function aims to express "qualities of being which can only be grasped by artistic creativity," there is a tension between the expression and the expressed, caused by the oscillation between reality and unreality.[73] Tillich thus acknowledges different ways in which knowledge of the world is revealed to humans, and suggests that some aspects of the truth might only be possible through experience of certain aesthetic forms.

Truth, for Tillich, is an encounter of the mind and world, and is thus an expression of that which is otherwise hidden. Overcoming the gap between the subject and the object is what we call truth in Tillich's view. Thus, in bridging this gap, the aesthetic forms of culture can be revelatory of otherwise hidden truth.[74] If this is so, with Tillich's belief that the "knowledge of revelation, directly or indirectly, is knowledge of God,"[75] then the aesthetic can reveal truth in knowledge of God. This contrasts with Balthasar's understanding of revelatory truth, which for him, must come through God's revelation in the Christ-form. For Tillich, there is no particular form that is necessary; revelation is a meeting of subject and object. This is particularly relevant to music which brings together the human subject and divine object in a way that temporarily suspends the boundary between the two.

Tillich notes, "nothing is excluded from revelation in principle because nothing is included in it on the basis of special qualities."[76] For this reason, "almost every type of reality has become a medium of revelation somewhere."[77] It is not the form of that reality that denotes whether it is a mode of revelation, but the qualities it has which "determine the direction in which a thing or event expresses our ultimate concern and our relation to the mystery of being."[78] In allowing every type of reality to become a

---

72. Lynch, *Understanding Theology and Popular Culture*, 102–3.
73. Tillich, *Systematic Theology III*, 62–65.
74. Ibid., 64.
75. Tillich *Systematic Theology I*, 131.
76. Ibid., 118.
77. Ibid., 118.
78. Ibid., 118.

medium of revelation, this allows all eras of music a place, regardless of the form that music takes.

Favourable Conditions for Revelation

David Brown's approach mediates the top-down and bottom-up approaches: God is already revealed, but revelation only occurs through human encounter with God. In order for musical revelation to communicate some truth about the reality of God, it must have an objective basis. However, it is also evidently subjective where it meets human experience. Brown accounts for revelation in hoping to understand how "features of the music help to communicate the presence of a God who is already there waiting to be experienced."[79] God's presence is a given, and God has already made possible the revelation. Brown notes, "it is not that God is forced upon anyone. Rather, it is a matter of favourable conditions being set under which experience of the divine does at least become a realistic possibility."[80] In other words, it is not particular qualities of a piece of music that allow for revelation, but the qualities of music in general, that allow for the prospect of revelation.

For Brown, music is one aspect of the necessarily fragmentary nature of revelation. More importantly, music can never wholly reveal God: "The partial character of all such musical experience seems . . . in no way to count against its veridical character. God could never in any case be experienced in his totality."[81] Revelation through music can only ever reveal aspects of God. All music is able to play some role in this revelation, as Brown notes that the human urge to deepen contact with God will permeate all forms of human creativity, of which music is one form. Music is not unique in terms of revelation, then, as all forms of revelation only reveal fragments of God's total revelation. Even different musical experiences allow for different aspects to be revealed: "inevitably, different aspects [of God] will be encountered through different types of musical performance."[82] Thus all forms of music may be revelatory and may reveal different partial truths of God.

Music, as one of many sources of revelation, should be brought into relation with other forms: "the ideal should be to allow all available sources of knowledge of God to interact, and not automatically to assume the absolute

---

79. Brown, *God and Grace of Body*, 222.
80. Ibid., 293–94.
81. Ibid., 222.
82. Ibid., 222.

priority of one over all the others."[83] The many sources of theological knowledge should be brought together for more complete knowledge about God, including scripture and tradition, which might be a source of knowledge of God, but for Brown they do not have absolute priority over other texts. No singular source of revelation has access to the complete truth of revelation. Therefore, revelation through music can add to and challenge existing forms of revelation.

Summary

It is evident that revelation is both God-given and is an ongoing process in human experience. Revelation must be given by God, and have an objective basis, in order for the truth content of claims about God to be measured. It is possible to understand accounts of revelation as a difference of emphasis of given revelation and human experience of revelation. Barth and Balthasar emphasize given revelation, holding to a definitive, objective form of revelation. Schleiermacher and Tillich emphasize human experience of God through culture. In accounting for human experience in revelation, existing forms of revelation may be challenged, as Brown allows in his theology.

Music is revelatory in two ways: in expounding truths of God's creation and in allowing an encounter between humans and God. Music is revelatory because it is a part of the created world, and therefore reflects something of the true nature of it. It may also tell us something about the creator of that world. Balthasar views creation as a continual source of revelation. Indeed, for Balthasar, music as a created object has the likeness of all creation and can thus be an analogy for revelation in creation. Music also allows an encounter between humans and God. In this sense, revelation is an ongoing process. Stone-Davis's work offers such a perspective on revelation: music suspends the boundary between the subject and object and therefore allows humans to encounter God.

Encountering God

God is transcendent. In other words, God is beyond human experience. Yet, humans do claim to experience God, and thus in some way encounter the transcendence of God. There are different theological understandings of the transcendence with regard to music, of which two general perspectives will be explored. As with revelation, the key difference is one of

---

83. Ibid., 246.

emphasis: whether the understanding begins with God or with humans. An understanding beginning with God stems from the theology of Barth and Balthasar, and emphasizes God as transcendent. An account of music from this perspective suggests that God transcends all of creation, of which music is a part. However, creation may offer a glimpse of God's transcendence. An approach beginning with the human, from the theology of Marsh and Roberts, and Lynch, emphasizes human experience of going beyond the self. Accounts differ as to whether transcending the self also involves encounter with the transcendence of God. In order for human experience of transcendence, or going beyond the self, to provide meaningful knowledge about God, or in other words to be revelatory, it must in some way be an encounter with the transcendence of God.[84]

Transcendence

Transcendence is a term that frequently appears in theological discussions of music.[85] The origin of the word "transcendent" is the Latin verb *transcendere*, meaning literally "to climb across" (from *trans*, "across," and *scandere*, "climb") or "to go beyond."[86] It has various meanings today, which range from describing an everyday experience—for example, "This issue transcends the remit of my job description"—to issues that might pertain more to spirituality—e.g. "This art work has transcendent beauty." In theology, the term has also been used in a variety of ways.

Contemporary American literature and religion specialist, Regina Schwartz, in the introduction to her edited work on transcendence, notes two applications of the word in theology: vertical transcendence, in which the subject goes beyond the immanent world, and horizontal transcendence, which is self-transcendence. Transcendence in general, however, for Schwartz is "a delirious rupture in immanence, an erotic claim made by it, a gap in the Real, a question put to subjectivity, a realm of the impossible that breaks into possibility."[87] In other words, transcendence is a step into the beyond that opens new potential for understanding reality. Experience of transcendence in music can be, as Schwartz notes, an experience which goes beyond the self, or an experience which goes beyond the usual reality of everyday existence.

84. Schwartz, *Transcendence*, x–xi.

85. Transcendence has been the focus of some theological accounts of music; for example, in Stone-Davis, *Music and Transcendence*, and Küng's *Mozart*.

86. Simpson and Weiner, *Oxford English Dictionary*

87. Schwartz, "Introduction," x–xi.

Other thinkers have also proposed that transcendence is a multifaceted concept. Philosopher Charles Taylor[88] claims three facets of the transcendent are that there is, firstly, "some good higher, beyond human flourishing"; secondly, it is the "belief in a higher power, the transcendent God": and, thirdly, that "our lives extend beyond this life."[89] Although this is not a theological account of transcendence, all three facets of the transcendent in Taylor's understanding overlap with theology. The first and last are characteristic of our approach of understanding theology from human experience, in that they are beginning with human experience and going beyond it, whilst the second is similar to the approach from existing theological truths, finding first the transcendent God.

Frank Burch Brown, American theologian and composer with an interest in religious aesthetics, particularly in relation to music, similarly believes that the transcendent is a concept with different aspects. He outlines four: first, the negative transcendent, in which God is not found but is still believed to exist, and therefore the presence of God is experienced as a sort of yearning; second, the radical transcendent in which God's otherness is found to be infinitely distant and cannot be represented; third, the proximate transcendence which is when earthly objects are used as a means through which God's presence is mediated;[90] and lastly, the immanent transcendent which affirms the everyday, and therefore that God is immersed in the ordinary.[91] The first two experiences emphasis the transcendence of God, whilst the latter two emphasize transcendence through human worldly experience.

These three accounts of transcendence show the difficulty of considering transcendence as a singular concept, as it has different dimensions. Schwartz's approach acknowledges the range of diversity in the human experience of transcendence: it may be horizontal, going beyond the self, or vertical, going beyond the world, neither of which necessitate encountering God. Taylor and Brown give insights into the different ways in which transcendence allows experience of God.

---

88. Charles Taylor is a Canadian philosopher and Roman Catholic, whose influential work *A Secular Age* explores his thought on the concept of transcendence.

89. Taylor, *Secular Age*, 20.

90. Marsh and Roberts recognize this as the sacramental form of transcendence. Marsh and Roberts, *Personal Jesus*, 87.

91. Brown, *Good Taste, Bad Taste*, 120–21.

God's Transcendence

A strong reading of God's transcendence stems from Karl Barth's[92] account of God's otherness. For Barth, transcendence describes the absolute difference between humans and God.[93] God is "wholly other," as Barth wrote in his early work *The Epistle to the Romans*.[94] This makes God fundamentally unknowable, except through God's own actions in revelation. For Barth, God is transcendent, completely different from all human cultures and creations, and all created categories such as human experience. Therefore, God's transcendence explains the unknowability of God: God is completely different from humans in transcendence, in that God cannot be known at all, except in God's act of revelation.[95] There is a qualitative difference between God and humans: God is fundamentally different from all of creation.[96] Therefore, for Barth, no culture gives access to God.[97]

Barth's theology is what might be termed a "top-down" theology.[98] Episcopal priest and theologian Paul F. M. Zahl defines top-down theology as that which "starts from revealed statements about God from God."[99] In other words, top-down theology begins with God's own actions in revelation. The stress on the linguistic form of revelation is also evident in Zahl's definition, and will return as an issue in later discussion. Revelation is given, and it is up to the church to respond to its form in the Word of God. The

---

92. Barth's early theology expresses this position more strongly than his later theology. An account of Kierkegaard's influence early in Barth's theology can be found in Lippitt and Pattison, *Oxford Handbook of Kierkegaard*, 535.

93. For Barth, God is "the unknown God dwelling in light unapproachable, the Holy One, Creator, and Redeemer" (*Epistle to the Romans*, 35).

94. Ibid., 49.

95. Barth writes that "We must be clear that whatever we say of God in such human concepts can never be more than an indication of Him; no such concept can really conceive the nature of God. God is inconceivable" (*Dogmatics in Outline*, 46).

96. Trevor Hart explains Barth's thoughts on the unknowability of God in Webster, *Cambridge Companion to Karl*, 37–56. He notes that, for Barth, "God does not belong to the world of objects with which human apprehension and speech ordinarily have to do and to which they are fitted to pertain. God's reality transcends this realm in such a way that human knowing could never aspire to lay hold of it and render it into an 'object.' God is beyond human classification, understanding and description" (*Cambridge Companion to Karl*, 42).

97. As explored by Palma in *Karl Barth's Theology of Culture*, 80. Palma holds that Barth does not go far enough in allowing human culture and work as appropriate responses to God's creation.

98. Moseley describes it this way in his chapter in Begbie and Guthrie, *Resonant Witness*, 242.

99. Zahl, *Short Systematic Theology*, 7.

first step is—and only can be—made by God, and this determines every experience of transcendence through given revelation.

Theology is limited by humanity, and Barth notes that "all theological thought and utterance" demonstrates its "necessary brokenness."[100] The radical difference between humans and God cannot be overcome by theological thought. It can only be overcome by God's revelation. The transcendence of God, in Barth's understanding, does not relate in any way to human experience, but is fundamentally different, such that humans cannot experience it. For Barth, theology is given, God is revealed decisively in Jesus Christ.

In addition, for Barth, there is a chasm between the human and the divine, a great dichotomy, and therefore no human culture can have access to God's transcendence. Music, as a part of the created universe, is a created category that God transcends. However, Barth gives a privileged place to Mozart's music in that, for him, it gives an appropriate theological response to creation.[101] However, Barth allows Mozart's music to give an insight into God's creation: it can tell us something about the nature of reality, beyond what we already know, and may in this way be called a transcendent experience.[102]

Barth's account of transcendence may allow for self-transcendence through Mozart's music. Mozart's music reveals something about the nature of God's creation, but it does not allow experience of God's transcendence. Barth's account means that no one human can be closer to God than any other, as all are qualitatively different from God. However, the music can never offer an experience of God's transcendence, or an encounter with God, as God is qualitatively different from all of creation. Therefore, for Barth, musical experience of transcendence cannot reveal anything of God: God's transcendence, or otherness, is not a greater or more extreme form of the transcendence experienced through music.

Human Creations

Unlike Barth's belief in the absolute qualitative difference between God in God's transcendence and humanity and human creations, Balthasar's understanding of God's revelation in the Christ-form allows God's transcendence to be at least glimpsed by humanity. Balthasar is more positive about culture than Barth, in that, for him, worldly forms can in some cases reveal God's transcendence through re-presenting the Christ-form, the form of

100. Barth, *Church Dogmatics III:3*, 293.
101. Barth, *Wolfgang Amadeus Mozart*, 55.
102. Ibid., 55.

God's self-revelation. In terms of music, then, it is only in replicating, to some degree, the Christ-form that music can be revelatory, and thus form becomes an important feature of music. A replication of this form of God's revelation may thus allow offer a glimpse of the transcendence of God.

Balthasar takes God's revelation in Jesus Christ as the starting point of his theology. He understands theological discourse to be limited by humanity, but it strives to overcome the separation between the transcendent God and humanity. Theology can only do this by using God's revelation in the form of Jesus Christ. Contemporary Anglican theologian Ben Quash, notes that "for Balthasar all worldly forms, word and thoughts . . . are measured by that which they exist to serve: the Christological *deus dixit* (God has spoken) which is presented to us in the underlying unity of the scriptural *Gestalt* [form]."[103] In other words, God's revelation, in the form of Christ, is the measure against which other created forms are held. They serve the purpose of God's revelation, through revealing something of the Christ-form they are measured against.

Balthasar and Barth both understand God's transcendence to be a pre-existing theological truth which is (almost, for Balthasar) beyond the remit of human experience. God's transcendence is fundamentally different from any transcendence in the created world: humans cannot experience it, given the fundamental difference between humans and God expressed in Barth's conception of the unknowability of God. This approach does not allow for a human experience of transcendence which could contribute to an understanding of God, except where it substantiates the revelation of God in God's self-revelation in the Christ-form, as revealed through the Word of God.

Barth and Balthasar's emphasis on the unknowability of God's transcendence leaves little scope for cultural creations, such as music, to allow experience of God's transcendence, though both have allowed a glimmer of possibility of self-transcendence through Mozart's music. Balthasar's theology tempers Barth's understanding somewhat, in there is a unity of the created world, through which God's transcendence might become accessible, at least in small part, to human experience, through God's prior revelation in the Christ-form. This does allow for a musical experience of transcendence, but only insofar as it expresses God's transcendence already present in creation.

---

103. Ford and Muers, *Modern Theologians*, 112.

Self-Transcendence

Clive Marsh and Vaughan S. Roberts have attempted to capture the theological meaning of human experience of transcendence through music in their work *Personal Jesus: How Popular Music Shapes Our Souls*.[104] For them, the concept of transcendence explains an important experience that occurs when some people listen to music. Their research, questioning people on their musical experience, suggests that people describe this experience in a variety of ways.

Their account highlights the experience of self-transcendence, without reference to God's transcendence, and offer little account of what might become known through the transcendent experience beyond knowledge of the self. They are concerned with the development of the individual's spiritual life, rather than the ongoing process of revelation, and their findings, therefore, are anthropologically important. For Marsh and Roberts, there need not be a transcendent Other in order for transcendent experience to be significant: transcendence "becomes a way in which we ascribe significance to what we feel or think."[105] In other words, transcendence is a matter of human experience and human spiritual development.

Marsh and Roberts write, "whatever transcendence may be, it is vital that we recognize the importance of the emotional, aesthetic, ethical, and cognitive work that occurs in the affective spaces inhabited by contemporary Western citizens when listening to and experiencing popular music, and acknowledge what is being termed transcendence in that space."[106] Their writing suggests that it is the listeners of music who term their experience as transcendent, and they take seriously the listeners' claims as to their musical experience. Whilst the listeners do not use this vocabulary, Marsh and Roberts suggest that listeners' reported accounts indicate that they experience a form of self-transcendence, which gives rise to their anthropological understanding of transcendence.

There is an overlap between certain facets of Taylor's and Frank Burch Brown's conceptions, outlined above, in that in some experiences of the transcendent there does not need to be a God. Marsh and Roberts highlight that the transcendent is then an experience of going beyond the self, and "There may be no Other as such to relate to, no objective reality of God."[107] Human experience of transcendence, then, is not necessarily an experience of the

---

104. Marsh and Roberts, *Personal Jesus*.
105. Ibid., 87.
106. Ibid., 85–86.
107. Ibid., 87.

transcendence of God, though an individual may understand it as such, but remains a significant experience: using the concept of the transcendence allows humans to name the musical experience as significant. Thus, even if transcendence is not revelatory of God, if God is not in any way mediated, it remains a significant and meaningful experience. However, this form of transcendence may still be theologically significant as the experience of it can allow better self-understanding and may help to answer theological questions, such as those posed by Lynch in his account of theology.[108]

An individual's spiritual life can develop regardless of whether God is a part of the transcendent experience, according to Marsh and Roberts. For them, the experience of listening to music is a spiritual practice, by which they mean "a practice in and through which people actively work on their development of an inner life."[109] That is not to say that people consciously listen to music to develop their spirituality, though some evidently do, but that listeners develop their inner lives "with different levels of awareness."[110] Whilst Marsh and Roberts make no claims for a theological experience, if listening to music is a significant spiritual experience during which one in engaged in a process of meaning-making in response to concepts that go beyond one's everyday life, this may overlap with making meaning of theological questions. This reflects Lynch's theology of popular culture, in that objective truth is not guaranteed, but meaning-making still occurs for the individual.[111]

Marsh and Roberts hint that the experience of the transcendent is an indescribable "tingle factor." They conclude that "The tingle factor puts us in touch with that which we cannot quite identify, but which is vitally important for human life, and which is very much the subject of theology."[112] In other words, the "tingle factor" expresses a feeling of indeterminate meaning. This is particularly relevant to music because meaning in music is always indeterminate: the "tingle factor" is a means of attempting to describe the ineffability of music. The idea of the "tingle factor," whilst unspecific in Marsh and Roberts' writing, might be further developed. It could be

---

108. For Lynch, theology is "the process of seeking normative answers to questions of truth, goodness, evil, suffering, redemption, and beauty in the context of particular social and cultural situations."

109. Ibid., 133.

110. Ibid., 133.

111. Lynch believes that theologians are always in pursuit of truth, without having special access to it. He writes, "the practice of theology leads, at its best, to the cultivation of care and humility in approaching tradition, and a moral regard for others in its interpretation" (Lynch, *On the Sacred*, 151).

112. Marsh and Roberts, *Personal Jesus*, 89.

that what they are describing as the "tingle factor" is in fact an experience that takes humans beyond their ordinary everyday experience. Through a musical experience of transcendence, something of the transcendent God becomes more accessible. The "tingle factor" might awaken that which Tillich would call our ultimate concern,[113] or Lynch would describe as theology, suggesting answers to our questions of truth, goodness, evil, suffering, redemption, and beauty.[114]

For Marsh and Roberts there is no need to claim universal knowledge through the experience of the transcendent, as it is an individual spiritual experience. Also, at least in terms of musical transcendent experience, they believe that rather than making assured statements about one's significance, the reverse happens, and one becomes more humble in the face of the transcendent: music "enable[s] people to discover that being human entails resisting self-absorption: entertaining some sense of otherness in one's life."[115] Music thus helps the listener to retain perspective of their place against the "other," whatever that other may be.

Marsh and Roberts' account is based on the self-reporting of listeners who have described their musical experience as experience of transcendence: music plays an important role in allowing them experience beyond themselves. Whether this experience of transcendence is an experience that can be related to God is the important issue for theology. As Marsh and Roberts note, "The existence of a universal spirituality of music, or of a single notion of God, does not follow from this."[116] Therefore, music cannot be used to affirm beliefs about God, or other religious beliefs. Rather, musical experience opens up diverse possibilities for beginning to suggest meaningful answers to theological questions that resonate with the individual.

For Marsh and Roberts, transcendent experience is an individual's experience in which they, consciously or subconsciously, develop their inner life—what some might call their spiritual life—and need not be a universal phenomenon. The experience may go beyond this into the different categories of the transcendent that some believe mediate something of God. However, this means that transcendent experiences, in and of themselves, are not dependent on God existing to validate them as transcendent. Thus, the experience is anthropologically important. To develop Marsh and Roberts' ideas theologically, however, it is important that the transcendent experience of music provides access to objective truth about God, rather than an

---

113. Tillich, *Dynamics of Faith*, 1–2.
114. Lynch, *Understanding Theology and Popular Culture*, 36.
115. Marsh and Roberts, *Personal Jesus*, 87.
116. Ibid., 88.

entirely subjective individual experience. In this, it could be a "bottom-up" approach to a search for the transcendent God.

Hierarchy of Transcendence

Lynch equates the transcendent with the numinous and with God in the conclusion to *Understanding Theology and Popular Culture*.[117] Lynch therefore mediates the two approaches somewhat, as, in his view, a transcendent experience is a meaningful experience humans have which is beyond the ordinary and may bring them closer to God on a personal level. In other words, horizontal transcendence is not experience of God's transcendence, but it brings individuals closer to God. Lynch asks of works of popular culture: "Does it make possible a sense of encounter with "God," the transcendent, or the numinous?"[118] The answers to this question forms an investigation into the theological value of popular culture. If humans can experience the transcendent through some medium of culture, such as music, it allows an encounter with God, and it may therefore be revelatory. Lynch affirms that there is a transcendent divinity, but allows for human experience to be self-transcendent and reach toward it through experience of music.

Lynch's account of transcendence in *Understanding Theology and Popular Culture* differs greatly from his account of transcendence as relating to the sacred, found in *On The Sacred*, which suggests that there is no objective basis for the sacred, but it is a social construct. His later work is more cautious about transcendence. Lynch highlights that all experience of transcendence is not necessarily experience of God, and only some of these experiences are of the true transcendence of the divine. This raises the issue of the basis of authority on which theology accepts an experience of transcendence as an experience of the transcendence of God rather than merely self-transcendence.

A potential effect of this understanding of transcendence is that it may create a hierarchy of religious elite who are thought to be pre-disposed to experiencing the transcendence of God. Moreover, Lynch cautions that it is possible to "use transcendence as a ground for legitimizing the exercise of ecclesiastical power, locating transcendence as the top rung of the ladder of sacred hierarchy with religious authorities on earth just a rung or two below."[119] In other words, experience of transcendence becomes a means of

---

117. The influence of Otto's account of numinous experience being an experience of the divine is evident here.

118. Lynch, *Understanding Theology and Popular Culture*, 190.

119. Lynch, *On The Sacred*, 152.

re-affirming the status of the religious elite. Lynch holds that an appeal to the transcendent at the peak of the theological hierarchy neglects or belittles ordinary human transcendent experience.

Lynch also highlights the potential sociological impact of such a stance, in that it gives power to the religious institution and this power may be misused or exploited—perhaps nowhere more so than in the clericalism of the Catholic Church. The stress on God as transcendent may lead some—against Barth's understanding of the radical difference and therefore complete incomprehensibility of God—to view transcendence as a ladder toward God; one which ultimately takes some people further up the ladder than others. This understanding may be used to privilege some forms of music over others: sacred music, or music with religious intent, may be held up as giving access to transcendence. The understanding of transcendent experience as climbing a ladder of transcendence toward God creates a hierarchy of the religious or cultural elite which may be abused by those perceived to be furthest up the ladder.

There is a further issue of over-confidence in the truth claims supported by transcendent experience. Lynch's caution that this over-confidence in transcendent experience may have a more sinister impact in legitimising destructive actions,[120] echoing John Carey's concern about claims to transcendence through given knowledge: "Claims to transcendence and universal knowledge are evidently a way of conferring significance on oneself and one's experiences and are likelier to occur to those already in possession of social confidence and economic power."[121] It would seem that claims about the transcendent could lead to the justification of theological truths that are hierarchical and oppressive for Carey.

For Lynch, transcendence ought not to be appropriated by particular groups who seek to use claimed experience thereof for negative, controlling or oppressive purposes. Lynch writes, "The true transcendence of the divine therefore stands over all attempts to utilize it to human ends through religious discourse and action."[122] In other words, if transcendence is appropriated by groups for their own ends, it can no longer be the true transcendence of the divine.[123] It cannot be a means of corroborating or legitimising

---

120. Ibid., 153–54.

121. Carey, *What Good are the Arts*, 126.

122. Lynch, *On The Sacred*, 153.

123. Lynch is writing here with reference to the terrorist attacks of 9/11 and using the response to those attacks by Rowan Williams to survey the use of the transcendent. He draws from Williams's theology, that those things that mediate the transcendent can help us to reimagine or to rethink our notions of the sacred, without resting in our certainty that we have already found theological truth. Lynch writes, following

pre-conceived theological ideas. Rather, whilst a transcendent experience might reflect a theological truth, it does not necessarily have to, and in fact may do the opposite. Perhaps it is only by corroboration with truths found outside of the experience of transcendence can its truth be evaluated.

Using music to justify truth claims goes against Gorringe's understanding of using culture to further humanity. Gorringe's thought suggests a different dimension to the approach to transcendence, which goes further than Lynch in removing the notion of a theological hierarchy. Like Lynch, Gorringe gives credit to individual human experience, whilst holding that these experiences do not bring one closer to God. Gorringe draws on Barth's understanding of God's transcendence as fundamentally different to humanity: God's real transcendence undermines all hierarchies because God is not at the top of the ladder, but that God is radically different from everything on the ladder.[124] This does not rely on any account of religious experience, but on a strong reading of the transcendence of God. Therefore, if God's transcendence works in this way, the religious and cultural elite are no closer to God than anyone else. However, Gorringe continues to stress the importance of human experience of culture in the development of humanity.[125]

Experience of the transcendent, then, is not a confirmatory experience of established theological truths, but should be a means of exploring said truths, holding them up for scrutiny, and re-evaluating them. Moreover, it is difficult to use experience of transcendence in music to affirm particular beliefs, given that the meaning of music is always indeterminate. Claims to experience of transcendence may be used to legitimize pre-existing beliefs, and such claims may be used to promote a hierarchy of religious elite who have more access to transcendence.

Summary

The focus of the concept of transcendence can be self-transcendence, of the transcendence of God, perhaps as revealed at least partially through the human experience of transcendence. Barth and Balthasar both approach transcendence from an account of the transcendence of God, but differ in

---

Williams's thought, that "there are particular symbols that stand as direct mediators of transcendence and become the means through which the comfortable certainties of our sacred systems of meaning are disrupted." In other words, transcendent experiences can also undermine established beliefs as well as confirm them (ibid., 154).

124. Gorringe, *Furthering Humanity*, 123–26.

125. Ibid., 265–66.

their approach to transcendence in culture and music. For Barth, experience of transcendence will never be able to tell humans anything of God, whereas Balthasar's theology offers the possibility of some glimpse of God's transcendence, in the replication of the form of God-s self-revelation.

Marsh and Roberts provide an account of transcendence from the perspective of reported human experience of transcendence in music. For them, transcendence is an anthropological concept, and has to do with the spiritual development of humanity, without reference to God. There is no objective basis for their account of transcendence. The experience of transcendence, of going beyond the self, does not necessitate an experience of God, unless there is an account of how God may be encountered. Lynch highlights that accounts of human experience of transcendence which do not include an encounter with God are problematic: a theology based on experiences of transcendence risks establishing a hierarchy, suggesting a ladder toward God. Moreover, this is dangerous as it may legitimize incorrect or damaging pre-existing beliefs. Experience of transcendence in music through its lack of determinate meaning, would perhaps avoid some of the potential to use it to affirm truth claims. Instead, experience of transcendence could be framed as an encounter that does not require language.

The exploration of the musical experience as experience of transcendence in this book begins with human experience in relation to God. In the human experience of transcendence through music, lies the possibility of the suspension of the boundary between human subject and divine object. This approach recognizes the individual or personal experience of transcendence, but with reference to an objective source. Therefore, the musical experience of transcendence is a means of encounter with God. In the sacramental experience of music, there lies the possibility for the humans to go beyond themselves. This is an experience of transcendence through music, in which the otherwise unknowable God is made known, the impossible breaks into possibility, in the individual going beyond their ordinary reality, and perhaps catching a glimpse of the transcendence of God.

Liminality

Experience of transcendence in music makes something of God known. It does not imply an upwards trajectory toward God, as God remains ultimately transcendent, but an encounter with the mystery of God in all its ineffability. It is possible to overcome the hierarchical understanding of transcendence by understanding the experience in terms of liminality.

Several theologians have employed Arnold van Gennep's concept of liminality[126] in explaining how experience beyond the ordinary, or experience of transcendence, impacts human understanding and way of life.[127] The term, coined by van Gennep in 1909, is derived from the Latin *limen*,[128] which means threshold, and was originally applied to rites of passage which marked transitional moments. It was further developed by anthropologist Victor Turner in relation to religious rituals.[129] The idea of liminality, of crossing thresholds, can be applied to the concept of transcendence.

Affective Space

Christopher Partridge, researcher of religion and popular music, argues in *The Lyre of Orpheus: Popular Music, the Sacred and the Profane* that the emotions evoked by music are a power to be explored theologically.[130] Partridge analyses music from the starting point of the text, or its written form, rather than the experience, which is added into his account afterwards.[131] He argues that music is "less an object and more an event, in the sense that it is an experience shaped by the reader, but under the guidance of the text."[132] For Partridge, music is an experience of a text, an enactment of the written work.

Partridge therefore considers music as an experience, but abstracts it from the body by developing an idea of a non-physical, or conceptual, space

---

126. Gennep's *Rites of Passage* introduced the concept of liminality in relation to rituals such as birth and marriage.

127. Thomassen gives a detailed account of the history of liminality in *Liminality and the Modern*. An example of theology that draws on the concept of liminality is found in Boff's *Faith on the Edge*, which uses the concept of liminality in a liberation theology. A specific example of theologians using the concept can be found in Jobling's understanding of the body in terms of liminality in Hannaford and Jobling, *Theology and the Body*, 105–22.

128. Simpson and Weiner, *Oxford English Dictionary*

129. Scottish cultural anthropologist Victor Turner renewed interest in the concept of liminality more than half a century after van Gennep first used the term in his work *The Forest of Symbols*, in which he includes an ethnographic study of liminal rituals in Zambia. Turner continued to use the term "liminal" in relation to his ethnographic fieldwork, but in discussing thresholds in modern contemporary society, such as in theatre, coined the term "liminoid" in his later work "Liminal to Liminoid in Play, Flow, and Ritual: An Essay in Comparative Symbology" published in the book *Process, Performance, and Pilgrimage*.

130. Partridge, *Lyre of Orpheus*.

131. Ibid., 41–43.

132. Ibid., 171.

in which music impacts on those experiencing the music. Partridge uses the term "affective space" to describe the place in which music is at work, conceptually. For Partridge, this intangible space allows the a person to cross the threshold from what they already know to further religious knowledge. This reflects a desire for knowledge to become disembodied, to enter a non-physical space, rather than as a bodily encounter. Partridge's affective space attempts to abstract music from the reality of its physicality. In preferring the abstract to the embodied, it treats knowledge and disembodied and conceptual, which it can never be.

For Partridge, in crossing thresholds in a liminal transcendent experience "the very possibility of openness and change emerges."[133] Against the concerns that music, once it is considered a mediator of transcendence, may provide justification for existing values, Partridge believes the experience of music has the opposite effect: "Moments of ecstasy, transgression and creativity ignite passion and stimulate vitality through a temporary release from social and cultural structures that might otherwise become dry and oppressive."[134] In other words, music does not—or cannot, with its meaning being indeterminate—confirm pre-formed judgements. Rather than reinforcing pre-existing beliefs, music opens up "enchanted affective spaces" within which one can experience emotions, liminality, and "transcend quotidian routine."[135] Music is a creative process that allows humans to cross the threshold of the ordinary and expected.

Partridge develops the idea of liminality in relation to the whole community through music. Experience of transcendence through music, in its liminality, may allow for theological re-evaluation not only for the individual, but also in social terms. As well as a movement across the threshold between humans and God, however, some theologians have also noted the transgressive transcendent at work in music, though this may not be the term they have used. Partridge relates the concept of liminality to the whole community, and in ways that may be destructive of boundaries before they are re-evaluated and rebuilt: "Liminality identifies a temporary disorientating period of reflection during which a community experiences a form of "acceptable disorder" when conventional structures are suspended and questioned; everyday values and behaviors [sic] are challenged; transgression is not merely tolerated, but celebrated."[136] Partridge finds music to be

---

133. Ibid., 74.
134. Ibid., 74.
135. Ibid., 144.
136. Ibid., 73.

particularly useful in breaking conventions and creating imaginative spaces for disorder to ensue before order is re-built.

Partridge lacks an understanding of the physicality of musical experience: music is conceived to be beyond the bodily realm due to its supposed creation of a conceptual affective space. This is an intangible imaginary space, which is opened up in a liminal moment which ignites passion and stimulates vitality by crossing the threshold of everyday existence: it is an individual or collective experience. This account allows self-transcendence, but not an experience of God's transcendence, as there is no sense of liminally crossing a threshold between humans and God, but between everyday life and the extraordinary.

Whilst this understanding of liminality limits its potential to allow for knowledge of God, it may be a means in which human communities are developed. Liminality is an important part of community rethinking for Partridge, who highlights the value of music as challenging established conventions and creating imaginative spaces, allowing the progress of humanity, without reference to God. Experience of self-transcendence through the liminality of affective spaces—in other words, imaginative and challenging conceptualisations—in music opens up a creativity which has potential to change the way humans and human communities live in relation to the world.

Liminal Encounter with God

If a transcendent experience is revelatory, it may be so by crossing or suspending the threshold between the human and the divine. The idea of liminality can be developed by Stone-Davis's idea of postponing the boundary between the subject and object in musical experience, in order to account for the "Other" in transcendent experience. It is in the liminal experience that the pre-reflective moment may occur. The idea of liminality is key to an account an experience of God in transcendence, as it includes an "other" which is a source of objective truth.[137]

For Schleiermacher, religion is based on intuition and feeling. These are not states that can be generated by the individual, but have a source outside the self, an objective basis in God. In the movement away from the self in religious intuition or feeling, it is because of an "other."[138] Likewise,

137. Cobussen's *Thresholds* provides an extensive argument for an understanding of the concept of the liminality of music in spiritual terms.

138. The continuity in Schleiermacher's thought on religious feeling in it always having a "whence" from which it is derived is explored by Dumbreck in *Schleiermacher*

for Stone-Davis, music is never entirely subjective. It is always a meeting of subject and object. Stone-Davis holds that the experience of music allows for a temporary suspension of the boundary between subject and object. In other words, experience of music is a liminal movement, suspending the threshold between the subject and the object, for Stone-Davis, the human and the beautiful. This account of liminality in musical experience can be developed further: the merging of subject and object in music is an encounter between humans and God.

Experience of transcendence in music may therefore be a liminal crossing of the threshold, a suspending of the boundary, between the human self and God. This is a pre-reflective moment in which humans meet God. In this way, a liminal experience can make known something about God, as it has an objective basis. Transcendence, as a liminal suspension of the threshold between humans and God, is therefore revelatory.

Liminal Music and Time

Cobb draws on van Gennep's research into liminality, and concludes that liminality is suspending the usual structures, "crossing through a ritual threshold slip between their society's normal categories of classification."[139] He notes that it has the same "intangible but lasting effects" of liminality as described by Turner.[140] Cobb highlights the rock concert as another place in popular culture for liminality: "In rock concerts we enter liminal time and space, we enter a ritual of anti-structure that has some capacity to cleanse our interior consciousness and enable us to imagine new ways of being."[141] In other words, music allows people to enter into time in a way that crosses the usual thresholds of time. This need not be exclusive to music, as perhaps a similar effect is achieved in theatre, or film—though music may also play a role in these—where alternative ways of being in time are entered into.

There is no objective "other" in Cobb's account of liminality, no source of the experience, and therefore it is self-transcendence that does allow encounter with God, though it may help to answer theological questions, in imagining new ways of being. Cobb is focused on the ritualistic aspect of crossing thresholds in music, using liminality in its original sense. This is one of few examples of Cobb's application of his theology to music, and is useful in helping to understand music's relation to time in theological

and Religious Feeling.

139. Cobb, *Blackwell Guide*, 125.
140. Ibid., 183.
141. Ibid., 235–36.

terms, an important feature of music also highlighted by Begbie. Perhaps the liminal time entered into in the experience of music is the pre-reflective moment suggested by Stone-Davis, in which the subject-object boundary is suspended. In other words, the threshold of the subject-object is momentarily overcome in the liminal experience of music.

Begbie also discusses the way music changes one's perception of time. Although Begbie may not relate this experience in terms of transcendence and liminality, this may be construed as a liminal experience of transcendence, liminally suspending the realm of ordinary time. Begbie is keen to note that this is not a special quality of music, that it has access to a particularly transcendent form of time, but rather that it "can 'take our time' and give it back to us, enriched, re-ordered in some manner."[142] In other words, there is a liminal experience of crossing the threshold of the usual everyday experience of time. Begbie views this as an enriching experience, in which humans participate bodily in a dynamic field, and, through this, their theological understanding of time is developed.

Summary

The concept of liminality assists to understand the way in which musical experience can allow for a human encounter with God's transcendence. Partridge's account has shown that liminality, without reference to God, may develop human life, particularly in community, but self-transcendence without reference to an objective source cannot provide any knowledge of God. However, with reference to Schleiermacher and Stone-Davis, liminal musical experience can also allow the pre-reflective suspending of the threshold between the human and the divine. When musical experience of transcendence is a liminal experience, the individual not only goes beyond the self, but suspends the threshold between the subject—the self—and the object—God. Through the application of liminality to transcendence, there is a given in transcendent experience; an objective basis for knowledge of God. If liminal transcendent experience reveals knowledge of God, it is thus revelatory.

Conclusion

Music is theology because of its sacramental potential, which is not limited sacred music, or music with explicitly religious intent. There is not a

142. Begbie, *Theology, Music and Time*, 19.

particular form of sacred music which connects with God; rather, all music has sacramental potential. The concept of sacred music unnecessarily excludes non-religious forms of music from theological conversation, when in fact all of creation can be in meaningful conversation with theology. Music only exists in relation to the human subject and should not be treated as an abstract object to be studied by theology, and to be measured against theology. As a sacramental form, music reveals something of the otherwise hidden God.

God relates to humans through the human body. God's form of revelation, the incarnation, took bodily form. Moreover, all human experience and knowledge is through the body. Humans strive to connect to God through the body, as God connects with humans through God's body in the incarnation. Music is always an embodied experience, not an abstract form. It exists in the relation of its musical form to the human subject. As an embodied form, music acts on the physical senses, evoking feelings and emotions, and allowing particular modes of attention. Moreover, music is always experienced in a particular place, by a particular person, who has a particular history. The context of the experience is therefore also important. There is a need to acknowledge this situatedness of humans attempting to investigate theological concerns in a particular time, place and culture, as will become evident in the following three case studies.

If music can properly be described as revelatory, musical experiences must have their source in God. Embodied musical experiences are therefore the sacramental way in which music operates, in revealing something of the otherwise hidden God, the object of the experience, which leaves open a path to understanding something new about God. However, because of music's indefinite meaning, or ineffable nature, it allows encounter the mystery of God in a way which does not require language. Musical experience of transcendence was seen to be a liminal experience, in that it was a pre-reflective suspension of the boundary between human subject and divine object. This may allow for a deeper knowledge of the self and its place in creation, and it might also allow an encounter with God.

The ongoing nature of the process of revelation in human experience has been highlighted. God is already present and has been revealed in the incarnation, but revelation is primarily a continuous progression. It is an ongoing development of human knowledge about God. Revelation, in human terms, can only ever be fragmentary. Understanding of God and religion develops alongside knowledge and culture, and thus revelation is always an ongoing process as well as an objective given. This stresses the role of embodied human experience in revelation. Different genres, eras, or types of music may therefore be revelatory in different ways, all of which are equally valuable. Each piece of music can only ever present an aspect of God, as God could never be fully known to humans.

"Another turning point, a fork stuck in the road
Time grabs you by the wrist, directs you where to go
So make the best of this test, and don't ask why
It's not a question, but a lesson learned in time
It's something unpredictable, but in the end it's right
I hope you had the time of your life."

—Green Day, "Good Riddance (Time of Your Life)"

3

The Incarnate Form
The Classical Era

Having explored theologies of music generally in chapters 1 and 2, the following three chapters will be used to explore theologies of music more specifically, taking into account the context and nuances of particular examples of music from three different eras. If, as is assumed in this book, music is revelatory, it is one source in the ongoing process of revelation, and is bound up by necessity with human experience. Some music is better able to convey a particular aspect of the divine, as all revelation is fragmentary, limited by human capacity to know God; David Brown writes, "experience of the divine will inevitably be multifaceted, with some composers better at inducting us into one aspect rather than another."[1] Therefore, each musical example will be discussed in terms of the particular aspects of theological revelation it makes possible, and how it does so through the relation between embodied experience of the musical form.

The music discussed is not necessarily religious, following the sacramental account of music outlined above. Music is not an abstract written form, nor is it created in a cultural vacuum, and, as Epstein argues, theologies of music must not decontextualize music, but take it seriously as a cultural document.[2] Therefore, the context of the works will be discussed as a backdrop to their interpretation. Any discussion of specific musical examples is always a selection which leaves much music untouched, but in many cases the works discussed are in some regard representative of a particular

1. Brown, *God and Grace of Body*, 293.
2. Epstein, *Melting the Venusberg*, 44.

characteristic of classical music, and therefore the insights are relevant to other works. Moreover, the works chosen allow significant dialogue at the intersection of music and theology.

The focus of this chapter is the era of Classical music, from the years 1750 to 1810.[3] I will discuss first the work of Joseph Haydn (1732-1809), a key Classical composer of today's repertoire. In particular, I will focus on Haydn's oratorio work *The Creation*. Wolfgang Amadeus Mozart (1756-1791) is the primary composer of the era, and several key twentieth-century theologians have written about his work, notably Karl Barth and Hans Küng.[4] Mozart has also been the subject of nineteenth-century Danish theologian Søren Kierkegaard's satirical work *Either/Or: A Fragment of Life*. However, it is the theology of Hans Urs von Balthasar which will underpin this discussion of Classical music, as his theological aesthetics will be seen to exalt form, a key feature of the Classical era.

The Classical era brings its own particular insights to theology, but an exclusive focus on music of this era on the basis of one characteristic to the neglect of others, its form, leads to a narrow theological interpretation, which does not allow for possible insights through other characteristics of the music. Form is undoubtedly an important feature of Classical music, and is not exclusive to the Classical era, but is not the only character by which the music should be judged. However, even in Classical music, form cannot be the only determining factor, as music is never solely form, although it is an integral part of the music. Moreover, a focus on form encourages an abstract analysis of music, interpreting it in its written form, rather than an experiential account, an understanding of the way in which music impacts on embodied human beings.

---

3. There is debate about the exact dates of the boundary between the Classical and Romantic eras in music, which is not a key concern here, as the examples in this chapter are firmly within the Classical era. Gradual stylistic changes over this period make it impossible to discern an exact point in time in which the Classical became the Romantic. Joseph Haydn, whose work is securely in the Classical style, wrote his last major work in 1802, a mass. Ludwig van Beethoven (1770-1827) is the key composer whose work spans the Classical and Romantic eras, and is often classified by academics in three sections: his early, middle, and mature periods, of which the middle spans the transitional years between the Classical and Romantic, roughly 1803 to 1814. The important factor is that there are shared features of the idiom of composers of the time, rather than a particular number of years.

4. Barth, *Wolfgang Amadeus Mozart*, is a collection of Barth's writings on Mozart; see also Küng, *Mozart*. Pope Benedict XVI also commented that "Mozart thoroughly penetrated our souls, and his music still touches me very deeply, because it is so luminous and yet at the same time so deep. His music is by no means just entertainment; it contains the whole tragedy of human existence" (Ratzinger, *Salt of the Earth*, 47).

Balthasar has a preference for Classical music, exploring form in the Classical era, and its relation to beauty, with regard to his theological aesthetics. The idioms of Classical form will then be examined in key works, applying Balthasar's theological aesthetics to music through the concept of form and the Christ-form. Form is a determining factor in the meaning of Classical music, but its relation to the Christ-form should allow an account of the embodied nature of the musical experience of form, rather than abstract the form to study it intellectually, apart from experience. Form must be considered in relation to embodiment in order to understand music as it is experienced by humans.

Haydn's *The Creation*, written late in his life, after the death of Mozart, has the explicit aim of portraying creation. This work reflects the concerns of the Classical era, and the overarching form and order of this work has been seen to reflect the perceived order of the created world. Haydn presents chaos in the prelude, through undermining musical expectations, whilst maintaining a traditional Classical form. This work also demonstrates an archetypal example of the musical sublime, with the theological implications that entails.

The following two musical examples demonstrate the theological insights the Classical era has beyond musical form. Two contrasting works from the late period of Mozart's life are discussed, his opera *Don Giovanni* and his *Requiem*. As an opera, *Don Giovanni* is an embodied form in more than one way. Singing uses the body's own instrument to make music, but in opera, the body is also used to act; the narrative is enfleshed by drama as well as music. *Don Giovanni* narrows the focus from the whole of creation to the human, as it focuses more specifically on the nature of being human.

Mozart's *Requiem* is the first of three examples of the requiem form in the second part of this book. The *Requiem* is a setting of the Catholic Requiem Mass, and as such is an encounter with death. Its context is important as it is bound up with legend surrounding Mozart's death, which continues to affect how it is received and experienced today. It also relates to the sublime, a concept established during the Enlightenment period, and, I will argue, shows that the sublime is not subsumed by the beautiful, as may be the case in a focus on form.

Balthasar's Theological Aesthetics and Classical Music

This section will explore form, a key feature of Classical music, in relation to the theology of Balthasar and embodiment. Balthasar's conception of the incarnate Christ-form has implications for theological accounts of Classical music. There is an underlying connection between Balthasar's theological aesthetics and his favourite music, that of Mozart. Balthasar's theological aesthetics make little mention of music, but can be applied to music, in particular his understanding of beauty.[5] His understanding of the Christ-form as the means of God's revelation is also significant to a theological account of musical form. The Christ-form is Balthasar's archetypal form in relation to musical form, a key musical feature of the Classical era. Balthasar's understanding of the Christ-form as the ultimate form of beauty leads to an emphasis on form to the neglect of other musical features.

An approach which emphasises musical form in the abstract not only neglects the content of the music, but overlooks the fact that musical form only ever exists in relation to an embodied human subject. Moreover, a Christological understanding of music should lead to more emphasis on the embodied experience of music because of the importance of the body to the incarnation. However, by focusing on the beauty of the Christ-form, which is the form of God's self-revelation, Balthasar's theological aesthetics objectifies revelation. When applied to music, this approach encourages an interpretation of music in its written form, or as an abstract form, rather than music as embodied experience.

Classical Music, Form, and Theology

In the Classical era form was an important part of musical composition, and it governed musical decisions on both a small and a large scale, for example, from the tempo of a movement, whether it is the right place in a symphony for a slow or fast movement, and tonality of a movement in terms of keys related to the tonic, to determining the overarching structure of a work, such as the number of movements. The music of Haydn and Mozart is representative and exemplary of Classical music and its principles. Even in musical representation of that which is without form, composers stuck to existing formal expectations, as will be explored with regard to Haydn representing chaos in *The Creation*.

The idealism of the Classical era was expressed in large part through form. The fundamental form of the era was sonata form. In later periods this form was expanded, subverted and developed in expected ways, as will become evident in Beethoven's use of sonata form in the Romantic style in the next chapter. Balthasar is wary of the dissolution of the form. He writes,

---

5. Balthasar's theological aesthetics in *Glory of the Lord* does not often deal explicitly with music, but he does comment on music, and explicitly Mozart, in his other works, notably *Truth is Symphonic*, which uses music as a theological analogy.

"Our first principle must always be the indissolubility of the form" and that, if "form is broken down into subdivisions and auxiliary parts for the sake of explanation, this is unfortunately a sign that the true form has not been perceived as such at all."[6] Classical music thus fits his theology comfortably, conforming to formal expectations, never breaking down form. Indeed, it often is strongly affirming of musical expectations, especially with regard to form, and those features which fit within it such as tonality.

Tillich, in contrast, opposes an emphasis on the Classical, because of the idealism that runs through the Classical arts. He differs from Barth and Balthasar, in that he views Classical music as striving for "an ideal without realistic foundation [which] is set up against the encountered reality, which is beautified and corrected to conform with the ideal in a manner which combines sentimentality and dishonesty."[7] In other words, the idealism of Classical music means that it no longer reflects an authentic account of reality. However, Tillich concedes that Classical music "still expresses something, although not encountered reality."[8] In other words, Classical music has meaning, even if that meaning is not representative of our experiences outside of music. In this account, the perfection of form that Classical music strives toward does not reflect human experience of the world.

Abstract Form

Balthasar understands beauty as a transcendental, an objective form that reveals God, relating to his conception of the Christ-form, the archetypal form of both beauty and revelation. Balthasar's theological aesthetics are also coherent with giving theological priority to music of the Classical era due to his emphasis on form, as a fundamental characteristic of Classical music is the precision of its form. Balthasar's theological understanding of form reflects his personal musical tastes: he was extremely fond of Mozart's music,[9] which is held up as the principle example in the introduction to *Truth is Symphonic*.[10]

---

6. Balthasar, *Glory of the Lord*, 26.

7. Tillich, *Systematic Theology III*, 72.

8. Ibid., 72.

9. As McCosker notes, Mozart's music played a key role in several of Balthasar's friendships, including, most influentially, those with Karl Barth and Adrienne von Speyr (McCosker, "Blessed Tension," 81–95).

10. Balthasar, *Truth is Symphonic*, 7, 15.

For some theologians of the past, such as Augustine and Aquinas, the Transcendentals were thought to reveal something of God to humanity.[11] The concept of beauty has also made a resurgence in contemporary theology[12] and philosophy.[13] Balthasar, for one, regrets the loss of the Transcendentals in theology, and goes some way to reinstating them in his theological aesthetics. Beauty, for Balthasar, is a transcendental; it is a characteristic of God, which is therefore objective. In other words, beauty is a God-given feature of the created world which reveals something about God, truths which are already revealed in the very fabric of creation: the Glory of the Lord is revealed in the beautiful. Thus, where beauty is of use to theology, it is in reflecting and exploring a characteristic of God.[14]

Beauty has two facets, form (*species*) and splendour (*lumen*).[15] Of these, Balthasar places most emphasis on form. Following Balthasar's understanding of beauty as form and splendour, musical beauty must be related to its musical form. For Balthasar, all beauty lies in the representation of the Christ-form, the ultimate form of God's revelation. In the *Gestalt* of Christ, God is made manifest. Mozart's music is that which comes nearest to perfection of the musical form. Christ is himself the perfection of form, and Mozart's music strives toward the perfection of form. Therefore, as Balthasar notes in the opening of *Truth is Symphonic*, Mozart's music leads

---

11. The history of the transcendentals has been explored in Goris and Aertsen, "Medieval Theories of Transcendentals."

12. For further accounts of beauty in recent theology see Forte, *The Portal of Beauty*; Harries, *Art and the Beauty of God*; Hart, *The Beauty of the Infinite*; Murphy, *The Beauty of God's House*; Navone, *Toward a Theology of Beauty*; Treier et al., *The Beauty of God*.

13. Attempts have also been made in philosophy to grapple with musical beauty; for example, by philosopher Roger Scruton, who has written much on aesthetics and music, in his book *Beauty*. For Roger Scruton, beauty and morality are also related. Scruton believes that one is free to reject a valid "judgement of taste," which is based on critical argument. On what grounds, then, can a disagreement of a judgement of beauty be made? A judgement of beauty brings with it certain value judgements which denote worth as, in some respect, it *does* make sense to say, "That is evidently true but I don't like it," but it does *not* make sense to say, "That is evidently beautiful but I don't like it." In this way, as Scruton notes, "there is as much objectivity in our judgements of beauty as there is in our judgements of virtue and vice. Beauty is therefore as firmly rooted in the scheme of things as goodness. It speaks to us as virtue speaks to us, of human fulfilment." As with Balthasar, Scruton conceives of beauty as a transcendental, though in Scruton's conception, a secular transcendental (Scruton, *Beauty*, 147).

14. This idea is found in relation to the Glory of God in Balthasar, *Glory of the Lord*, 37. For Balthasar, beauty is an attribute of God which surpasses all human conceptions of beauty, and can only be defined by God. In a similar way, for Viladesau, who draws on Balthasar, all beauty has its source in God (*Theological Aesthetics*, 138).

15. The *species* is the actual form of the beautiful object, whilst the *lumen* is the splendour or glory of God that shines through it (Balthasar, *Glory of the Lord*, 117–18).

to Christ.[16] Applying Balthasar's theological aesthetics to music means that the nearer music comes to reflecting the beauty of the Christ-form, or the closer to perfection the musical form is, the more the music is revelatory, in reflecting the beauty of God's self-revelation in the Christ-form.

God, who cannot otherwise be perceived, has made perception of himself possible through the Incarnation: "He who is formless takes form in the world and in history, and can be encountered and experienced by the whole man in this form which he himself has chosen and put on."[17] The Christ-form is, for Balthasar, the form of most perfect beauty, to which worldly beauty can only aspire. It is the measure of beauty. Worldly beauty is beautiful because of its (poor) imitation of the Christ-form; it is precisely in its *form* that it is beautiful. For Balthasar, "if beauty is conceived of transcendentally, then its definition must be derived from God himself. Furthermore, what we know to be most proper to God—his self-revelation in history and in the Incarnation—must now become for us the very apex and archetype of beauty in the world, whether men [sic] see it or not."[18] In other words, God has provided the perfect model of worldly beauty in his revelation through Incarnation in Jesus Christ. Balthasar stresses the incarnate form of Jesus, writing, "as the Word of the Father that has come to us, Jesus is a man with body and soul and with all the experience proper to man [sic]."[19] Human experience is thus also a part of God's existence.

Christ, in his humanity, experiences God as all humankind experience God. Balthasar writes, "Christ, the full and perfect man, has in his own totality the experience of what God is. He is, with body and soul, the embodiment of this experience. And, as God-become-man who reveals God to man, Christ, even as God, has the experience of what man is."[20] In other words, Jesus is inseparable from his humanity in the same way that all humans are inseparable from their humanity. Balthasar highlights here the importance of human experience to Jesus. Christ is an archetype for human experiences of God.[21] Victoria Harrison writes that Christ as archetype means "the perfect way in which a human being relates to God and, therefore, the perfect way of being human."[22] Christ as archetype is what

---

16. Balthasar, *Truth is Symphonic*, 15.
17. Balthasar, *Glory of the Lord*, 301.
18. Ibid., 69.
19. Ibid., 324.
20. Ibid., 304.
21. Ibid., 321.
22. Harrison, *Apologetic Value*, 12.

embodied human life should aspire toward. Therefore, human experience is important, as it is essential to the Christ-form.

Balthasar writes that "in Christ the *species* and *lumen* coincide—as manifest, personal love."[23] The form is perhaps the prerequisite for the splendour, given that the splendour radiates through the form; "only through form can the lightning-bolt of eternal beauty flash."[24] Balthasar thus conceives of form as the splendour and glory of being: "We are 'enraptured' by our contemplation of these depths and are 'transported' to them" via the form.[25] Though never do we "leave the (horizontal) form behind us in order to plunge (vertically) into the naked depths."[26] For Balthasar, then, form plays a continuous role; it cannot be overcome or transcended.

Balthasar's thoughts on music are Christologically shaped in the correlation of beautiful forms. However, his interest in music also influences his theology: he uses music as an analogy to explain the relation between Christ's divine and human natures.[27] This begins in Balthasar's *The Development of the Idea of Music*, where McCosker perceives that in music, for Balthasar, "plenitude and presence goes with a complete inability to articulate that presence (presence and a certain absence commingle, or indeed, are *identified*, in the form of music)."[28] Music can in this way hold together a seemingly contradictory unity of presence and absence; it is the border between the apophatic and cataphatic. As music is "the meeting place of opposites, or at any rate contraries,"[29] so is Christ in holding both the divine and the human in one being.

It is in Christ that human subjects can encounter God, the object, or, as Balthasar notes, "in Christ subject and object coincide."[30] Leahy notes that it is through form that Balthasar is able to bring together the subjective and objective evidence for the Glory of the Lord,[31] and the definitive form is, of course, the Christ-form. Thus, the Christ-form must, as such, hold in tension the subject and object, humanity and God.[32] The Christ-form is both human subject and divine object; the two coexist in one form.

23. Balthasar, *Glory of the Lord*, 235.
24. Ibid., 32.
25. Ibid., 119.
26. Ibid., 119.
27. Balthasar, *Truth is Symphonic*, 8.
28. McCosker, "Blessed Tension," 90–91.
29. Ibid., 81–95.
30. Balthasar, *Glory of the Lord*, 308.
31. McGregor and Norris, *Beauty of Christ*, 30.
32. Balthasar, *Glory of the Lord*, 324–25.

Indeed, for Balthasar, music sits on the cusp between humanity and divinity: "music is a borderland of the human, and it is here that the divine begins."[33] If the subject and object coincide, it must be through Christ. The music must therefore reflect the Christ-form. In this way, for Balthasar, musical form allows human subject to encounter divine object. In leading to Christ, then, Mozart's music must present the Christ-form which allows the human subject to coincide with the divine object. In this way, the music is revelatory.

Balthasar is concerned with the form of revelation as well as the form of music. The Christ-form is God's form of self-revelation, and therefore is the archetypal form through which revelation occurs. For Balthasar, the experience of a member of the church "is but a privileged participation in Christ's all-sustaining experience of God."[34] In other words, individual experience is subsumed into the Christ-form, God's form of self-revelation; the subjectivity of the revelatory experience is always secondary to the objectivity of the Christ-form.

Balthasar's understanding of archetypal experience[35] stems from his concern with form; if revelation is contained within the formal boundaries of the archetype, revelatory experiences must be seen to be formally correct before being accepted as revelation.[36] This is a means by which to measure experience, and control what falls under the banner of Christian revelation. The form of revelation must therefore fit into existing revelation, which would not allow music to challenge it.

In summary, in Balthasar's thought, beauty has two facets, form and splendour. As a transcendental, beauty reveals a characteristic of God, but God is also revealed in particular through one archetypal beautiful form, the Christ-form. Following Balthasar's thought, it is through its form that any aspect of creation may be revelatory, in replicating the Christ-form, God's ultimate form of self-revelation and the objective form of beauty. In application of Balthasar's thought to music, particularly in the Classical era, musical form is a convenient measure of beauty in music, as form as analysed in written music is perhaps the most objective part of a composition as a whole. Treating the Christ-form as a form and measure of objective beauty, however, risks abstracting it from its embodied humanity with all that entails. It must be remembered that Jesus is the Christ-form, and he

---

33. Balthasar, *Development of the Idea of Music*, 57.
34. Balthasar, *Glory of the Lord*, 350.
35. Ibid., 301–65.
36. Ibid., 350–65.

has embodied human experience, he is the content of revelation as well as the form.

Incarnate Form

An emphasis on the form of revelation neglects the content and experience of music. In musical analysis, it is possible to take a formalist approach, but this approach may overlook the levels of meaning provided by the musical content. Form can be and is occasionally also disputed, though less so in Classical music than that of later periods.[37] It is not as objective a category as initially taught in early stages of musical learning.[38] Formal boundaries may be unclear or absent, which is often deliberate on the part of the composer, as a means of humour, delaying or subverting musical expectations, and both Mozart and Haydn use this compositional technique. An experiencing subject is therefore required for a musical joke to take effect in form.

Formalism removes any individual input in the musical experience, and removes also the subjective human experience of the musical form. It suggests that if form is correctly discerned, all will find the same meaning in the music. Thus, the only variable lies in the ability of those who experience the music to discern the form and the parts which make up that form. Individual musical experience is not a consideration, as the form and beauty of the music is objective regardless of the context. Formalism subsumes any subjective experience into the objectivity of the form.

Philosopher of music Leonard Meyer supports the notion that a focus on musical form leads to abstraction: he writes that the "concept of a form involves abstraction and generalisation," which is not derived from any one work, but from a number of works, out of which an ideal type grows, which becomes the basis for expectations.[39] The perception of form becomes an intellectual activity, based on the acquisition of knowledge of many works of similar form, rather than an experience, and becomes, as Meyer holds, an abstraction. It is no longer reliant on the experience of the music, but on the perceived structure, or even the structure as analysed in its written form.

---

37. For discussion of musicological perspectives to form, which highlights the context and perspective of the analyst, see McClary, *Conventional Wisdom*. For an account of three different approaches to analysing musical form, see Caplin, Hepokoski and Webster, *Musical Form, Forms & Formenlehre*. Caplin has also analysed the formal functions of Haydn, Mozart and Beethoven's instrumental music in *Classical Form*.

38. Rosen makes this clear in *The Classical Style*, claiming that there is not so much a form as a style of Classical music (*Classical Style*, 19, 370).

39. Meyer, *Emotion and Meaning*, 57.

Moreover, it is difficult to take a formalist approach to music whilst acknowledging the importance of the physical embodied experience. Other features, such as mood, style, even genre, are more important in experiencing the music, and yet are more subjective as they are influenced by context and expectations as well as the written score. Not only is the analysis of written musical form an abstraction or generalisation, but it can overlook the subject matter and content of the music. Tillich holds that formalism empties art of its content and meaning; it "disregards the content and meaning of artistic creations for the sake of their form."[40] For Tillich, even the most perfect form is empty if it does not express substance in its content.

Balthasar's account of the Christ-form recognizes the importance of the human body, but instead of accounting for human experience, his emphasis on its form leads toward an analysis of musical in the abstract. For Balthasar, it is the whole person that is affected by revelation, not just the intellect or mind. Balthasar writes "it is the whole man [sic] who has to respond to the whole form of revelation as it appears within the whole of the created world, and it is God who empowers him to give such a response."[41] The human response to revelation is in embodied form. Music, likewise, requires a response with the entirety of one's being: "all our senses are engaged when the interior space of a beautiful musical composition . . . opens itself to us and captivates us: the whole person then enters into a state of vibration and becomes responsive space, the 'sounding box' of the event of beauty occurring within him."[42] This is an acknowledgement that music reverberates physically in the body, and the form of beauty is embodied by those experiencing the music.

In Balthasar's personal interactions with music, creating the music himself was an important aspect of the musical experience. For Balthasar, Mozart's music became embodied in his own person: in later life, instead of listening to recordings of Mozart's music, he would play it for himself, from memory, on the piano.[43] Performing the music makes for a more intense physical experience of it. The form of revelation and the form of music affect us physically as human beings.

Therefore, although Balthasar identifies the physical experience of music here, his thought always moves beyond the subjective experience of music to the objective beauty which reflects the Christ-form. The subjective

---

40. Tillich, *Systematic Theology I*, 90.
41. Balthasar, *Glory of the Lord*, 297.
42. Ibid., 220.
43. He would also play Mozart from memory to his students (Schindler, *Hans Urs von Balthasar*, 16).

experience of the individual is always subsumed by objective categories. These categories relate to the form of the beautiful, the Christ-form. As the Christ-form is the measure against which all forms are measured, they must strive for perfection. This encourages an understanding of music based on its form, which is highly ordered and precise in Classical music.

Epstein's Christological understanding of music supports the approach to music from the incarnation, without the formalism of comparison with beauty as transcendental, as she claims that music is a "more palpable rather than imaginary translation of Christ's bodily presence."[44] In other words, music, like Christ's bodily presence, is wholly physical. Therefore, the relation between music and the incarnation is not based on abstract properties, but on physical resemblance. Music relates the importance of the incarnation through its incarnate existence.

A Christological account of musical form should help toward acknowledging the bodily nature of all musical forms. The incarnation should lead toward a consideration of the place of the human body, both Christ's body as part of the incarnated form of revelation, and our bodies, for which the Christ-form was revealed. Balthasar's emphasis on the incarnated Christ-form as the perfect form leads to an abstract consideration of form at the expense of content. This content includes, most importantly, embodied human experience. Therefore, following form as the sole point of reference between music and theology leads toward a more abstract conception of music.

The issue with an approach to music from a theological aesthetics that takes beauty to have an objective form is that it makes form abstract rather than embodied. A focus on the beauty of musical form leads to the abstraction of music from the musical experience to analysing the notes on the page. It neglects the embodied experience of music. In treating the Christ-form as a beautiful form, the embodied human experience also present in the incarnation is neglected. As the consideration of the Christ-form in the abstract neglects the content of the incarnation, the embodied revelation of God in a particular human being, Jesus, a consideration of music as form also neglects the musical content. Moreover, the similarity between the incarnation and music is in their embodied nature, which allows the human subject to coincide with the divine object. Analysing music as form neglects the experience of music and becomes an abstract, intellectual exercise, which overlooks the embodied nature of musical experience.

---

44. Epstein, *Melting the Venusberg*, 148.

Summary

Theology that measures music against an objective form of beauty approaches music as an abstract written form. It also neglects music's content and fails to account for it as embodied experience. Form is merely one of music's many facets which contribute to the overall experience of it. Balthasar's understanding of the Christ-form as the once-and-for-all form of revelation is a reminder of the enfleshed nature of revelation. However, it does not go far enough in recognising the importance of human embodiment in grasping that revelation. An account of the importance of the human body to God's revelation, as seen in the form of that revelation, the Christ-form, ought to lead to an emphasis on the embodied nature of all knowledge of God.

Due to the Christ-form's inextricable connection to the form of beauty in Balthasar's theology, it leads an account of music toward abstract formalism rather being grounded in the embodied experience of music. Moreover, by treating the incarnation as a form, the content, or the embodied human person of Jesus, is neglected. Music, as embodied experience, reveals the importance of the incarnate revelatory content of the person of Jesus, not through resembling the abstract Christ-form, but through being of the same nature as it, embodied. The particular relation of the embodied human and the musical form in Classical music emphasizes the written score, whereas in later music from the Romantic and Modern eras, the emphasis moves more toward the embodied experience.

The Creation: Embodied Participation in Musical Form

The first musical example of this chapter is Haydn's *The Creation* (1798), which represents a musical effort to expound theological truths of creation. This has been deliberately chosen as a work which uses traditional Classical forms, but shows a depth to those forms which goes beyond formal analysis and exists only in relation to the experiencing human subject. In other words, there is more to the form than seen, literally, in the musical analysis of the score. Two particular examples of how this occurs will be the focus of this section: firstly, the presentation of chaos in strict sonata form will be considered; secondly, this will be seen to give way to a sublime moment of musical experience at the start of the first day.

The Historical Context

Haydn did not hold back on resources in this work, its instrumentation going beyond the usual size of the Classical symphony orchestra: *The Creation* uses the full orchestral resources available to Haydn, with a full wind section alongside the usual Classical strings. A choir is also essential, as this is an oratorio form, as well as the three soloists, playing the role of three angels narrating the story. Musicologist Nicholas Temperley notes that approximately 180 musicians were required for the first public performance.[45] The usual size of orchestras at the time Haydn conducted his symphonies in London was approximately 60, and his Esterhazy orchestra was less than half that, and has been estimated at 21 players.[46]

Such a grand scale work is governed overall by the form of the libretto Haydn set to music. The libretto also includes biblical texts from books other than Genesis, from the Psalms, woven with text from John Milton's Paradise Lost. It was given to him first in English on one of his visits to England, and translated into German by Baron Gottfried van Swieten.[47] The libretto is a mixture of the sacred and secular, and portrays how the search for meaning in human life is not confined to the "religious." Thus, the text uses religious and secular accounts of creation combined in one text. Temperley believes that it is the libretto by the unidentified librettist that gives the work its theological character.[48] Thus, if Classical music is well-suited to elucidating the theological truth of creation, this explicit attempt to expound a partly scriptural account is the obvious place to start.

Form, Embodiment, and *The Creation*

Haydn's *The Creation*, which was written six years or so after Mozart's death, is wholly Classical in style and conforms broadly to Classical formal expectations. The presentation of creation is not only a presentation of an ordered created world; it also presents chaos before creation. There is more to creation than its form, but the scriptural account of creation guides the overarching form in this work. The overall form of the first two parts draws on the biblical account of creation in six days, into which the libretto is split

---

45. Temperley, *Haydn*, 36.
46. Clark, *Cambridge Companion to Haydn*, 258.
47. Ibid., 151.
48. Temperley, *Haydn*, 9. He also gives an account of the religious background in Georgian England, from whence the text was derived and an account of Catholic Austria where Haydn was living and working (ibid., 10–16).

where, as musicologist James Webster notes, "each Day as a whole points toward a triumphant chorus as climax."[49] It is thus guided in its form by the scriptural account of Creation that it is presenting. This overarching structure reinforces the text that the music is delivering. Arthur Peacocke and Ann Pederson, in their work *The Music of Creation*, suggest that Haydn's music in this work "splendidly tracks the Genesis text."[50] Haydn's music elucidates the theological meaning of the text.

It is paradoxical that chaos can be evoked in ordered form, as it is in the prelude: "The Representation of Chaos" follows the Classical idiom of sonata form. Haydn conveys chaos by undermining the formal expectations of those who have prior experience of sonata form, in a way that is most evident in the experience of the music rather than in the score. This movement, analysed in the abstract, meets formal expectations of the typical Classical sonata form. However, analysed with regard to the musical experience of the time, it is perplexing and disturbing as it repeatedly undermines other unwritten rules of Classical composition. The form is undermined only because of musical expectations with regard to harmony, tonality, phrasing and cadences. In other words, in the experience of the music, it is chaotic. These do not sound as severe to musicians of the twenty-first century as they would have done to musicians of the Classical era, and therefore there is less evocation of a sense of chaos than at the time of writing due to the change of context.

Haydn's prelude acts upon an experiencing subject's expectations of sonata form, and represents chaos by subverting or delaying expected musical occurrences, for example in the delayed cadences, which Haydn noted as a key feature of this movement, because there is no form yet in the universe.[51] Composers attempting to represent chaos today may resort to more obvious compositional techniques, such as the removal of key structural features such as tonality and time signature, but in this orchestral movement Haydn uses sonata form in C minor. Haydn uses shifting keys with modulations to unexpected and distantly related keys, deferred and unfinished cadences, suspensions, and the alternation of loud and quiet dynamics to upset expectations and create a sense of formlessness.[52] It opens with a series of dissonant sustained chords. This would have been highly unusual to those experiencing the music around the time of its composition, for

49. Clark, *Cambridge Companion to Haydn*, 153.
50. Peacocke and Pederson, *Music of Creation*, 4.
51. Temperley, *Haydn*, 32.
52. For a more detailed musical analysis, see Rosen, *Classical Style*, 370–73, and Peacocke and Pederson, *Music of Creation*, 11.

whom the dissonance would have been more unexpected and disturbing, more chaotic, given its abnormality.

Haydn achieves the presentation of chaos within an ordered form to such an extent that musicologist Charles Rosen suggests in his analysis that for Haydn "the 'sonata' is not a form at all, but an integral part of the musical language, and even a necessary minimum for any large statement that can be made within that language."[53] The form is an essential part of the construction of musical formlessness, but it is the backdrop to the experience, rather than the determining factor in the meaning of the music. The chaos is experienced in the undermining of musical expectations in the experience of the music, which demonstrates that analysis of musical form is changed by considering it in relation to an experiencing human subject.

Beyond elucidating the biblical text, Peacocke and Pederson believe that Haydn's music in this movement represents the theological interpretation of this text in creation *ex nihilo*.[54] For them, Haydn represents the non-existence, "timeless and without order, a chaos where no forms have duration warranting their being described as existent."[55] Indeed, this is reinforced by the fragmentary nature of the short themes. However, this sense of formlessness is created within a strict form: it is precisely because of the expectations of form in the Classical era, in the expected cadences, that Haydn was able to represent chaos within such strict form.

In dramatic fashion, the C minor key of the prelude is resolved on this first "day," in the first movement, in unusual fashion for the form, into C major. Webster writes, "The Creation of Light is overwhelming not in its own right, but because it resolves the disjunction and mystery of the entire Chaos music, as it resolves an unstable c minor into the radiant purity of C major."[56] The association of the major key with brightness is suggestive, but the force of the moment is in its excess of the sudden fortissimo on the word "light." This is a sublime moment in which disorder resolves resoundingly into light.

The Sublime Moment

Haydn's *The Creation* uses an extremely sophisticated and well-organized overarching form, and employs traditional Classical forms in each movement. It is extremely well-constructed in terms of form, and a follower of

---

53. Rosen, *Classical Style*, 370.
54. Peacocke and Pederson, *Music of Creation*, 10–11.
55. Ibid., 10.
56. Clark, *Cambridge Companion to Haydn*, 150–63.

Balthasar's theological aesthetics may therefore expect to find beauty in it. However, the meaning of this work is perhaps found in one sublime moment, in the disintegration of the chaos, in the moment that encapsulates the whole content of the work. This moment is found only in the embodied experience of the music: it is only after the distressing chaos of the prelude that the overwhelming effect of the moment of light can be sublime.

The opening of the first "day" in particular is held up as an example of the work arousing the sublime, in the sense of being overwhelmed by the force of nature as it is presented.[57] The sublime as presented in Haydn's *The Creation* is a typical Kantian presentation of humanity against the created world.[58] Haydn evokes the created world, and fear of nature, but from a position of power, where nature does not have dominion. Brown notes that "Order on its own can all too quickly become predictable and therefore boring" and therefore Haydn and Mozart's search for "the creation of the sublime in music . . . [is] through simple evocation of majestic power."[59] Brown gives this moment of *The Creation* as an example.[60] It is a moment of enlightenment, but it is also unexpected and therefore unsettling to those experiencing it. The sublime moment effects the riddance of chaos. It is a moment of unexpected clarity, in which the chaos is immediately disintegrated by the sudden interruption of one pronounced chord, the unexpected C major. In this work, Haydn has based his compositional technique on the feelings aroused. The musical form is experienced as an enactment of the theological meaning of the work. For Balthasar, the sublime moment is a moment of enhanced objectivity, in which reason is not negated or surpassed, but enlightened and developed: "The experience of sublime beauty is overwhelming and can be enrapturing and crushing."[61] The sublime is thus an event which informs reason in the same way that beauty is "enlightening."

Whilst the sublime moment is, in some way, revealing, it is also a moment of surplus of indeterminate meaning. The meaning of Creation, which cannot be captured by language, is evoked in the experience of the sublime moment in the music. This understanding of the sublime draws on philosopher Hans-Georg Gadamer's (1900–2002) account. Gadamer holds that the sublime can never be wholly conceptualized; discussion of its

---

57. Sisman, *Haydn and His World*, 66
58. Kant, *Critique of Judgment*, §27, 258.
59. Brown, *God and Grace of Body*, 254.
60. Ibid., 255.
61. Ibid., 320–21.

meaning cannot be exhausted. The sublime is an experience with an excess of meaning.[62]

The pastoral theme which runs through the work allows creation to be presented simply. Musical analyses highlight the pastoral nature of *The Creation*. For Rosen, it is this style that allows Haydn to grapple with issues of major import. He writes, "The imposed simplicity of the pastoral style was the condition which made it possible to grasp subjects of such immensity."[63] Moreover, the "subject of pastoral is not Nature itself, but man's [sic] relation to nature."[64] For Rosen, then, Haydn's work allows for greater understanding of humanity's relationship to the created world. This relationship is ultimately conceived as "other"; one is drawn into the music, but through the musical sublime, stands as other to the awesomeness of creation. For Temperley, *The Creation* is "a statement of warm optimism about the world and our place in it."[65] However, it presents a bold and overpowering view of nature, which is consistent with understandings of the sublime in Haydn's time.

Haydn's sublime moment presents an all-consuming moment of clarity in the illustration of the moment of creation. This presentation of creation ultimately presents the natural world as "other" through its evocation of the sublime. The musical experience plays out over against the created world, rather than in the midst of it. This will be seen to contrast the presentation of the natural world in the Romantic era, in which the individual is encouraged to explore the place of the self within creation.

Summary

Haydn encapsulates the biblical account of creation in the experience of the musical form. It is evident in *The Creation* that even when music does follow a strict form, it can also paradoxically convey formlessness if the form is considered in relation to an experiencing human subject. The experience of formlessness and chaos within a distinct sonata form highlights that a theological musical analysis cannot only take into account the score. Reference to the context of the time highlights the different feelings Haydn's contemporaries would have had in comparison those experiencing the music today.

This analysis of Haydn's *The Creation* takes into account the context of the embodied experience of the music. The context is important in taking

62. Gadamer, *Truth and Method*.
63. Rosen, *Classical Style*, 372–73.
64. Ibid., 373.
65. Temperley, *Haydn*, 46.

experience into account. Haydn's contemporaries would have been far more disconcerted than someone in the twenty-first century by his then radical compositional techniques. The lack of resolution at the end of phrases would have been a key feature in the Classical era, as would the extravagant harmony, as the dissonance and lack of resolution would have been unexpected.

Moreover, without physically experiencing the music, the theological message is lost. An analysis of a coherent traditional sonata form on paper does not very well represent chaos, and the moment of clarity provided by the sublime appearance of the C major chord at the beginning of the first "day" is only present in experiencing the music. This marks the early stages of the development of the relationship between the embodied subject and the musical form. Haydn's construction of the musical form here causes those experiencing the music to feel a sense of chaos; however, degree of chaos perceived is variable due to differing expectations and contexts. There remains an excess of indeterminate meaning in the experience of the sublime moment of clarity, which eludes theological reasoning.

This example of the relation between musical form and embodiment impacting on the meaning of the music is a precursor to the development of musical form in the Romantic era, in which meaning becomes more indeterminate as more emphasis is placed on the experience. The individual's subjective knowledge comes to play a greater role in determining musical meaning in Romantic music.

Understanding Human Embodiment through Opera: *Don Giovanni*

Analysis of Haydn's *The Creation* has shown that musical form is not always a straightforward tool in music, and can hold contradiction within itself. The content of creation was also seen to be important in that it dictated the overarching form, as well as compositional details within the form. Mozart's late opera *The Rake Punished, or Don Giovanni* (1787)[66] is an example of where content in music is at least as important as form in determining meaning; its content guides discussion into an exploration of what it means to be human. This is not only explored in the musical content, however, because, as an opera, it includes staged drama as well as music. Therefore, it takes us beyond Haydn's work, incorporating actions of the body as well as its sounds. Music in opera is very much embodied: not only is it played on

---

66. The full title is *Il Dissoluto Punito, ossia il Don Giovanni* in Italian. Hereafter, I refer to it as *Don Giovanni*, as it is commonly known.

the most enfleshed instrument, the voice, but it also plays out narratives in human lives in its libretto and drama. Opera is therefore a musical medium that is integral in discussing human embodiment.

Several interpretations of *Don Giovanni* are based on the relationship between the content, or the narrative, and the musical form, opera. These will be examined first, before developing an understanding of the relation between embodiment and the form of the opera. This theological reading of *Don Giovanni* demonstrates that analysing the relationship between embodiment, content and form in the opera reveals a different interpretation to that based on the relation of content and form.

Content and Form: Explicit Meaning of *Don Giovanni*

Many theologians have engaged with Mozart's opera *Don Giovanni*, such as Kierkegaard in his pseudonymous satirical work *Either/Or* of 1843. In it, Kierkegaard's aestheticist, "A," states that "Mozart is the greatest among classical composers, and . . . his *Don Giovanni* deserves the highest place among all classic works of art."[67] For the aestheticist, a classic work is defined as one in which there is an absolute correlation between form and content.

Kierkegaard's account from the aestheticist "A" suggests the importance of the music in exploring the three erotic stages of Mozart's opera. George Pattison notes that Don Giovanni is the "very incarnation of sensuous immediacy" for the aestheticist.[68] In other words, Don Giovanni is the musical encapsulation of the sensuous human being. His existence affirms human life, in all its facets, including sexuality. Pattison notes that "The relationship between language and music thus exactly parallels the relationship between Christianity and sensuality, and it is in sensuous immediacy that music is said to find its absolute object."[69] If the absolute object of music is the sensuous, then it may reveal something about the nature of being human.

For the aestheticist, the perfect subject matter for the form of music is the sensuous. Brown interprets the aestheticist as arguing that a Christian reading "should find in the music a worthy celebration of the aesthetic, of the fervour and passion that Christianity has so often denied in its history but which rightly belongs to faith itself."[70] The opera also celebrates the sensuous nature of bodily existence, that has oft been denied by Christianity. The aesthetic and physical world is valuable; it is not the seduction away

---

67. Kierkegaard, *Either/Or*, 76.
68. Hannay and Marino, *Cambridge Companion to Kierkegaard*, 82.
69. Ibid., 83.
70. Brown, *God and Grace of Body*, 381.

from ethics or religion, but a fundamental part of human life. Theology should not neglect the sensual realm portrayed in both the libretto and music of *Don Giovanni*. The form of the opera is the ideal form in which to raise issues of human sensuality.

For Kierkegaard's aestheticist, this opera most perfectly unites narrative with music:[71] "The expression of this idea [of the spirit of sensuality] is Don Giovanni, and the expression of Don Giovanni is, again, solely music."[72] The narrative focused on human sexuality represents one facet of the fundamental human concern of embodiment, which unites with the operatic form. The music needs the narrative for the aestheticist, as without it, its indeterminacy is its greatest limitation: "the fact that it is indeterminable is not its perfection but a defect."[73] In terms of this aesthetic perspective, the sensual story is best expressed in and through Mozart's music, which makes the nature of human sensuality comprehensible. For "A," music is the only medium in which the sensuous can be presented: there is a perfect unity between the form and content.

The meaning of the opera is explicit because of the nature of story-telling in the genre: Don Giovanni, with the assistance of his servant Leporello, spends his days focused on increasing his number of sexual relationships. This interpretation is almost entirely based on the libretto, rather than the music. Mozart's sentimental ending following the death of Don Giovanni, a simple, cheerful ensemble in D major, seems to support the surface level reading that Don Giovanni's poor ethical choices in his sexual life are justly punished, whilst the other protagonists, victims of the Don's choices, are rewarded. The libretto supports the optimistic music: "the death of a sinner always reflects his life." The finale is contentious, as it may be perceived as undermining the tragedy, or as a lightening of the mood.

For Pattison it is "'fatuous" to call Don Giovanni immoral, because surrendering to the seductive power of the music occurs in an aesthetic context in which moral claims and actions do not arise."[74] In other words, any account that passes ethical judgement is meaningless. The fact that the narrative is in the realm of the artistic, rather than the realm of reality, makes any ethical judgement redundant, and therefore there is more to *Don Giovanni* than a moral tale for Kierkegaard's "A." Indeed, modern musicologists agree that the correct interpretation of *Don Giovanni* is not as a lesson in morality. Edmund J. Goehring writes, "One of the least satisfying inter-

---

71. Kierkegaard, *Either/Or*, 70.
72. Ibid., 94.
73. Ibid., 80.
74. Hannay and Marino, *Cambridge Companion to Kierkegaard*, 84.

pretations of *Don Giovanni* is to take seriously as a moral statement rather than a simple observation the other part of the opera's title, 'the libertine punished.'"[75] Indeed, the punishment is inconceivable when it occurs, with the Commendatore reciprocating the Don Giovanni's invitation to dinner posthumously, appearing as a statue and taking the Don to hell. Thus, whilst it is possible to analyse the content based on an ethical judgement of the actions of the protagonist, there is a deeper meaning that the surface level of the text. It is more than a deterrence to unethical sexual behaviour.

Against Kierkegaard's perceived three stages of life, the aesthetic, ethical and religious stages, enacted and represented by the characters A and B in *Either/Or*,[76] the opera *Don Giovanni* reminds us that these need not be distinct stages. The opera is not only a life lesson about being solely an aesthete—as Don Giovanni lives and dies in the aesthetic realm[77]—but is a reminder that sexuality is an integral part of what it means to be human, and therefore transcends the aesthetic.[78] The embodied experience of being human ought not to be neglected in any search for meaning, musical or theological.

However, there is a deeper reading which reflects Epstein's assertion that human sexuality should not be ignored in a theological consideration of music.[79] For Epstein, the Don's flaw lies not only in the fact that he has been seduced by women (though it is debatable whether he is seduced *by* the women, as he goes to great lengths himself to seduce the women), but that he has been seduced by seduction itself.[80] In this way, Don Giovanni's ethical failing has become abstract, no longer related solely to his physical desires.

Aside from the obvious criticism about the role of women in this opera, in following this conclusion, Epstein believes women are equated with music, as it too is, in Kierkegaard's aestheticist's view, the most sensuous seductress.[81] Epstein's interpretation therefore holds that it is not only mu-

75. Keefe, *Cambridge Companion to Mozart*, 141.
76. Epstein, *Melting the Venusberg*, 44.
77. Ibid., 44.
78. Musicologist Charles Ford has analysed the opera *Don Giovanni* with reference to sexuality and the Enlightenment, and provides background to the particular musical techniques used by Mozart, in comparison with the operas *Figaro* and *Così Fan Tutte* in *Music, Sexuality and the Enlightenment in Mozart's Figaro, Don Giovanni and Così Fan Tutte*. Ford's analysis focuses solely on understanding the context at the time the operas were composed, whilst I also want to consider their meaning in today's context.
79. Epstein, *Melting the Venusberg*, 43.
80. Ibid., 45.
81. Ibid., 44.

sic, but also women, that are conceived in the abstract in neglecting the embodiment of form. Thus, the aestheticist's conclusion that music speaks for itself is contradicted by the need for the embodied figure of the mythical Don Giovanni.[82]

The sensuous is not the object of the music, but its content. The true meaning of the opera is not found in its content, as moral claims are abstract, not embodied. The meaning is found in the relation between the human subject and the musical form. In the embodied experience of music, the object encountered is external to the music, it is not merely its content: in the embodied musical experience the human subject and divine object coincide.

Embodiment and Form: Implicit Meaning of *Don Giovanni*

The interpretation of the one of the key moments described above, the sentimental and optimistic finale, changes when the audience's embodied experience of the opera is accounted for in the analysis. Understood as embodied musical experience, for the audience the release of tension in this finale is a moment of catharsis. Sexuality is seen to be a fundamental part of human life, and the content of the opera leads to a questioning of how to live that out in relation to others. However, its meaning goes beyond an ethical lesson in behaviour toward others, as its simplicity draws those experiencing it into a moment of reflection on and immersion in their embodied being in relation to the other—the human other and the divine other.

The opera also raises the question of gender. Goehring notes how the tragic impact of the story on the women seduced by Don Giovanni is also rendered comic, for example by the use of Baroque-sounding melody in Elvira's aria of rage, evoking the passé sense to mock Elvira. This, Goehring notes, generates an ironic tone.[83] Mozart here uses music humorously, knowing the outdated Baroque sounds will resonate incongruously with the audience. This generates pathos for the women, who appear to be trapped by circumstance, like the Baroque melodies which are stuck in the past.

The meaning of the opera is found in the fact that the musical form, which is experienced through the human body, and which makes its meaning only in that relation, conveys content that is also conducive to consideration of embodiment. The content in this case supports the relation between the musical form and the human subject. In the merging of musical form, human embodied experience, and the content of human sensuality, the

---

82. Ibid., 46.
83. Keefe, *Cambridge Companion to Mozart*, 142.

human subject is able to develop understanding of the nature of embodied existence.

Revelation and Concealment in *Don Giovanni*

The relationship between embodiment, content and form in *Don Giovanni* is representative of the nature of revelation: the music enacts the theological claim that God's revelation is paradoxically revealed and concealed. Kierkegaard's aestheticist also describes the paradoxical nature of music's revelatory powers, stating "I am convinced that if Mozart ever became wholly comprehensible to me, he would for the first time become wholly incomprehensible to me."[84] This reflects the understanding of the fragmentary nature of revelation. Balthasar holds that the incarnation of the Word is the most extreme manifestation within the deepest concealment.[85] Jesus Christ is the means by which God chooses to reveal himself, but Jesus Christ also holds the deepest mystery of God. Thus, revelation allows humanity deeper knowledge of God, but also a deeper sense of profound mystery in the face of this revelation of God.

Balthasar compares the notion of simultaneous revealing and concealing in revelation with the composition of a work of art: "the artist will conceal himself in his work as much as he will reveal himself. To be sure, in so far as he gives shape to *his* world-view, the artist reveals something of himself: but in so far as, at a deeper level, he desires to manifest the world as he has understood it, he becomes unimportant to himself and treats himself as a mere medium which as such does not strive to reach any prominence."[86] Balthasar notes that the composer is simultaneously wise and ignorant in his creation of a work of art, in that he assumes an attitude of ignorance toward profound depths, but in doing so, is able to create a work that becomes an expression of the sacred unknown, without his intending to do so.[87] There is thus a deeper unity of creation expressed in the created piece of music, channelled through the composer's conscious and subconscious activity in creating the music.

For Barth, Mozart's music holds together different perspectives, institutes, and facets of human creation, and it is therefore necessary to quote him at length here: "Mozart is universal. One marvels again and again how everything comes to expression in him: heaven and earth, nature and man,

---

84. Kierkegaard, *Either/Or*, 72.
85. Balthasar, *Glory of the Lord*, 457.
86. Ibid., 443.
87. Ibid., 445.

comedy and tragedy, passion in all its forms and the most profound inner peace, the Virgin Mary and the demons, the church mass, the curious solemnity of the Freemasons and the dance hall, ignorant and sophisticated people, cowards and heroes (genuine or bogus), the faithful and the faithless, aristocrats and peasants, Papageno and Sarastro. And he seems to concern himself with each of these in turn not only partially, but fully; rain and sunshine fall on all."[88] For Barth, Mozart's music expresses the fundamental concerns of humanity and of theology through the representation of individuals, or of particular aspects of the world. Although Mozart focuses attention on the detail, Mozart's music is simultaneously representative of the whole of creation.

In *Don Giovanni* Mozart has explored the nature of humanity through the different characters of the protagonists. Barth suggests that Mozart's music expresses true freedom. In encapsulating freedom of choice in the superficial story, but more importantly the limitlessness of eternity in the music, in *Don Giovanni*, Mozart might thus be expressing this as an aspect of the human condition. The paradox of the finite human life, and the striving for something beyond it, is evident in the music.

Summary

The opera *Don Giovanni* combines a story told musically in libretto with the embodied portrayal of the story through drama. The narrative is literally enfleshed as it is acted out and sung on stage. Having definite content makes an analysis of the meaning of the story attractive. However, this particular opera shows that such a surface level interpretation of the narrative is inadequate in determining its meaning. The relationship between human embodiment and musical form is not only influenced by the music as it is performed, but also by the physical enactment of this relationship on stage.

Don Giovanni has been analysed through the relation of its content to its form. This has not produced a satisfying account of the meaning of the opera, as there is evidently a sense of irony in the story, and the finale has been interpreted as simplistic or trite. However, by incorporating the additional facet of embodiment into the analysis, the meaning of the opera has changed. A fundamental facet of human life is questioned in the opera, humans in relation through sexuality, and through the presentation of one permutation of a response in the Don's relations, those experiencing the opera are given freedom to come to their own conclusion. The opera is no longer about the Don exploring the limits of his sexuality, but offers, in the

88. Barth, *Church Dogmatics III:3*, 35.

relation between musical form, narrative content, and embodied experience, fertile ground for reflection. The audience is thus given space, within the opera, to consider the implications of the opera, its content, and their embodied experience of it as regards its implications for who they are as an embodied human relation in relation to the human other and the divine other.

Classical forms are self-contained, but the music of the finale extends the opera beyond the denouement, allowing for reflection within the form, before it has closure. Mozart's technique here is developed by Beethoven in the more condensed sonata form, as will become evident in the following discussion of Romantic music in relation to the heroic form.

Requiem

The final example in this chapter, the requiem, is a form that will return in the following two chapters, tracing its development through the Romantic and Modern eras. The requiem is used throughout the second half of this book as a common example between different musical eras, as it shows both the importance of the continuity of the form and the changing theological dynamics of using such a sacred form. This form brings together several of the themes that are key in this book. In particular, the requiem has much to contribute to the understanding of what it means to be human. It deals with embodiment, but also brings it together with the sublime, the excess of meaning in the embodied musical experience.

Mozart's *Requiem* is a reminder of the embodied nature of human experience, and explores the nature of the human condition. As a requiem, it is about death, but as a sublime work, following the Classical era's conception of the sublime, it is an in-the-moment experience which transports those who experience the music beyond the everyday in an excess of meaning that may be indeterminate, but is nonetheless enlightening.

The Legend: Mozart's *Requiem*

Mozart's *Requiem* is a work in which the context of its composition is bound up with its meaning, and has great impact on how the work continues to be experienced today. The *Requiem* was commissioned in the last year of Mozart's life, and was unfinished when he died in December 1791. Thus, his wife arranged for its completion, probably to fulfil the commission and take payment.⁸⁹ Most of the movements were at least sketched out by Mozart,⁹⁰ and only the Sanctus, Benedictus and Agnus Dei are believed to have been written without any input by Mozart, and are entirely the work of fellow Austrian composer Franz Xaver Süssmayr (1766–1803). The work now known as Mozart's *Requiem* was therefore the work of at least two people, and how far the completed work complies with Mozart's intentions for his work cannot now be known. As a work, though, it is influential and is worth discussing in its own right. Musicologist Simon P. Keefe notes that the performed *Requiem* can never be about Mozart alone.⁹¹ Indeed, the meaning of the work is not only to be found in the intention of the composer, but in the experience of the human subject, for whom the historical context is also important.

Keefe notes that the "legend" surrounding Mozart's *Requiem* has always had an impact on its reception, and there is a "deep seated desire to bring biography and music into perfect harmony" in our imagining of Mozart's foreknowledge of his own death.⁹² Although many have perceived a personal aspect of the *Requiem*, in that the "legend and work are mutually reinforcing,"⁹³ and although there is a trend toward a more personalized form of the requiem as will become evident in chapters 4 and 5, there is no evidence that Mozart was writing his own requiem. It is merely speculation to claim that Mozart was aware that his illness was fatal. Mozart was writing the *Requiem* as a commissioned work, to be performed in the usual manner as a Catholic Requiem Mass. As Keefe notes, it is unlikely that Mozart imagined his work being performed anywhere other than in a church.⁹⁴

Although there is little evidence to support the personalized understanding of Mozart's *Requiem*, the legend and the music are inseparable. The legend undoubtedly plays a role in the context of many people's experience

---

89. Indeed, the widowed Constanze Mozart's letters are the source of many false stories surrounding the *Requiem*. It may be that she fabricated stories about the work to gain popularity, in order to deceive others about the authenticity of the work's authorship, or for other unknown reasons. Keefe notes that Constanze considerably muddied factual waters (Keefe, *Mozart's Requiem*, 16).

90. The extent of Mozart's input into the movements which are not in his handwriting in the original score can only be speculated at this distance, but at any rate many movements are a collaboration between Mozart's melodies—in his own hand in the score—and Süssmayr's orchestration, some after an earlier attempt at orchestration by Joseph von Eybler. For a full account of the composition of each movement, see Keefe's *Mozart's Requiem*.

91. Ibid., 245.
92. Ibid., 22.
93. Ibid., 170.
94. Ibid., 3.

of the music. Keefe notes that "circumstance reinforce[s] musical experience and vice versa."[95] The *Requiem* need not be Mozart's swansong in historical fact for it to be perceived as such by individuals of the past, or of today. As it is the last work Mozart worked on, it is undoubtedly the height of his musical maturity, and his death meant that it could not be surpassed. It has therefore acquired a particular place in ongoing understandings of his music. As the *Requiem* has come to be known as a complete work today, it is can explored as such, without recourse to the details, so far as can be told, of exactly which parts were composed by Mozart and which parts were the work of another hand. Knowledge of the context of the work therefore contributes to our understanding of it today.

The Musical Sublime in Mozart's *Requiem*

The particular quality of the *Requiem* that allows it to speak theologically is its evocation of the sublime, a newly formed concept of the enlightenment, and explored in relation to Haydn's *The Creation*, above. Here, it is not the form that dictates the experience, but the haunting beauty of the melody, the text with which it expounds so fully, and the stridency which many have interpreted as Mozart facing his own death.

The relation between the musical form and the embodied experience of it is important in the analysis of Mozart's *Requiem*. The work is not best analysed on the basis of its abstract musical form, or the manner in which it represents the requiem form, but on the experience it gives the experiencing subject. This is recognized in musical analyses, such as in Keefe's comprehensive account of the work, which puts the musical performance before the formal analysis. In fact, only one chapter of the book is given to discussing the particular sounds and strategies that make up the musical form of the *Requiem*.[96]

Whilst Mozart does not break from the Classical style, the key to the particularly dramatic atmosphere of his *Requiem* is the manner in which he uses the chorus, frequently changing the textures to build and release tension. Mozart, from a tonic of D minor, uses flat keys rather than sharp keys, reflecting the dark, pensive mood of the requiem.[97] Particularly sublime,

---

95. Ibid., 88.
96. Ibid., 107–72.

97. D minor is a flat key, in that it consists of notes that are flat, being a semitone lower than the note named, rather than sharp notes. Flat keys have long-standing associations with sadness, grief, and death, whilst sharp keys have associations with brightness and happiness.

or holy, in Otto's sense of *mysterium tremendum et fascinans*, are the trombones in the "Dies Irae" which are simultaneously dark and terrifying, and *awesome*. Trombones are unexpected in an orchestral work of this time.[98]

The musical sublime, as defined in this book, is the excess of meaning found in experience of music, in which those experiencing it are drawn into a complete immersion in the music, which some have noted as an ecstatic mode of attention. Mozart's *Requiem* effects this in part by its dramatic representation of the form most closely associated with death. There is a paradoxical array of feelings evoked by the music of Mozart's *Requiem*. Brown writes "Apparent inconsistency in what is deduced from experience of instrumental music need not necessarily entail ultimate incompatibility. As with our experience of other human beings, terror and peace, for example, can come from the same source."[99] This account of terror and peace coming from the same source is experienced in the *Requiem*, which, perhaps because of the legend that has grown around Mozart's own death during its composition, focuses on mortality not only in general, but in relation to the individual.

There is, however, an aspect of the experience of the music of Mozart's *Requiem* where the music goes beyond the meaning of the text. In this, there is an excess of meaning, and it is this which is the musical sublime, in which music both reveals and conceals the revelation of God. The *Requiem* reveals something about human mortality through both the music and the context. The music is not ineffable; it has an obvious content which is its subject matter. Its meaning is there not as indeterminate as an orchestral work.

For Barth, that Mozart has been gifted a sort of prescient access to higher things, when his music "evidently comes from on high, where (since everything is known there) the right and left of existence and therefore its joy and sorrow, good and evil, life and death, are experienced in their reality but also in their limitation."[100] The paradox imagined by Barth is similar to the paradox in Haydn's *The Creation* in which formlessness is expressed through form; in Mozart's music eternity is expressed through the finite duration of sound.

---

98. The first major symphony in which trombones were used was in Ludwig van Beethoven's *Symphony 5*, composed in 1808.

99. Brown, *God and Grace of Body*, 224.

100. Barth, *Wolfgang Amadeus Mozart*, 33.

Summary

The requiem is a liminal form, on the boundary between life and death. As in Mozart's case, sometimes the context of the composer's life and death is bound up in the musical meaning of the requiem, through long-standing association. The particular circumstances of the composer, in this case, serve to make the *Requiem* a more awe-inspiring experience, being closely related to one individual death as well as to death in general. Those who experience this music are guided toward a consideration of their own death through the form, making experience of the *Requiem* a personal and unique musical experience, and therefore the meaning is determined by each individual person as they are in the moment of experiencing it. However, it also leads to a consideration of the universal concept of death, and its theological significance as enacting the finitude of human existence as we know it.

Mozart's *Requiem* illustrates the reliance on the sacred form of the Requiem Mass in conveying religious thought about death in the Classical era. As the Romantic era began, composers began to experiment with new ways of tackling the issue of death by developing the requiem form. Mozart's work predates the development of the traditional religious forms of the church. However, it does begin to expand the form, for example by the unusual inclusion of brass instruments, which marks a small but significant step toward the personalisation of the requiem form. This development is evident in the trajectory of the later requiems of the Romantic and Modern eras. The context of Mozart's *Requiem*, or what Keefe calls the legend surrounding it, is made more important because of the importance of the context of later Romantic works, and their relation to the lives of individual composers. The understanding of later works therefore impacts on today's understanding of Mozart's work.

Mozart's *Requiem* evokes an experience of the sublime in those who experience it, which creates an excess of indeterminate meaning, which may be enlightening or revelatory. The music is simultaneously beautiful and terrifying, leading to a contemplation of death, but more particularly, one's own death. This experience of the sublime is no longer a single moment, as in Haydn's creation, but lasts throughout the work, driven by the intensity of the chorus and orchestration. This experience allows one to consider the threshold between life and death, and in this way is a powerful liminal experience. Through the ecstatic mode of attention created by the experience of the sublime, the threshold may also be crossed between human subject and divine object, and therefore the music may be revelatory.

Conclusion

This chapter has explored the theological implications of features of the Classical era, with a particular emphasis on form, which underpins the Classical style. An emphasis on form in engaging theologically with music encourages a study of music in the abstract written score, and, although this is possible with the music of the Classical era, it misses layers of meaning that are developed in understanding form in relation to an experiencing human subject. This approach to music gives precedence to one musical era, the Classical, as later eras are less focused on form in the abstract. There are no particular qualities in music that should be value above others, as all music is sacramental, and therefore the Classical era cannot be held up as an archetype of the way in which music should reveal God because of the precedence of musical form.

Balthasar's theology gives a positive account of God's revelation through beauty in the world. However, his account of the Christ-form as the ultimate revelation of the objective form of God's beauty risks treating the incarnational form of God's revelation as an object, rather than as an experiencing human person. This overlooks the content of the incarnation, its human person, and abstracts God's revelation from human experience. This is evident in discussing God's self-revelation as the Christ-form, rather than the human person Jesus. The Christ-form is treated as an object, and discussed in impersonal terms, which takes the focus away from the human person of Jesus. The Incarnation is therefore discussed as an objective form of beauty, rather than as an embodied subjective form. As the incarnation is made abstract by the focus on form rather than embodiment, so too is music. Moreover, in making form the determining measure of music's worth, artificial criteria are imposed by which to judge music, whereas form is not necessarily a determining factor in an individual's experience of music.

Rather, a Christological account of music as theology should look to the embodied nature of the incarnation, acknowledging that it is only through the bodily, and in particular through one body, that humans can know God. Though form is easily analysed in the abstract in the Classical era, the three musical examples in this chapter have been analysed in relation to a potential experiencing human subject. In this way, the meaning of the musical forms of the Classical era are considered in relation through experience.

Haydn's *The Creation*, with its content grappling with the theological issue of creation, shows how, paradoxically, formlessness can be musically represented by a fairly strict form. Music is able to to juxtapose and hold in tension what seem to be opposites. This too is representative of revelation, in simultaneously revealing and concealing. Haydn does not deny order to create the semblance of chaos, but is able to do it within form. Haydn's portrayal of chaos does not evoke a sense of the chaotic without accounting for an embodied human subject experiencing the music. As a written form, it remains a traditional sonata form. This work is also useful in illustrating the different experiences of a listener based on the context of the time of listening. What Haydn's listeners would have perceived as unnerving and chaotic appear less so today. Musical expectations based on prior musical knowledge therefore have an impact on the interpretation of the meaning of the work. However, the meaning of the work has not changed across the eras; this work demonstrates that in the Classical era, although musical forms have layers of meaning only accessible in relation to the experiencing human subject, the content of the work continues to dominate the interpretation of the meaning more than the subjective experience of the listener.

Opera is perhaps the most enfleshed form of music. The integration of song, the use of the body's own instrument, with drama through the form of the opera has made it an embodied enactment of a narrative. By highlighting the aesthetic realm of Mozart's *Don Giovanni*, Kierkegaard's aesthete has in fact opened up the embodied realm, in understanding how the impact of the aesthetic works. Epstein has argued that music takes the place of woman in this story, as the Don is seduced not by women but by seduction itself, which takes musical form. This opera in particular highlights the sensuous nature of being an embodied human.

Mozart's *Requiem* marks a moment of change in the understanding of the relation of the composer to the musical form of the requiems, but it does so without challenging Classical form. Experience of the sublime in Mozart's *Requiem* shows that there is an excess of meaning that goes beyond beauty and is never resolved. There is no resolution of death in Mozart's *Requiem*, but an acceptance of it. The work is explicitly transient, as human life is, but the beauty only lasts as long as the final chord. This *Requiem* therefore coordinates beauty and the sublime in relation to mortality. It does so by merging the sublime and the beautiful, in suggesting a resolution which does not exist in actuality, and is as fleeting as the music.

The *Requiem* is not best analysed on the basis of its form, as the form of the music is only important in relation to those who experience it. It is better analysed as an embodied liminal work, crossing the boundary between the subjective and the objective, on the threshold of life and death. Its content therefore has as much impact on its meaning as its form. This *Requiem* brings together the individual and the universal. In dealing with death, the universal feature of life, the music is relevant to every person, but in its context as Mozart's last work, it is also personal to him. Mozart's music evokes an experience of the sublime, in holding the listener in an ecstatic mode of attention in consideration of the universal concept of death and their own death, in which there is an excess of indefinable meaning. Whilst the experience is important in understanding the meaning of Mozart's *Requiem*, the formal elements of the music are not as personal, and therefore do not impact as greatly on the musical meaning as the individuality of form of the requiems of the Romantic and Modern era.

If music is firstly an embodied experience rather than a written text, the way in which the human subject relates to the musical form is important even in music in which the determining feature is form. The Classical era has offered one potential means of relating musical form and embodiment. The musical form in this era is paramount, and in itself is able to speak to theology, as for example in the form of Haydn's *The Creation* demonstrating theology account of creation, but it is in relation to a human subject that it fully reveals its potential. The embodied experience of the musical form will be seen to be more important in determining the meaning of the music in the Romantic era, and yet more important in Modern music.

"This is our time, we can't rewind
Our place to shine out, we can live it anyway
This is our time, to feel sublime
Our place to shine now, and we can do it anyway
We can't rewind."

—Feeder, "We Can't Rewind"

4

The Transcendence of the Self
The Romantic Era

This chapter will focus on the Romantic era of classical music. The early Romantic movement, begun in the late eighteenth century, had an impact on the development of theology and this filtered into the composition of music. Romantic thought continues to affect how the music of the Romantic era is interpreted today. For the purpose of this chapter, the Romantic era is taken to mean approximately the years 1800 to 1910[1] for musical reasons, as it is the Romantic style, rather than the dates, that are of importance in analysing the music. Context continues to be important, as Romantic music is influenced by the thinking of Romantic movement, just as the Classical era was influenced by the thought of the Enlightenment. The influence of Enlightenment thinkers continued, demonstrated through the Romantic desire to create experiences of the sublime. The sublime, as an enrapturing experience of an excess of meaning, is an experience many Romantic composers attempted to evoke through their music.

The concept of the self is important in Romantic thought, as seen above in Schleiermacher, and it is also important in Romantic music, which becomes more self-reflective than music of the Classical era. The Romantic

---

1. Romantic thought began at the end of the eighteenth century, but took some time to filter into musical compositions. There is an overlap with the Classical era, as change did not happen overnight, but gradually, as composers developed their practice. Beethoven's style of music changed gradually between 1803 and 1814 to that which we now recognize as the Romantic style. By 1910, Modernism was taking over the musical scene. One of the great Romantic composers, Mahler, died in 1911, and Stravinksy's *Rite of Spring* of 1912 confirmed the appearance of the modernist style.

era is the time in which the individual experience comes to the fore in music, with composers beginning to write more personally, which is evidenced in the requiem form. Gordon Lynch holds that the Romantic movement used written texts to develop non-rational perspectives on life.[2] Romantic composers also use music, a non-linguistic source, to develop individual perspectives on life. Transcendence is a key theme here, and it splits into the two forms, going beyond the immanent world, or transcending the ordinary in encountering God.

Ludwig van Beethoven (1770–1827) transitions the Classical and Romantic eras, and his music was a forerunner of the Romantic style. Beethoven's oeuvre therefore sits on the boundary between the Classical and Romantic eras of music: he began his musical career composing in the Classical style, and finished firmly in the Romantic. Beethoven's compositional style shifted over a decade or so around the turn of the century, and his works exhibit the transformation of the use of form between the two periods.

Beethoven wrote the *Symphony No. 6: "The Pastoral Symphony"* op. 68 (1808) in the midst of this stylistic shift toward the Romantic. Natural theology is important to understanding this work, in particular as it relates to the cultural context of the Romantic era, as Beethoven was using a widespread trope of the time to explore the human place in the natural world. Nature is often seen to hold many of the qualities attributed to the sublime. The pastoral in music can captivate us with a presentation of nature, summed up in sound. Creation is encapsulated in music in an excess of meaning that goes beyond words. This allows the individual human life to be seen as a small yet significant part of creation. The experience of transcendence allowed through this musical work is based on the pastoral, taking account of the self as a fragment of a greater whole, as a part of the natural world. This pastoral form of self-transcendence therefore encourages us to re-evaluate the place of the individual in a wider context of God's creation.

Musicologist Scott Burnham identifies that form begins to include the participation of the listener, and the key issues his analysis highlights—the re-evaluation of the self, understanding the self as part of a greater whole, and the merging of subjective and objective in the musical experience—are means of allowing the experience of transcendence in the musical analysis. A focus on the human life encourages composers to map out human journeys in their music. Romantic music also focuses on how the self relates to the wider world.

---

2. Lynch, *Understanding Theology and Popular Culture*, 82.

The requiem, which was identified in the previous chapter as a key form of encounter between music and theology, is an important form in Romantic music. The requiem is a key liminal form: it is always about a liminal event, the threshold between life and death, a universal feature of all life. This is paradoxically both personal—in the sense that every person's death is their own—and universal. The requiem form holds this paradox; it is personal to the composer, but universally relevant to those who experience the music, whilst allowing them a personal forum in which to encounter death. The experience of the sublime in this context relates to a fundamental aspect of human life, death, and the excess of indeterminate meaning found in consideration of it. The value of the requiem form in conveying the sublime musical experience might be seen in the many extraordinary requiems that were written during the Romantic era.

Romanticism in Music and Theology

Romantic music becomes more self-reflective than Classical music, following the trend of Romantic thought: with the composition of music comes a focus on aspects of life, from birth to death. The journey of the human life becomes a theme of Romantic composition. According to American literary critic M. H. Abrams, there are five key ways in which the Romantic era differs from the period before: 1) a stance against traditionalism; 2) the arts are a "spontaneous overflow of feelings" (as Wordsworth described poetry); 3) nature is a stimulus for human thought; 4) the audience is invited to empathize with the protagonist; and 5) it was an age of new beginnings and human potential was viewed positively, with "limitless aspiration toward the infinite good envisioned by the faculty of imagination."[3] Abrams's summary of these five Romantic thoughts form the backdrop for much of the theological thought of the era, as well as the themes of many musical compositions.

Romantic Music

A brief overview of the general trends in Romantic music is helpful in understanding its relation to similar movements in theological thought. In the Romantic era, more focus is given to the individual's experience. Therefore, the concept of the individual self is important in the Romantic era, which is evident in the theology of Schleiermacher outlined, and undoubtedly influenced the nature of musical compositions. It is linked with the development

---

3. Abrams, *Glossary of Literary Terms*, 127–29.

of form, in that the forms are personalized and begin to reflect the individuality of the composer. Composers began to create self-reflective music. This encourages composers to treat form as a part of the embodied musical experience. Form therefore becomes an interaction between the written music and the listener.

Romantic music was also concerned with the journey of the self. The journey of childhood plays a role in Schleiermacher's *Christmas Eve Celebration*, a fictional story which examines the meaning of Christmas. One of the characters, Friederike, accompanies the evening's discussions, playing the piano to suit the mood of the orator's speech.[4] In the story, music is seen to be a formative part of the life of the youngest character, Sophie, the only child. Music, both religious and non-religious, is seen to be influential in her development, and delights in the book of sheet music she is given as a Christmas present,[5] which she immediately plays on the piano whilst the others talk, before the more lengthy speeches begin.[6]

This childhood journey through music is also reflected in the piano works of Robert Schumann (1810–1856), *Kinderszenen*, or Scenes from Childhood. Composers not only wanted to reflect their "self," but to go beyond themselves, particularly the parts of the self that are not pleasurable, for example illness, suffering and death. Through the exploration of the self in music, and the horizontal transcendence of the self, composers explored the place of the individual in relation to the whole of creation. It is here that the Romantic theme of the pastoral is integrated with the emphasis on the individual. Self-transcendence allows the individual to re-evaluate their place within the whole of creation. Whilst the composer's intentions can be useful in contextualising the music, and giving some degree of meaning to it, they are not the only influential factor in the musical experience.

Romantic music begins to push boundaries of accepted form, often expanding, developing, subverting or undermining Classical form, and therefore does not fit a theological aesthetics that is based around the perfection of form. Within these new forms, composers became more aware of the possibility of representing non-musical objects and circumstances through instrumental music,[7] and a genre of programme music became popular. As

---

4. Schleiermacher, *Christmas Eve Celebration*, 44.

5. Ibid., 6.

6. Ibid., 36.

7. Musicologist Daniel Chua believes that gender understandings influenced the development of the musical sublime, meaning that instrumental music was perceived as more masculine, particularly the symphony. This form of the sublime is similar to that conceived by Burke, in which beauty is feminine and the sublime masculine, as discussed in chapter 2, but whilst it may be the understanding of the sublime followed

theology became more receptive to the possibility of religious experience in secular context, composers also began to write music with religious content designed to be performed in non-religious contexts. Brown writes, "it was the nineteenth century that saw with the Romantic movement the growth of programmatic instrumental music and so more explicit discussion of the possibility of various types of religious experience through instrumental music."[8] As Brown highlights, some composers intentionally sought to create religious experiences through the narrative, or programme, of their music. As will be discussed with regard to the requiem, these musical experiences may include a traditional religious form, but composers began to adapt the form to suit the particular needs of their composition.

Rosen notes that the Romantic form requires the listener to use the imagination in order for the form to be complete. The form cannot be perfected in an abstract way, as it can only be complete in relation to an experiencing embodied. It is, then, a realisation that musical form is not complete in the abstract, only in the experience. Beethoven, as the first Romantic composer, understood this: "More than any composer before him, Beethoven understood the pathos of the gap between idea and realization, and the sense of strain put on the listener's imagination is essential here."[9] The discontent with form, and understanding of its incompleteness, may be seen as part of the malaise of the Romantic outlook. It is also an acknowledgement of the incompleteness of human experience. Following Balthasar's theological aesthetics, the incarnation of God's revelation highlights the importance of the embodied experience in all its limitations in encountering God in the Christ-form.

Romantic music, through the transformation of traditional Classical form, transcends written form and takes the participant, through active involvement and use of their expectations, memory and imagination. In this way, the musical form of the Romantic era admits it is fragment of a greater whole. It is completed only in relation to the embodied experience, who brings to the work their understanding, drawn from their individual, social and cultural context. This completes the form for that individual but does not preclude completion in different ways by different listeners. The suspense of the sense of incompleteness in itself draws those who experience it beyond the music to feelings of a greater entity.

---

by some composers at the time, it is not the definition of the sublime observed in this book (Chua, *Absolute Music*, 136).

8. Brown, *God and Grace of Body*, 247.
9. Rosen, *Romantic Generation*, 3.

Form in Romantic music is transformed: it is adjusted, remodelled, or subverted to construct new modes of meaning in music. Not only were the Classical forms reconstructed, but new forms emerged, particularly ones that focused on the individual, such as the song cycle for solo singer. As well as the imagination, composers also used musical memory as a tool in their construction of form. A degree of complexity is added to the form in its ability to make "an earlier movement intrude on the domain of a later one," and, in this way is a dislocation of the traditional form.[10] This use of memory to dislocate form is inspired by the Romantic emphasis on memory as a physical experience of calling up the past within the present, not, as Rosen says, merely a sense of loss and regret, but a physical re-experiencing.[11] This is similar to Rosen's understanding of the Romantic fragment which characterized early Romanticism: a fragment that is complete in its own right, and yet is felt to be torn away from a larger whole.[12]

Romantic Thought on Music

Romantic theologians were influenced by the thought of the post-enlightenment era, in which scientific or empirical evidence was being sought to corroborate knowledge. Schleiermacher's theology begins from the point of religious experience. The natural world is an important part of human experience, which takes account of experience of the divine through the created world. Schleiermacher believes God is revealed in the created world. However, Schleiermacher's theology is not a form of natural theology, which is for him too universal. He strives to achieve a balance between the individual and universal forms of religion, or, the revealed "positive" religion and natural religion.[13] It is through his philosophical theology, which takes account of and critically understands human experiences, that he attempts to bridge the gap. Klemm writes "Philosophical theologians are free, by the power of imagination and understanding, to enter into the intuitions and feelings of the universe found in the historical religions, while being free from their particular claims to truth."[14] They can, then, take traditions and reimagine them; they can re-evaluate tradition in light of the times. The religion of the traditions continued to have meaning for Schleiermacher,

---

10. Ibid., 88–89.
11. Ibid., 183.
12. Ibid., 48.
13. Schleiermacher, *On Religion*, 98–99.
14. Marina, *Cambridge Companion*, 261.

and it was to work alongside what is newly revealed in the ongoing progress of theological thought.

Schleiermacher's thought closely links religion and music. For Schleiermacher, religion is the feeling of absolute dependence.[15] That music is often free from words means that it speaks directly to the feelings, in Schleiermacher's understanding, and therefore it feeds directly into religion, which is itself feeling. Schleiermacher evidently thought about the relation of music to religious feeling, as his character Eduard discusses it in the *Christmas Eve Celebration*. Eduard claims music is most closely related to religious feeling.[16] Eduard also states that "particular events are only the passing notes for music. Its true content is the great chords of our mind and heart."[17] In other words, music's true subject is feeling, and for Schleiermacher, so is religion's. This feeling of absolute dependence could be ignited by one of the key themes of Romantic music, the pastoral, encouraging the feeling that humans are dependent upon nature. This is most likely to occur when the sublime is experienced through pastoral music. This is supported by Schleiermacher's claim that music is a self-contained revelation of the world.[18] This feeling of absolute dependence is also, for Schleiermacher, consciousness of God.[19] Therefore the feeling of absolute dependence is a fundamental response to God that is pre-reflective. Experience of transcendence in music is a place where this reflection can take place, in the merging of the human subject with the divine object.

Although Romantic thought often places importance on the experience of the individual, Schleiermacher's thought reminds us of the place of the community, both in musical and religious experience. Schleiermacher imagines a "music among the saints that becomes speech without words, the most definite, most understandable expression of what is innermost."[20] Music represents the relationship between the community, an unspoken reflection which makes it no longer necessary to speak in words. Schleiermacher's *Christmas Eve Celebration* also portrays music as a device which binds together a group of friends.

It is evident in *Christmas Eve Celebration* that Schleiermacher understands the importance of particular experiences of particular music in the tunes played by the child on the piano, performing to the adults as her

---

15. Schleiermacher, *Christian Faith*, 12.
16. Schleiermacher, *Christmas Eve Celebration*, 29–30.
17. Ibid., 32.
18. Schleiermacher, *On Religion*, 41.
19. Schleiermacher, *Christian Faith*, 17.
20. Schleiermacher, *On Religion*, 75.

Christmas gift to them, and also in Friederike's musical accompaniment to the narratives of her friends. The music is used in this context to bind the group together as a community involved in the experience of this particular music. Schleiermacher also expresses an acknowledgement of the more universal aspect of music, however, through the mouth of Karoline, who claims that "never does music weep or laugh over particular circumstances, but always over life itself."[21] Music encapsulates something important about the whole of life. It is both a fragment of the whole, and an encapsulation of the whole. Whilst this is a fictional work, and the words cannot be put in Schleiermacher's mouth, these claims are not refuted by any of the characters in the dialogue.

If, as Schleiermacher suggests through characters in his *Christmas Eve Celebration*, music could encapsulate the feelings of an experience particularly well, then the feelings which arise from the intuition of listening to a piece of music are a way of experiencing the particular revelation through music. As Eduard says, "every fine feeling comes completely to the fore only when we have found the right musical expression for it. Not the spoken words, for this can never be anything but indirect . . . but a real, uncluttered tone."[22] The feelings evoked by nature only come completely to the fore when encapsulated by music.

In summary, Schleiermacher gives importance to the individual experience, but also as it fits into a greater whole. This bigger picture may be religion or society in his thought, but it may be the natural world. The pastoral is a key theme of the Romantic thinkers, and nature was idealized particularly because of the negative impact of the industrial revolution on the landscape and natural world, but also on the quality of life of those living in polluted cities. In the Romantic era, the natural world also became a focal point of composers in their music, as it did also in other forms of art. This preoccupation with nature is a reaction against less wholesome features of the industrial revolution, in turning, aesthetically at least, to healthier parts of the world. The man-made features of the industrial revolution encouraged a focus on the beauty of nature, such that the natural world became idealized.

Romantic Music and Self

The idea of being at once complete and yet part of something greater is a prevailing sense of one particular form used by Romantic composers—the

21. Schleiermacher, *Christmas Eve Celebration*, 31.
22. Ibid., 29.

song cycle.[23] The song cycle, for example, is, in Rosen's view, "the most original musical form created in the first half of the nineteenth century."[24] Schumann's *Dichterliebe* song cycle is one example given by Rosen of the Romantic fragment. Each song is a complete song in its own right, and yet forms a part of the song cycle, which is, in its entirety, built up of these complete songs. Not only that but the first and last songs of the song cycle bring a sense of the entire song cycle being a part of a greater whole: "The form is not fixed but is torn apart or exploded by paradox, by ambiguity, just as the opening song of *Dichterliebe* is a closed, circular form in which beginning and end are unstable—implying a past before the song begins and a future after its final chord."[25] The form sounds paradoxically complete; it is finished, and yet incomplete, in that there is more to it than presented. The song cycle draws the listener into the embodied experience of the form. The listener puts themselves at the heart of the story in the role of protagonist, and the song cycle becomes part of a personal journey.

Composers of the song cycle form were not the only ones to take traditional classical formal elements and transform them. Felix Mendelssohn (1809–1847), like Schumann, continued to use "traditional elements of classical form to achieve a deeply unclassical effect."[26] Mendelssohn attempts to dispel the illusion of the perfect form in his exploitation of traditional Classical form in the first movement of his *Eb Major Quartet*. Here he subverts the effect of satisfaction produced by the return of the main theme, by means of the preparation for its return: "Harmony, rhythm, and texture conspire to produce an effect of extreme exhaustion after an access of passion, and it is with the sense of exhaustion, of wasted energy, that Mendelssohn reintroduces his main theme and the tonic harmony."[27] This is a similar technique to that which Haydn employed in creating frustration by the evocation of chaos in the prelude to *The Creation*, which uses the listener's feelings in the construction of form. However, whereas for Haydn this was deliberately representative of a particular concept, for Mendelssohn it was a compositional tool without external reference beyond the music. There is a sense of futility about the return of the theme at this point, a surrendering to the greater whole on its return.

---

23. The song cycle is a form that came to prominence during the Romantic era. It is a set of related songs which are designed to be performed either as a whole or individually. They often feature a solo singer and accompaniment.

24. Rosen, *Romantic Generation*, 194.

25. Ibid., 51.

26. Ibid., 583.

27. Ibid., 583.

The self is reflected in the music: the self is always complete in itself, but also striving for self-development, to be more than it is, and to be in relation. The journey of the self is never complete until the self ceases to exist. There are also obstacles to self-development, such as suffering, which are both a part of the individual and a hindrance to their progress. Physical suffering is a reminder of the failings of the body. Composers often explored such issues through their music. The personal experience of the suffering of composers themselves often inspired them in their music, for example Beethoven with the onset of deafness over a long period of time, Franz Schubert (1797–1828) with syphilis, and Schumann's mental illness, leading to him voluntarily entering an asylum two years before his untimely death at the age of 46. The suffering encountered by such composers was not physically overcome by their music. For such composers, we might imagine there was a process of meaning-making in exploring their suffering through music. Moreover, the Romantic reminder that the music is only a fragment of the whole is perhaps a means of transcending the suffering in the sense of it being taken up into some greater reality.

For Brown, Beethoven and Schubert confront and resolve issues to do with human suffering through their music. Brown holds that whilst Beethoven overcame suffering by reaffirming a resolution beyond the grave, Schubert's resolution occurs in his life-time.[28] In other words, Schubert is comforted or reconciled with his illness through his music, but Beethoven looks forward to a time without suffering beyond death. Brown focuses on the acceptance of suffering in the knowledge that it is worthwhile for the value of the grace in this life or the afterlife, but it is not a means to remove it. The bodily nature of music does not offer a permanent resolution to suffering, but the help to accept it as a part of human life. The liminal experience of self-transcendence through music that deals directly with the issue of suffering is a means of understanding the place of suffering in the world, without denying it or striving to overcome it, which would be futile. Similarly, music does not resolve issues with the finite nature of bodily being, but affirms bodily transience and limitations.

In Schubert's *Winterreise*, the listener is encouraged to project themselves onto the protagonist, they are immersed in the journey and become the protagonist, as in Beethoven's heroic form explored above. In this form, it is achieved partly through the use of a lone singer accompanied only by piano. Schubert, known primarily for his songs and song cycles, guides toward the issue of death in his song cycle *Winterreise*. Based on a set of poems by Müller, the protagonist makes a solitary journey away from his

---

28. Brown, *God and Grace of Body*, 267.

beloved. It was more common at the time of writing for individual songs to be performed than the whole song cycle, though Kristina Muxfeldt notes that it is documented that Schubert did play the whole cycle of *Winterreise* for his friends.[29] Muxfeldt notes that the frequent modulations of the music reflects the inner experience of the wanderer, through memories, fantasies and present experience.[30]

The main theme of the music is loneliness, but the wanderer's journey may also be interpreted as the private journey toward death.[31] The Romantic characteristic of *Sehnsucht*, or intense longing, is present in the cycle. It is mixture of a longing for the love of the wanderer's beloved with a longing for death, changing from the former to the latter during the cycle.[32] The wanderer is denied both of these. Schubert was ill during the composition, and was perhaps coming to terms with his own mortality. Toward the end of this journey on which Schubert takes the listener, the song "Der Wegweiser," the signpost, metaphorically points toward the inevitability of death. The signpost points down a path from whence there is no return. The last verse can be interpreted as the culmination of this journey, the protagonist's death, as he goes his way with the hurdy-gurdy man.

The Self in the *Pastoral Symphony*

The experience of transcendence through music not only allows humans to reflect on their concept of self, but also to re-evaluate their place in the world. It is in being taken outside of the everyday that allows for such a wider reflection. This can be achieved when the created world is encapsulated and presented in musical form, as in Haydn's *The Creation*. However, this becomes more prominent with the emphasis on the self as a fragment of the natural world in the pastoral works of the Romantic era. The Romantic concern with the self shifts the focus from an illustration or representation of creation to presenting the self within creation; Romantic music is concerned about the place of the self within the natural world, rather than nature as an object to be represented by music.

The Romantics were undoubtedly concerned with nature and attempted to discover meaning in nature, but this theme continues to be important in contemporary theology. Nature plays a role in Brown's theology and he

29. Gibbs, *Cambridge Companion to Schubert*, 123.

30. Ibid., 126.

31. A detailed analysis of the protagonist's attitude toward death is found in Lauri Suurpää's *Death in Winterreise*.

32. Ibid., ix.

explores "the range of sacramentality available through nature."[33] Brown advocates a re-enchantment of place—of natural and man-made places. If one particular aspect of the material or natural world can stand for all of reality, then it can speak of a universal truth. For Brown, only through the Romantic movement is "the finding of the divine in nature at its most majestic or awesome."[34] Brown notes that "some sets of historical circumstance make it easier to experience God in one way rather than another"[35] and thus perhaps the industrialisation of the time allowed for God to be accessed more easily through the natural world, which was perceived to be more innocent, more beautiful, more pure.

Beethoven's *Symphony No. 6: Pastoral Symphony*, premièred in 1808, which exemplifies the focus on the natural beauty of the world. Unusually for Beethoven, it is explicitly programmatic, and each movement has a title that links it to nature.[36] It is written in the middle of Beethoven's transition to a more Romantic style of composing, and was undoubtedly influenced by Romantic thought. Beethoven wanted the symphony to remind the listener of nature. He wanted the symphony to be titled *Pastoral Symphony or Reminiscence of Rural Life: More an Expression of Feeling Than a Painting*, showing the relation between music and feeling, as discussed in chapter 1 in relation to Schleiermacher's thought. Beethoven's symphony arouses the feelings associated with experiencing features of the natural world, rather than describing them in music.

The third movement of the *Pastoral Symphony*, "Merry Gathering of Country Folk," is focused on the country people. The folk style of country dancing is portrayed: it is a scherzo, or a dance, that uses the theme from the first movement. Its place as the central movement of the work puts human life at the heart of nature. The use of themes from the first movement shows the importance of the relation between the people and nature: they are not distinct entities, but connected. A dance is an extension of the embodied form of music, responding physically to the sounds. The theme of country living returns in the fifth and final movement, in which the life of the shepherd is portrayed in peaceful relation to nature. In this way, Beethoven introduces individual life experiences into his music, and, in this way, it is easier for the listener to empathize and thereby put themselves in the music.

33. Brown, *God and Enchantment of Place*, 84.
34. Ibid., 85.
35. Ibid., 87.
36. The titles of its movements, given by Beethoven, are 1) Awakening of Cheerful Feelings on Arriving in the Country, "Allegro ma non troppo"; 2) Scene by the Brook; 3) Merry Gathering of Country Folk; 4) Thunderstorm; and 5) Shepherd's Song—Happy and Thankful Feelings After the Storm.

This work contrasts with Haydn's portrayal of nature in *The Creation*, which objectifies creation, presenting it as an other, whereas Beethoven introduces the subjective self to nature. As the musical form requires more input from those experiencing it in constructing the meaning of the experience, the listener is placed in the midst of creation, rather than as an observer of creation, as they are in Haydn's work. In contrast to the Classical presentation of nature, the listener is therefore allowed the opportunity to evaluate their place in the midst of the natural world through the Romantic evocation of nature.

The Sublime in the *Pastoral Symphony*

The understanding of the sublime is demonstrated by the trope of the uncontrollable force of nature in Beethoven's *Pastoral Symphony*. Human life is threatened in the fourth movement by the thunderstorm. The fifth movement of Beethoven's *Pastoral Symphony* represents a dramatic thunderstorm which passes away and leads to a section of thanks to God. However, unlike Haydn's sublime moment in *The Creation*, the sublime moment of the thunderstorm is surrounding by ordinary activities of everyday life, in the forms of entertainment and work, or specifically dancing and shepherding. The thunderstorm in Beethoven's *Pastoral Symphony* illustrates that nature is beyond human control and is another means in which musical experience of the sublime may guide one to reflect thought on the divine.

Such a use of the thunderstorm may be interpreted as the traditional battle of good overcoming evil, or as expressing the notion that God is in control, despite apparent lapses represented by the storms. These storms are reminiscent of the nineteenth-century conception of the sublime, in Burke's view by an overwhelming natural incident causing fear, or Kant's by the imagination of morally overcoming the overwhelming natural event. Nature is used to represent the breaking apart of form when music transcends the form. The thunderstorm may represent the chaos, as the form breaks down.

The sublime is closely related to nature in the Romantic era, due partly to Kant's strong links between the dynamical sublime and the overwhelming parts of the natural world. Crowther writes that "Kant's emphatic linking of the sublime to nature has left it profoundly associated with the Romantic era."[37] The definition of the sublime as a captivating experience of an excess of meaning, gives more emphasis to the individual's experience than the natural world. Moreover, if this experience allows the threshold

---

37. Crowther, *Kantian Sublime*, 163.

between the human subject and the divine object to be liminally suspended, experiencing the sublime in the overwhelming presentation of the natural world through music is also a place of encounter between humans and God.

The created world in Beethoven's *Pastoral Symphony* differs from Haydn's presentation of creation, in that Beethoven presents it in relation to human life rather than against an "other." No longer is the human subject against creation, as in Haydn's sublime moment of being overawed by the moment of creation out of chaos. In Beethoven's work, the sublime moment is in the natural world of God's creation, but always in relation to humans: the dance of the country people in the third movement, and the shepherd of the fifth movement, "Shepherd's Song—Happy and Thankful Feelings After the Storm." The sublime moment is therefore always in relation to human protagonists of the story, much like the musical sublime only ever exists in relation to the embodied human subject.

Summary

In the Romantic era new musical metaphors were developed which incorporated nature and similarly allowed God to be found through these representations of the natural world. However, the pastoral as a theme in Romantic music is no longer concerned with presenting nature as it is, but with illustrating the place of humans within nature. In musical terms, the experiencing human subject embodies those presentations of humans in nature, and is therefore able to evaluate their place within the created world.

Beethoven's presentation of the sublime moment in the thunderstorm demonstrates the centrality of the human life in nature, as it is surrounded by music illustrating the everyday lives of country folk. This contrasts with Haydn's presentation of creation, in which his sublime moment is evoked by a created world viewed as other, over against humans. However, in Beethoven's sublime moment, the created world is seen in relation to the human protagonists. Those experiencing the music enact the human participation represented in each movement, in participating in the dance and the shepherd's song surrounding the thunderstorm.

The Individual Self and Embodied Form

Scott Burnham's identifies the idea of the self in the heroic form in Beethoven. Burnham's reading of Beethoven draws on Hegel's understanding of self-development.[38] This use of Hegel's understanding of self-development leads to an account of form that, whilst acknowledging the place of human experience, remains too generalized. It is an ethical, rather an aesthetic form, but assumes that the form will be experienced the same way by all: in this way, it is idealistic. Schleiermacher's thought can be used to develop Burnham's idea of heroic form toward an account of embodied form. Burnham's understanding of form begins to take account of the experience of music based on the feelings it produces rather than the abstract written musical score, the basis for many analyses of musical form, but that it does not go far enough in its account of the individual self that experiences the music.

Burnham calls his analysis of form "ethical" as opposed to the usual "aesthetic" way of analysing the written score, but it is in fact a step toward an embodied way of understanding musical form, beyond the abstract approach of much musicology to written musical form. Burnham's analysis incorporates feelings and emotions aroused by music, as well as the notes written on the page. Burnham seeks meaning in the works, and identifies three key themes that are relevant also to theological discussion of Beethoven. These are the evaluation of the self, the place of the self as part of a greater whole, and the merging of the subjective and objective through the musical experience.

Heroic Form in the *Eroica*

Beethoven's music strives to go beyond the Classical, and, in his transformative middle period, he develops what Burnham has identified as a trope, the heroic: "This trope shares significant features with the quest plot, or hero's journey, and as such carries significant mystic and ethical force."[39] According to this trope, Beethoven's music tells a story, or rather takes the listener on a journey, which is both indeterminate and heroic. In other words, the form is embodied in the experience of the music. There is no protagonist in the story of the hero's journey, it does not describe a particular event, but the listener is drawn into putting themselves in the place of the hero in the journey. Burnham highlights the dual role of the music in that it is both telling a story, but is also an enactment of that story through the listener's participation.[40]

---

38. I will not engage in the argument between Hegel and Schleiermacher here, as I am interested in Burnham's use of Hegel to interpret Beethoven's musical form.

39. Burnham, *Beethoven Hero*, 24.

40. Ibid., 24.

In his musical analysis of Beethoven, Burnham identifies a particular means of the development of form in Beethoven's composition through a form he identifies as the heroic form. This form is a development of the Classical sonata form. It is significant that his analysis is not based on merely looking at the score, but at considering the feelings that are aroused by the music. It takes account of the experience of the music. Indeed, the heroic form is not possible without the relation of the musical form to a human subject: without an account of the experience of listening to the music, it remains a sonata form. This reflects the trend in Romantic thought toward a consideration of the feelings aroused by religion and music, as discussed with regard to Schleiermacher in chapter 1. Burnham believes that music's "communicability is contingent upon the fact that as citizens of the same era and tradition, we are not so different from one another as we might imagine."[41] In other words, the sorts of feelings aroused by the experience of music will be similar, if we come to the music from similar contexts.

A musical example of the heroic form is the first movement of Beethoven's *Symphony No. 3 "Eroica,"* or the "Heroic Symphony," op. 55 (1804). For Burnham, the heroic trope is effected particularly through the coda.[42] In the Classical era codas were typically short passages that reinforced the final cadence by extending it. They did not include thematic material from the movement. Beethoven extends the coda, and reflects on what has gone before by the use of earlier themes. Therefore, Beethoven is able to make much greater thematic use of the coda, which allows it greater impact on the listener's feelings. For Burnham, "in the coda the idea of retelling the movement is merged with the culminating release, or telos, of the movement—the distancing implied by the readings of the coda as a narrating summation of the entire movement is paradoxically at the same time a moment of complete identification."[43] Beethoven sustains the intensity of the story in-the-moment whilst also pointing toward the ending. The coda points forward to the ending, which is the main role of the coda in the Classical style, but in concluding and encapsulating the narrative in the Romantic style, it points back to the journey as well as forward to the ending.

---

41. Ibid., 165.

42. The coda is the concluding section of a movement. As such, it represents a point of reflection on the movement that has gone before. In Classical form, it is often an extended cadence, the concluding phrase of a passage. It makes evident the end of the movement, and noticeably does not necessarily use thematic material from the movement. Beethoven develops the place of the coda, extending it beyond its Classical remit, giving it more importance in the overall form.

43. Burnham, *Beethoven Hero*, 23.

Moreover, the coda re-presents the whole of the story in summary, and is therefore both a fragment of the whole story, and an encapsulation of the whole. It is particularly the heroic form that lends itself to this, as the listener is drawn into the story through the Romantic notion of the projection of self. As the listener is taken on a journey with the music, they imagine themselves embroiled in whatever it is the music encounters on the way, and thus the experience becomes more real. In using the heroic form, Beethoven is drawing the listener into the quest for the self, which, through identification with the story, but retaining the distance of a non-participant listener, the self is able to become more conscious of itself and is perhaps changed by this. Empathy is a key part of the imaginative entering into the music for the heroic form, as indeed it is for much Romantic music.

The coda, as the end point of the movement, is a useful point at which the listener can reflect on the whole of the story, alongside their participation in it. The impact of the coda of the first movement of *Eroica*, in its ultimate sense of closure using the technique of retelling and encapsulating the story with great intensity, and in its *telos* being "not just an end but an end accomplished," had a lasting impact on Romantic music and critical thought about music thereafter. Burnham believes that the "phenomenological momentousness of closure in the heroic style reinforced this idea of the closed work: because of the feeling of end-orientation enforced by such closure . . . one could not hope to interpret the details of the ongoing temporal flow of a piece without a knowledge of the whole, without a perspective that closes off the work as a whole."[44] This extended coda allows for reflection before the closure of the whole, as part of the musical experience, rather than in memory. This musical technique was identified in the finale of Mozart's *Don Giovanni*, where, similar to Beethoven's coda, the listener is given musical time to reflect on the journey, whilst still remaining in-the-moment of the music.

However, whilst Burnham highlights closure of the work in the coda, an understanding of the listener's experience in determining the musical form leaves it open to differing interpretations. Moreover, the idea that the narrative is re-enacted in the listening experience of every new listener denies the possibility of a closed musical form. If musical form is always in relation to an individual embodied human subject, Beethoven's heroic form must therefore be open to new interpretations with every experience of it.

The traditional use of sonata form remains discernible in any musicological analysis of the written score, but such an analysis that does not account for the embodied experience of listening to the music would overlook

---

44. Ibid., 67.

Burnham's heroic form, more so an account of embodied form. The embodied experience of the music allows for reflection in-the-moment of the coda, without the need for prior knowledge of musical occurrences, though that may of course deepen the level of interpretation. The heroic form as an embodied form acts in the moment and does not require existing musical knowledge, though such knowledge may be helpful in recognising traditional formal markers. The listener's experience of the musical form allows for reinterpretation of the form with every listening: there is no guarantee that the same person will experience the form the same way twice.

Heroic Form and Self-Development

Schleiermacher's understanding of the individual self contrasts with the understanding of self-development proposed by Burnham, who reads Beethoven through Hegel. Burnham concludes that self-development is about imagining the self both in a story, and also being able to stand outside the story. In the heroic form, there is a simultaneous feeling of distance and identification, the self is simultaneously at a remove from the music but is also in the music. Burnham likens this to Hegel's discussion of the human consciousness, in self-awareness being, in Burnham's view, that one is both the self and can stand apart from it to be aware of it.[45] This dialectic process is, for Hegel, a means of the development of the self. In being drawn into the story of the music, experiencing human subjects are able to be themselves whilst standing apart from themselves and thus have a new perspective that may lead to a different or developed self. This is the basis for understanding the form as ethical rather than aesthetic, because it is concerned with the development of the self.

The ethical pull of the music draws the listener into participating in the musical experience, according to Burnham. He believes that this ethical pull is "the sense of an earnest and fundamental presence burdened with some great weight yet coursing forth ineluctably, moving the listener along as does the earth itself."[46] Music is always progressing in its necessary movement through time, but for Burnham it also moves the listener. For Burnham, the experience of the heroic form is almost a call to action, which develops the self, in light of some objective ethical presence. Therefore, if the music is to have a meaningful effect, there must be an objective form with which this embodied form merges. This progress is inevitable if the music produces the same effects, however whilst this may be the case in

45. Ibid., 23.
46. Ibid., 65.

Burnham's abstract ethical form, an understanding of embodied form means that each individual will not experience the music in exactly the same way. By drawing on Hegel, Burnham's account suggests that everyone will follow the same pattern of self-development. This approach is idealistic, and does not take account of the individual self. Rather, it considers "the self" in general. However, the self is always an individual self, and therefore the development of the self is always about a particular self.

In contrast, approaching musical form following Schleiermacher's thought leads to an emphasis on the feelings aroused by the music. Following Schleiermacher, the music is theologically valid because of the feelings it evokes, the same feelings that are evoked by religion. Following this understanding, music is not ethical in terms of guiding the individual's self-development, but is an embodied religious experience, in evoking a feeling of absolute dependence. There is no empirical data gathered from the experience as to how to live better, but in relation to the religious experience it may be a form of self-development. Therefore, an account of Romantic form which draws on Schleiermacher rather than Hegel accounts for subjective individual experiences of the form. Self-development is not a single trajectory, in this account, but has multiple paths.

Heroic Form: Ethical and Embodied

An ethical form drawn from Hegel's remains abstract, and is expected to give the same results for all. Therefore, a full account of the human participation in the musical form is better understood as embodied form, drawing on the approach to music from embodiment outlined in chapter 2. Burnham's understanding of ethical form over-formalizes the Romantic form as there remains one interpretation of the form. This was also the issue with formalism in Classical music, as highlighted in chapter 3, in which form was abstracted from musical experience. Form in Romantic music is more incomplete than Burnham's ethical form suggests. It is ever-changing due to the individual contexts in which people experience the music, which was seen to be important in theologies of popular culture in chapter 1.

In analysing ethical form rather than aesthetic form, Burnham has highlighted how an experience of what is perceived by the individual to be the heroic form leads to a re-evaluation of the self as a part of a greater whole. However, there is an underlying assumption in Burnham's analysis of the heroic form that different people will experience the same heroic journey through the music. For Burnham, through the ethical heroic form, the listener joins the hero, participating in the hero's journey. It is the experience of the individual self that makes for a particular experience of the heroic form for each person, which takes into account the feelings evoked by the themes and tropes of the music, but also the individual's context. This understanding of ethical form therefore remains abstract in that it does not take account of the individual self in the experience of the musical form.

Burnham's understanding of self-development, drawing on Hegel's thought, imagines the self in general, rather than the individual self. However, it does not make sense to talk about the self as in general, as the self must always be a particular self. Therefore, self-development must always relate to a particular individual. A reading of Beethoven's heroic form through Schleiermacher, rather than Hegel, suggests that the individual self in the story makes the form always particular to that one experience, and therefore it is not about participation in the same heroic journey for everyone. In an understanding of this embodied form there is no generic hero, but it is the experiencing subject who takes on the role of the protagonist in their experience of the music. The heroic journey is therefore no longer the same story for every individual.

Summary

Burnham's desire to analyse Beethoven's ethical form, through the feelings it evokes, rather than aesthetic form based on the abstract musical score, stems from an understanding that form is more an experience of the music than the reading of a written score. Burnham does not go far enough in accounting for individual experience, however, as he suggests that all will encounter the same story. An understanding of the self in relation to form must always place the self in a particular context: the self is not a general concept, but is always an individual self. The concept of self-development is therefore idealized, suggesting the same journey for all. Burnham's ethical form does not take account of the individual self as they experience the music, and therefore remains an abstract rather than embodied account of form. The heroic form allows for a deepening understanding of the self in itself, but also as a part of a greater whole, drawing on Burnham's account of self-development through Hegel.

Burnham's understanding of the heroic form in Beethoven's music has been developed toward an understanding of embodied form, rather than aesthetic or ethical. This movement in fact sounds similar to the development of humanity as represented by the different characters of Kierkegaard's *Either/Or*, from the aesthetic to the ethical, to the religious. Burnham has developed the traditional understanding, drawing on Hegel, to understand form as ethical. This has been developed further in accounting for the context of each individual, to understand musical form as embodied, which, following Schleiermacher's understanding, is religious. The musical form is religious in the sense, in that it evokes the feeling of absolute dependence in those who experience it. This allows for self-development through experience of embodied forms of music allow for deepening understanding of God, because the feelings evoked by the music, similar to religion, can be feelings of absolute dependence.

Death and the Self

In the Romantic era, the requiem is a key religious work that exhibits the tension between individual religious experience and revealed religion as a whole. Composers' requiems became a way of expressing and communicating their beliefs and feelings about death. The requiem was thought of less as "sacred music" bound within the church, and found its way into the concert hall. The requiem does not transcend death, it is no resolution to the transience of life, but affirms the reality of both. In the Romantic era, composers develop this further: in adapting and eventually abandoning the text of the requiem, they stray further away from a religious resolution to death. The requiem form progressed after Mozart's *Requiem* to Brahms's *Ein deutsches Requiem*, op. 45. The shift of thinking away from the category of sacred music means that transcendence comes to the fore: transcendence of the self and transcendence in encountering God.

The Development of the Requiem Form: Individualisation

The individualisation of the requiem was developed in the Romantic era. The requiem grew in scale during the Romantic era, from Mozart's relatively small orchestra and chorus, to a number of performers too large for an average church setting. The scale of the requiem pushed it into the realm of the concert hall, outside the realm of established religion. This takes the formerly religious form to a body of secular listeners in a secular context. The requiems of Hector Berlioz (1803–1869) and Gabriel Fauré (1845–1924) exemplify this dramatic increase in scale. Composers also began to adapt the text of the requiem to suit their own composition, as Johannes Brahms (1833–1897) did in 1865, and Fauré in 1887 to 1890. Giuseppe Verdi (1813–1901) wrote his *Requiem* (1874) in memory of Italian poet

Alessandro Manzoni. The trend toward secularism is evident in his use of operatic techniques, for which the *Requiem* was criticized.[47]

Berlioz's 1837 *Grande Messe des Morts* uses the traditional requiem text. However, it has four off stage brass ensembles and is conceived as a concert work, which is evident in the stage directions. The scale of this work makes it impractical to perform it in a church setting, and has far surpassed the orchestras of Haydn and Mozart. Berlioz's directions allow for up to 800 singers in the chorus. Similar to Mozart's *Requiem*, but in greater forces, the brass have a menacing but powerful role, again in the Dies Irae, where they are used to portray the final judgement. The sinister mood is dominated by the brass. In the Lacrymosa, the brass again depict a pain that is also sweet. As in Mozart's *Requiem*, Berlioz uses alternating textures to build tension, but the magnitude of his resources allows this to have a much greater effect.

Berlioz did not intend his requiem to be liturgical, as Mozart's was, and he did not write it out of religious motivation. The requiem was commissioned to commemorate soldiers who had died and, as such, was subject to approval by the state. Berlioz writes in his memoirs that the characteristics of his work, as exemplified by his requiem are "passionate expression, intense ardour, rhythmic animation, and unexpected turns." These, then, are the secular features that Berlioz allowed to encroach on the religious form of his *Grande Messe des Morts*.

Fauré's *Requiem*, op. 48 (1890) was begun two years after the death of the composer's father, and was in progress when his mother died in 1887. It is scored for a full orchestra, again, and a choir that splits into six parts. Like Brahms, Fauré also has a male and female soloist, and, though it is not obvious if the composer intended these soloists to represent anyone in particular, as may be contended with Brahms, perhaps the use of the soloist allows individuals a point of access to the music, layering their own meaning on to these powerful solos.

Brahms: *Ein deutsches Requiem*

In the middle of in the Romantic era, Brahms began to compose his *Ein deutsches Requiem*, op. 45, following the death of his mother in 1865, and completed it in 1867. Brahms's composition exhibits the full extent of the personalisation of the traditional form of the requiem: it does not use the standard requiem text; rather it consists of Bible passages from the Lutheran Bible chosen by Brahms himself. The text can thus be seen to reflect Brahms's own religious motivations, and his personal circumstances in

---

47. Kreuzer, *Verdi and the Germans*, 60–61.

regard to his mother's death: it evidences the privatisation of the Requiem Mass. Brahms, in his correspondence with Carl Reinthaler, claimed that the work could have been titled "A Human Requiem."[48] It is clear that Brahms did not intend the work to be a traditional Christian requiem.

This *Requiem* is on a much larger scale than anything Brahms had composed before, and he did not surpass it with his later works. It marks not only the pinnacle of Brahms's orchestral and choral forces, but also a key moment in Brahms's life as a composer. Daniel Beller-McKenna notes that the composition of this work marked a "monumental step forward on every level in Brahms's development as a composer."[49] The requiem form took Brahms further in his compositional life.

Schleiermacher's character Eduard, in the *Christmas Eve Celebration* believes "we can well dispense with particular words in church music but not with the singing itself. A miserere, a gloria, or a requiem: what special words are required for these? Their very character conveys plenty of meaning."[50] This supports Schleiermacher's understanding of music as feeling, as the text is not necessary in evoking feelings and therefore conveying the meaning of the music. This reflects the Romantic thought that no longer are the standard sacred texts untouchable, hence composers begin to change them to suit their own personal circumstances. Brahms's *Requiem* expresses symmetry through both music and text, as Beller-McKenna's musical analysis highlights.[51] It is a complete response to death as a rounded work, and therefore seems not leave anything unsaid, for Brahms. It does not reconcile one with death, it does not overcome death, but it gives a complete response to death.

The text of Brahms's *Requiem* is in German, hence its title, and not Latin, making this personal religious expression through words accessible to a wider population of German speakers. This requiem does not use the traditional text, but Brahms personally selects texts from the Lutheran Bible, which itself made religious texts more accessible to a wider population, and brought the Bible into secular contexts outside of the church, rather than use the traditional Latin text that is all but inaccessible to the secular population.[52] As Brahms felt free to choose his own text, though still a Christian text, there is a shift toward the secular through the language and content of

48. Steinberg, *Choral Masterworks*, 70.
49. Musgrave, *Cambridge Companion to Brahms*, 178.
50. Schleiermacher, *Christmas Eve Celebration*, 30.
51. Musgrave, *Cambridge Companion to Brahms*, 183.
52. Musgrave charts the passages in the Bible from whence Brahms's text is taken in *Cambridge Companion to Brahms*, 14. He also provides an English translation of Brahms's text.

the texts chosen. The use of the term secular may seem surprising, but this is because the text uses secular language in the sense of being the vernacular, the language of the people, German, rather than Latin. The biblical text has become accessible outside of religious contexts, in the secular world, in the concert hall. Scholar of German Romantic music Michael Musgrave believes that the choice of texts which are interknit exhibits Brahms's deep knowledge of the Bible.[53] These texts relate to all of humanity, rather than just the Christian, and stay away from Christian dogma. There is no reference in the text to salvation through Christ, as is expected in the requiem.

The Self and *Ein deutsches Requiem*

Ein deutsches Requiem focuses on the living rather than the dead, and attempts to speak to all. It begins "Blessed are they who mourn," with this text replacing the traditional "Grant them eternal rest." This shifts the focus to the mourners, and suggests that the purpose of this requiem has more to do with dealing with grief than about praying for the eternal life of the souls of the dead. It is focused on this world, not the next.

It inhabits a secular context, supported by religious texts that are made through personal choice, not dictated by the church. Musgrave notes that what Brahms omits is as important as what he includes in the text: he includes texts themes around "comfort, hope reassurance and reward for personal effort," whilst he avoids "judgement, vengeance, religious symbols and—above all—the sacrifice of Christ for human sin."[54] Through his choice of texts Brahms is evidently moving away from Christian doctrine toward a more universal response to death. The first baritone solo is a lamentation: "Lord teach me, Ah how in vain." This could be interpreted as expressing Brahms's own grief in the solo male voice, but equally the listener easily empathizes with the lamentation. This reflects the Romantic concern with the self, and the listener is drawn into this particular expression of grief.

His choice of soloists may also be relevant, as the female soloist plays a motherly role. In a Catholic requiem, this female comforter may be interpreted as Mary, but as Brahms had claimed that he was not writing a Christian requiem, it is more likely to be representative of his own mother. A text more traditionally associated with reuniting with Christ could be interpreted as a longing for reunion with his mother. It is easy to relate to Brahms's text, particularly in those parts which express a longing for reunion, such as when the female soloist sings from John 16:22: "Now it's your

53. Ibid., 18.
54. Ibid., 21.

time to be sad. But I will see you again. Then you will be full of joy. And no one will take away your joy." In this context, the reunion is perceived to be between the deceased and those who grieve for them, rather than the traditional interpretation of a reunion with Christ. The solo female singer singing these lines alternates with the choir singing a passage explicitly about motherhood, from Isaiah 66:13: "As a mother comforts her child, I will comfort you." Given his personal circumstances, and the situation of the text within passages about motherhood, the text from John could be interpreted as a longing for a reunion with his recently deceased mother, who died in 1865.[55] The result of Brahms choosing these texts and changing their context is, as Musgrave notes, "a personal hymn to consolation and comfort which removes the words from a Christian context, the voice of a God figure or Christ, and gives them by implication to the voice of a mother, realized in the music by a soprano solo."[56] As well as his mother's death, Brahms had experienced the death of his close friend Robert Schumann a decade earlier in 1856.

Summary

Whereas Mozart used the traditional liturgical form of the requiem in the Classical era, composers of the Romantic era felt able to adapt the form to suit their composition. Some composers, for example Berlioz, continued the trend started by Mozart in expanding the orchestral forces, such that performance in a church was no longer a realistic possibility. More importantly in terms of determining musical meaning, composers began to change the text that accompanies the music. This meant that the texts chosen could represent the particular circumstances of the composer, or the particular occasion for which the music was written. The requiem forms are thus less dependent upon traditional sacred forms and become more personal. This development is a precursor to Takemitsu's *Requiem for String Orchestra* in the Modern era, which dispenses with the text altogether.

Brahms's *Ein deutsches Requiem* reflects the thought of the Romantic era that life is no longer governed from above by religion, but that theological meaning can be found outside the church as well as within. The composer is given more freedom to search for meaning in the so-called secular world, and incorporate this into their understanding of the requiem form. While the listener senses the personal in Brahms's *Requiem* and empathizes

---

55. Beller-McKenna notes that Brahms's mother's death in this year was an immediate impetus for him writing the *Requiem* (*Cambridge Companion to Brahms*, 179).

56. Musgrave, *Cambridge Companion to Brahms*, 22.

with him, the music touches us beyond that at a more universal level. That the requiem is at once personal, reflecting the composer's experiences with death, but also on some level universal, allowing any listener to place themselves as "self" in the work, is a reflection of the words spoken by Karoline in the *Christmas Eve Celebration*, quoted above, that music does not weep or laugh over particular circumstances, only over life itself.[57] Brahms may himself be weeping over certain events, but the listener hears this as universal, allowing them to put themselves in the music.

In Schleiermacher's terms, then, Brahms's *Ein deutsches Requiem*, and the requiem form in general remains religious because of the feelings it evokes. The requiem form has moved toward individualisation but it is the self that is required to experience the music in order for it to be religious. The requiem no longer needs the traditional text in order to explore the liminal concept of death. Music is not religious because of the content of a traditionally religious form, but because of the way the individual body responds to it.

Conclusion

Romantic thought is interwoven with Romantic music. Schleiermacher's emphasis on feeling in religion and music is also a concern of Romantic composers, for whom the feelings of those who will experience their music begin to play a more prominent role in the construction of musical form. The particular context of the Romantic era focuses theological attention on certain issues, as the issues that are important at the time become a part of the fabric of artistic creations. These issues of selfhood and the individual's relation to the world are reflected in music of the era. Musical composition in the Romantic era has become more self-reflective than in the Classical era, encouraged by the move toward individualisation.

The development of Classical form in the Romantic era has shown a change in the relation between musical form and the embodied listener. It was possible to fully analyse form without considering a human subject in the Classical era, but it has become more difficult in the Romantic era. Musicologists Rosen and Burnham have identified compositions in which composers use feelings evoked in the listener to convey musical form. Rosen notes that composers employ the listener's imagination and memory in order to complete forms that otherwise remain incomplete. Romantic forms are incomplete without relation to an experiencing human subject.

---

57. Schleiermacher, *Christmas Eve Celebration*, 31.

Burnham identified the heroic form in Beethoven's music, relating it to the concept of self-development drawn from Hegel. This is also a recognition of the role of the listener in completing the form. However, as Burnham classifies this as an ethical form and expects it to convey the same meaning for all, it remains abstract. Burnham's understanding of this form was developed, drawing on Schleiermacher, in relation to the individual self. The self is always an individual embodied human being, therefore the musical form becomes a new form for each person. The idea of self-development is not only found in the heroic form as the journey of the human life is a trope in Romantic composition.

Exploring the self also encourages a re-evaluation of the place of the human in the world. The Romantics had a particular concern with nature: the industrial revolution led to the idealisation of nature, and the pastoral found its way into many musical works. In contrast to the Classical era, in which the natural world was objectified in a formalized way, the Romantic era was concerned with the individual self in relation to the natural world. Instead of presenting nature in itself, it explores the human place in nature.

The requiem form also reflects the move from objective form in the Classical era to embodied form. Musical requiems are no longer the objective requiem form but are individual forms constructed by composers to reflect their own feelings. These have been seen to relate to their personal experiences, which can be conveyed through the choice of text, as well as through the music. Brahms's *Deutsche Requiem* will always be an expression of Brahms's contemplation of death, which reflects his grief over the death of his mother. However, it is also a more accessible exploration of death than the traditional requiem form. In other words, the requiem can no longer be analysed as an objective form of sacred music, but must be considered as sacramental music.

In the Romantic era music becomes more closely associated with feelings. Musical forms are constructed in relation to an experiencing, embodied human subject, in such a way that without embodied engagement the musical forms remain incomplete. The individual self therefore directs the completion of the created musical form, which has content, but no fixed meaning. This relation between the musical form and embodied human determines the meaning of the music.

> "Slip inside the eye of your mind
> Don't you know you might find
> A better place to play?"
>
> —Oasis, "Don't Look Back in Anger"

5

The Self-Reflective Self
The Modern Era

The twentieth century is characterised by a greater diversity of musical styles than any other century previously. Toward the end of the Romantic movement, composers began experimenting with new ways to develop music: some looked to the past for inspiration, and developed a style now known as neo-classical; others developed new techniques attempting to break from the constraints of the past, composing for modern electronic or modified instruments, using new technologies, and overcoming tonality in the twelve-tone scale. There is enormous variety in music of the Modern era, as composers sought to creatively develop music beyond what some thought of as the stagnant musical restrictions of the past. One of the musical techniques that some composers experimented with was a self-conscious use of silence as a musical tool.[1] Whilst musical silence is not the defining feature of modern music, it would not be possible to discuss such a great diversity of musical styles and genres that exist in this time period. Moreover, musical silence is a feature of Modern music which has great theological depth, and will be the focus of this chapter.

Experimentation in anechoic chambers has shown that human life does not and cannot exist without sound. Therefore, the definition of silence I employ is not dependent on the literal absence of sound, but on the perception of its absence. I will explore negative readings of musical silence in theology, as a form of negation or as a desire for disembodiment through

---

1. The use of musical silence is discussed more fully in Losseff and Doctor, *Silence, Music, Silent Music*; and Bokyan, *Silence and Slow Time*.

the musical form. However, I will suggest a positive theological reading of musical silence, and I will argue that this approach affirms and celebrates the body, in all its limitations.

I will begin with discussion of theological understandings of silence in reference to the primary concepts of this understanding of music as theology: form and embodiment. I will then explore the history of the use of silence in the twentieth century, to understand the context out of which it arises as one of the many features of experimentation in the Modern era, before analysing two specific works, John Cage's *4'33"* (1952) and Toru Takemitsu's *Requiem for String Orchestra* (1957). Cage composed *4'33"* as a serious piece of music in which there is not a single musical note played. It was not written for any particular instrument, though it was premiered on piano by David Tudor.[2] The lid of the piano was closed and opened to delineate the three movements. Cage composed a sequel to this work, *o'oo" (4'33" No. 2)* in 1962, which is also silent, but this piece is of indeterminate length. Takemitsu's *Requiem for String Orchestra* is a requiem without words which, although it is not an entirely silent work, makes pronounced use of musical silence.

Cage and Takemitsu not only used silence in their music as a compositional tool, but also wrote at length to explain their use of silence. Cage, in particular, explored silence—unlike in the definition used in this book, in the sense of absence of sound—physically and philosophically. He was also interested in Zen Buddhism and its quest for silence as a means of going beyond the everyday. Takemitsu and Cage shared philosophical as well as musical ideas, but Takemitsu was also influenced by Japanese culture, and in particular, the liminal concept of *ma*,[3] the moment of transition between sound and silence. In this chapter I will bring the writings of Cage and Takemitsu into dialogue with musicological understandings of their work, and the contemporary theology on the issues of embodiment and liminality.

Theology and Musical Silence

There are two key theological concerns in this book: musical form and embodiment. The relation between musical form and embodiment is

---

2. The score which Tudor played from has been lost, and there is some dispute over what was actually written for Tudor to perform from. Tudor claims that it was written on staff paper (the traditional form of musical manuscript). See Nicholls, *Cambridge Companion*, 174–75.

3. This is the intense moment of silence that occurs just before sound. See Takemitsu, *Confronting Silence*, 51.

fundamental to a theological understanding of musical silence. I have outlined in chapter 2 that music is a bodily form of communication. Silence, too, is a bodily form of communication. There cannot be an experience of silence without the body, and therefore experience of silence does not negate the body, but affirms it in all its limitations.

Philosopher Bernhard Dauenhauer also holds that silence is active, not passive: it is not only a general feature of human activity, but it is also a form of communicative activity.[4] A silence is not a lack of communication, but a form of communication that opens up possibilities: in music, there is no silence that is not also a form of embodied communication. As John Potter writes, "There can be no dead silence until the end of the piece, and even then the silence is a rhetorical one in which either performers will be estimating when to start the next piece or the audience will be judging when (or if) they should applaud."[5] In other words, silence is always loaded; it is never an inert state, and it is through interpreting the nuances of the silence that meaning is found. This is reflected in the Japanese concept of *ma*, which is a particular moment of silent tension before sound breaks silence. This concept will be explored in relation to Takemitsu's *Requiem for String Orchestra*.

Rachel Muers, following Dauenhauer, argues that "Silence is both something we encounter or discover—the silence of a deserted place, an empty room—and something we do, and experience as done by others—conversational silences, silences in response to questions."[6] In other words, silence only exists in relation to the human subject. Similarly, in listening to music, silence is both discovered in a work and often kept by the listener, in the experience of classical music at least. As a performer, there is a balance to be struck between creating sounds and creating silence.

There is also a binding element to silence in music between the performer and listener, or amongst a group of listeners, which gives musical silence a communal or social aspect. This is reflected in Muers's notion of silence as an enactment of "the reality of a given and non-verbalised common ground."[7] It is a sharing between related human beings: in music, this is particularly important with regard to the relation between composer, performer(s), and listener(s). Musical silence is particularly effective at challenging the relationship between these groups, as is evident in Cage's 4'33".

---

4. Dauenhauer, *Silence*, 6–7, as noted by Muers in *Keeping God's Silence*, 4.
5. Losseff and Doctor, *Silence, Music, Silent Music*, 164.
6. Muers, *Keeping God's Silence*, 4.
7. Ibid., 153.

When a listener experiences a silence, this is an experience of something deeply fundamental to creation. This would make the experience of silence an experience that gives the listener a deeper experience of the created world. This may occur through a transcendent experience, in which the threshold between the realm of sounds and the realm of silence is crossed. Ward has argued that "with respect to the discourse of negative theology, there are not then 'fissures opened by our language' that are not simultaneously bound and constructed by that language."[8] Similarly, the silences in music are not autonomous sound chasms, but are created by the sounds: they are bound to the sound. Without reference to musical sounds, it is difficult to create an experience of musical silence: thus, listeners may not find themselves immersed in the silence. Perhaps this is why many struggle to recognize Cage's 4'33" as musical silence, or indeed as music, as the silence is not created by sounds but exists in and of itself.

Ward argues that it is necessary to "rethink . . . the relationship between language and silence in a way that recognizes silence as integral to communication; silence *as* a form of communication."[9] In other words, silence is a fundamental part of human communication. In the silence, time is taken to communicate what is left unsaid by the words. For this understanding of music as theology, the silence communicates what is left unsaid by the music, which is already communicating in a more indeterminate manner than language. For Ward, in terms of language, the "empty spaces here establish a certain tension between the arrangement of the letters, the words and the syntax into a communication and the empty margins which create a space for the cessation of intellection. It is a space for/of breathing."[10] Similar to the concept of *ma*, Ward holds there to be a tension in the silence. The tension is created by the expectation of what might break the silence. In musical terms, the tension between the sounds and the pauses, or the notes and the rests, creates such a space for and of breathing. Indeed, musicians—both performers and listeners—often do breathe deeply in such pauses. This emphasizes that silence is a bodily form of communication.

For Dauenhauer, silences can be interpreted as gestures toward God.[11] In his discussion of Balthasar's thought and its relation to Eastern and Western thought, Raymond Gawronski notes that Balthasar believes all religions to have a "tendency to word-weariness." Gawronski notes that all religions

---

8. Davies and Turner, *Silence and the Word*, 179.
9. Ibid., 179.
10. Ibid., 179.
11. Muers, *Keeping God's Silence*, 6.

aspire toward silence: "spiritual man [sic] tends to want silence."[12] There are many differing reasons for this, but primarily silence connects on a deeper level to God: Gawronski writes, "For Balthasar, the interplay of word and silence in God is part of the mystery of God himself. The tension between these points to the fullness of God."[13] Similarly, it would seem to make sense that the tension between word and silence in humanity has something to do with the fullness of being human: it is part of the revelation of God, and therefore is much to do with the relationship between humanity and God. Only in relation to God is humanity fully human.

Modern Music and Silence

Silence is an integral part of music; music almost always emerges from silence and finishes in silence. Silence, as a perceived lack of sound, can play an important role in music. It is not the opposite of sound, but is a complementary part of music that is put into use by composers. Picard holds that in music, silence is "parallel" to music.[14] Silence is integral to music; it is not the reverse of music. I will first outline the backdrop to the use of silence in modern music out of which emerge the two key examples in this chapter, Cage's *4'33"* and Takemitsu's *Requiem*. As with these two examples, these works are either wholly silent, or silence is intentionally integrated with sound to create a lasting effect of silence.

Silent Music: Allais

The first readily available example of a silent work is found before the Modern era, though it is not entirely serious as a piece of music. The humourist Alphonse Allais (1854–1905) composed a work of 24 bars entitled *Funeral March for the Obsequies of a Deaf Man* (1897) with the instruction "Great sorrows being mute, the performers should occupy themselves with the sole task of counting the bars, instead of indulging in the kind of indecent row that destroys the august character of the best obsequies."[15] It would seem, if we were to take the work and the instructions seriously, that the purpose of the silence is to allow a place for sorrow in its right temperament without

---

12. Gawronski, *Word and Silence*, 1.
13. Ibid., 3.
14. Picard, *World of Silence*, 27.
15. Whiting, *Satie the Bohemian*, 81.

the interruption of sound.[16] There is no intention, however, that this be treated as a serious piece of music.

As a light-hearted form of requiem, then, it is a further step removed from the form employed by Brahms, as discussed in the previous chapter, and pre-empts the development of the requiem form in the twentieth century, as will become clear in discussion of Takemitsu's *Requiem*. This goes against the increasing personalisation of the requiem form, as seen in the Romantic era, and evident in Brahms's *Ein deutsches Requiem*. This silent expression of grief may be interpreted as a parody of the sentimentalism of the expression of feeling in the Romantic era.[17] The composer directly states in the preface that the great sorrow of grief is mute, and therefore so should the music.

Moreover, he cautions against counting out time, the pun in the French is that *tapage* means "beating" or "tapping out time," as a conductor would, and rowdiness or disturbance. Allais's instructions mean that instead of beating time the performer should count the passage of the bars. This means that the performer steps back from the minutiae to facilitate and comprehend the greater musical form.

Silent Music: Schulhoff

In 1919, the Czech composer Erwin Schulhoff also composed a silent piece that is a movement of a larger work, *In Futurum*. This work is notated in great detail in rests and has many intricate rhythms and changes of time signature. The treble and bass clefs also change places from what the performer would usually find in a score, with a bass clef on the first stave and a treble clef on the second. These details of course cannot be heard in performance, though rhythms and exclamations may sometimes be inferred from the movement of the performer. The rests are deliberately written with movement up and down the stave, with a tie marking outlining the trajectory of

16. The one-page score consists of a single stave without clef or key markings, indeed with no markings at all save the tempo marking "lento rigolando."

17. The preface reads: "L'Auteur de cette Marche funèbre s'est inspiré, dans sa composition, de ce principe, accepté par tout le monde, que les grandes douleurs sont muettes. Les grandes douleurs étant muettes, les exécutants devront uniquement s'occuper à compter des mesures, au lieu de se livrer à ce tapage indécent qui retire tout caractère auguste aux meilleures obsèques." This translates, without the puns present in the original, as "The author of this composition was inspired, in this composition, by the principle, accepted by everyone, that great sorrows are silent. As great sorrows are mute, the performers should only occupy themselves in counting out the bars, instead of engaging in tapping out time, which negates the solemn character of the best funerals" (my translation).

the rests in several places. Four exclamation marks hover over a fermata in bar 9, presumably to give effect to the pause, whilst the final note heads on both staves are shaped as a content and sleepy-looking smiley face—what would now be called an emoji—which is larger than a usual note head, each with its own fermata.

The reference to the future in the title of the work perhaps hints at the direction the composer thought modern music was heading. Schulhoff had recently been awarded the Mendelssohn Prize for composition in 1918, so it is incongruous that he would follow this by writing a silent work. It could be argued that this work is representative of a pessimistic outlook on music in the modern era. Having served in the Austro-Hungarian military for four years during the First World War, and having been wounded and captured, the impact of Schulhoff's personal experiences may be seen in his silent work. This may be more of a statement about the future of Europe after the First World War, in that the horror of it leaves little to say. The energy of the feverish musical rests is futile: the same silence is communicated. On the other hand, the silence need not be interpreted as negative: perhaps in the wake of the war, Schulhoff is optimistic about prospects following the war and the frenetic energy is productive rather than going to waste; or perhaps Schulhoff is providing space to reflect on the impact of the war in the silence.

Like Schulhoff's *In Futurum*, Cage's work also has visual elements, which are also present in the performance. It has three movements, which again must be visually marked if marked at all. In Cage's score (probably produced after David Tudor performed its premiere), the instruction is that the lid of the piano will be closed during the performance but opened briefly between movements to mark the end of one movement and the start of the next. This is Cage's attempt to clarify the form of the work, in three separate movements, with a set time each. The clarity of form is important when the theological implications of form are taken into account, as will be discussed in due course.

Schulhoff's somewhat frenzied silent score, with all its intricacies that in some performances are symbolized by a great deal of movement without sound—for example moving the hands on the piano keys in the rhythm marked but without sounding the notes—is in contrast to Cage's attempts to achieve a Zen-like contemplative silence where his performers are often very still. The performer in Schulhoff's work must also interpret the exclamation marks and the faces on the score. Cage's performer, in contrast, has a minimal score to interpret.

Silent Music: Messiaen

Olivier Messiaen (1908–1992) wrote the *Quartet for the End of Time* (1941) during the Second World War. The preface states that the work was inspired by the Book of Revelation, which is also suggested in its title.[18] It also gives a detailed movement-by-movement programmatic account of the images and scenarios Messiaen was presenting in the music. Many biblical references appear in the descriptions. The fifth movement is to be played "infinitely slow" to represent the eternity of the Word.[19] Music theorist Anthony Pople notes the passing back and forth between movements which represent eternity and movements which are concerned with the apocalypse.[20] This endlessness is woven in and through the whole *Quartet*.

Messiaen intends for the silence to be experienced on a religious plane. He writes of the first movement: "Between three and four in the morning, the awakening of birds: a solo blackbird or nightingale improvises, surrounded by a shimmer of sound, by a halo of trills lost very high in the trees. Transpose this onto a religious plane and you have the harmonious silence of Heaven." Messiaen uses birdsong, or rather fragments of birdsong, in the clarinet and violin over the sustained notes of the piano and cello. Pople notes how straightforward it is to interpret the continuous notes as a representation of heaven and the birds are held in this musical frame.[21] Messiaen here uses the pastoral to evoke silence. Nature often has associations with tranquillity or peacefulness, and Messiaen channels these through his music.

Alongside the religious interpretation, The *Quartet* can also be interpreted as a response to war. Messiaen was imprisoned in a prisoner-of-war

---

18. "And I saw another mighty angel coming down from heaven, wrapped in a cloud, with a rainbow over his head; his face was like the sun, and his legs like pillars of fire. He held a little scroll open in his hand. Setting his right foot on the sea and his left foot on the land, he gave a great shout, like a lion roaring. And when he shouted, the seven thunders sounded. And when the seven thunders had sounded, I was about to write, but I heard a voice from heaven saying, 'Seal up what the seven thunders have said, and do not write it down.' Then the angel whom I saw standing on the sea and the land raised his right hand to heaven and swore by him who lives forever and ever, who created heaven and what is in it, the earth and what is in it, and the sea and what is in it: 'There will be no more delay, but in the days when the seventh angel is to blow his trumpet, the mystery of God will be fulfilled, as he announced to his servants the prophets'" (Rev 10:1–7, NRSV).

19. For a fuller account of the theological inspiration for the work, see Pople, *Messiaen*, 11–14.

20. Ibid., 14.

21. Ibid., 11.

camp when the majority of the work was written,[22] and its unusual combination of instruments was dictated by the musicians available for its performance. Again, different interpretations are possible with regard to its relation to the war. Firstly, there is a longing for eternity since war has brought the end of time, or even the world, as we know it. However, as clarinettist Rebecca Rischin notes, the *Quartet* is not a work of despair expressing the absence of God, like others written at the time, but is hopeful: the message of the *Quartet* is, for her, a "resounding reaffirmation."[23]

In both musicological and theological accounts, analysts have identified a quality of silence in Messiaen's *Quartet*, although there are no great pauses or rests in the score. Musicologist Jan Christiaens notes that "Messiaen's theological music confronts us with a paradox: sounds moving in time are being used as an evocation of a silent eternity."[24] In other words, the listener's experience and the score appear to be contradictory: whilst the music is sounding, the listener perceives silence, even the silence of eternity. This interpretation is based on analysis of the experience of music, rather than the score of the music. The music makes it a theological representation of eternity only through the relation of the embodied human listener and the musical form.

One way of thinking about Messiaen's silence comes from the musicologist Zofia Lissa, whom Darla Crispin considers in relation to Cage's silence. According to Crispin, Lissa "articulates one view of silence—that it may be characterized as an omnipresent factor in a work, but one that advances and retreats from the perceptual surface depending upon the nature of the material that is heard or read over it."[25] Messiaen could instill an impression of silence in the listener by frequent recourse to silence at surface level, and by creating sounds that flow across this silence, not jolting the listener out of the experience of silence but perhaps prolonging a quality of it in the sound. This is an embodied experience of silence that does not exist in the analysis of the musical score.

The musicologist Jan Christiaens writes: "Music as an evocation of silence: it's hard to imagine a stronger paradox. As such, it is closely related to the theological paradox that most fascinated Messiaen: the dogma of the incarnation of God in Christ, the fusion of the Eternal with the temporal."[26]

---

22. The third movement had been written earlier, whilst Messiaen was in a transit camp (ibid., 8–9).
23. Rischin, *For the End of Time*, 6.
24. Losseff and Doctor, *Silence, Music, Silent Music*, 56.
25. Ibid., 127–35.
26. Ibid., 57.

This is an insight into Messiaen's reasons for trying to instill an inner silence into his music. In musical silence, the incarnation is best represented, as both are embodied paradoxes: the impossible occurring in human experience. Christiaens argues that Messiaen can do this because silence is a presence not an absence: the music flows in and out of silence in a natural way, giving the listener an impression of silence.[27]

Christiaens notes that Messiaen wants to "bring the listener closer to eternity and infinity."[28] For Messiaen, giving the listener this impression of the presence of silence is his aim, as for him this experience is an earthly experience of the eternal in a temporal musical form. Silence is particularly appropriate for expressing ideas of the eternal because of its perceived continuous state, despite the sounds, that Messiaen creates in the embodied experience of the listener. This expresses the hope that humans will be able to participate fully in the eternal, and reflects the theological claims of the incarnation, that the eternal was fully present in the temporal. In other words, it is a hopeful appraisal, despite the limitations of human existence, of participating in the eternal.

Silent Music: Denver

Many musicians working in the world of popular music have adopted the idea of silence.[29] John Denver (1943–1997) and John Lennon (1940–1980) are two famous popular musicians to have written silent popular works. Denver has written a silent work which lasts six seconds, and appears on his first album, with the title "The Ballad of Richard Nixon" (1969). This track is easily interpreted as a silent political criticism. The silence may be a reference to the silence desired by Nixon in ordering the destruction of the tapes that implicated him in the Watergate scandal. This is contrary to the technique used by Nixon himself, in taking the concept of silence metaphorically in his speech now known as the "Silent Majority Speech," to respond to criticism of America's military involvement in Vietnam. Nixon's turn of phrase has been said to be lifted from the politician George Meany's speech in support of the war.[30] The silent majority that Nixon addressed were the silent supporters of his message: silence in this case is not a cover up, but

---

27. Ibid., 53–69.
28. Ibid., 56.
29. Osborne, "Sounds of Silence."
30. Varon, *Bringing the War Home*, 330.

an affirmation of support. Denver's political activism was reported in the popular media in 1986, but comments only briefly on this silent work.[31]

Silent Music: Lennon

Lennon wrote two silent works. The first, "Two Minutes Silence" (1969) he wrote with Yoko Ono, and they dedicated it to the baby the couple lost by miscarriage, perhaps expressing the grief that the couple could not put into words following this tragic event. Without knowledge of that context, it could also be interpreted as a reference to the usual tribute or memorial of silence, such as the widely held silences of remembrance, as in Remembrance Day observance, and in doing so uniting with a more universal sense of human loss. This uniting in silence is one of the features of the social conception of "sacred" according to Gordon Lynch.

The second silent work of Lennon is a three second work with the title "Nutopian International Anthem" (1973), which was, like Denver's, a political statement explained in the sleeve notes announcing the birth of the conceptual country Nutopia. This seeming negative reference to utopia—at once the good place and no place—reads like a refutation of this place, but in fact is said in the sleeve notes to have "no land, no boundaries, no passports, only people." In other words, it is, as the title suggests, international: in other words, it is a reference to the whole world. Perhaps, given that it is an "international anthem," it is a call humans all around the world to "keep silence" in the hope of realising a new future. "Nutopia" also suggests that it is new: it does not already exist. This silence leaves of the possibility of a creating a new understanding of humanity, based not on nations, only on the relation between individuals as they form an international community.

Two of these examples are short silent works with suggestive titles and explanatory sleeve-notes. Lennon and Ono's personal silence, however, is longer, and may be experienced like a tribute in the manner of silences kept in memorial of those who die. In keeping this silence, the couple unite with all those who hold the tradition of silence in remembrance. Silence is used to transcend the individual tragedy, and to take it onto the plane of universal human experience.

---

31. Smith, "Good Ol' Boy?"

Embodied Silence in Cage's 4'33"

I will consider the theological implications of the relation between embodiment and the musical form of silence through the music and writings of John Cage (1912–1992). I propose that Cage's musical silence of 4'33" is an embodied silence that affirms life and as such is open to a positive theological interpretation. I will bring Cage's own account of silence in his music, from his writing, into dialogue with contemporary theologians.

There are at least two possible approaches to Cage's use of silence. One possible approach draws on Pickstock's theology, and considers Cage's silent music as an attempt to transcend embodied limits of a world created *ex nihilo*, an ultimately futile endeavour to become disembodied. Interpreted in this way, Cage's musical silence has two implications: it does not acknowledge the nothingness that is present in embodied humans as part of creation; and it denies the material finitude of all human life. Rather than this negative theological reading of Cage's silence, drawing on Gawronski's reading of Balthasar, I suggest that an attempt to create musical silence, as in 4'33", in fact celebrates the complexity of the "in-the-moment" nature of embodied human life. This has two theological implications; this musical silence celebrates the limitations of the human body, by immersing the listener in those same limitations by creating a perception of soundlessness which is impossible in embodied being and acknowledging finitude in all its aspects, importantly through the fixed time period of the piece, 4 minutes and 33 seconds.

The relationship between the form, silent music, and the embodied human listener allows this to happen. Cage gives precedence to form, calling it the "highest truth."[32] For him, length or duration of notes is what governs the form, important in silent work as the only musical characteristic measurable by silence is duration.[33] Cage strips bare the music to pure experience of form, not of harmony, tonality, timbre; there are no distractions to the form. The listener is intertwined with the form in a way that cannot be achieved through musical sounds.

Through the experience of and participation in this musical silence, humans are able to encounter the mystery of God, thereby understanding themselves more in relation to God. Cage's work not only impacts on how theologians understand the human relationship with God, but also how to understand relations with other humans, in community. The relation between the composer, performer, and listener is challenged in that they

32. Cage, *Silence*, 186.
33. Ibid., 13–14.

do not fully assume their usual roles. The relationship, although initially uncertain, is ultimately reinforced by the fact that the audience does sit and listen, while the performer gives a performance, albeit more visual than sonic, following the instructions of the composer. As Larson notes, for the duration of the performance, "The hall is one body, one mind."[34] The composer and the performer do not control the sounds that the audience hears, and thus the audience has control over the sounds of the music. The individual listener, however, does not have total control over what they hear, as they are part of a larger audience, and they are in a particular place with ambient sounds, neither of which they can control. The sounds that are heard in the music, therefore, cannot be controlled by any one individual, whether they are composer, performer, or listener. The musical silence must be constructed in community.

Cage on Silence

Cage's thoughts on silence changed over time. He felt the desire to search for a place where he could experience a total lack of sound. In the anechoic chamber at Harvard University he continued to hear sounds. Cage writes, "There is no such thing as silence. Get thee to an anechoic chamber and hear there thy nervous system in operation and hear thy blood in circulation."[35] Experience in the anechoic chamber shows a limit of the human body: it cannot exist without making sounds. In this way, Cage discovered that "silence is not acoustic. It is a change of mind, a turning around. I devoted my music to it. My work became an exploration of nonintention."[36] The presence of such sounds in the best technologically possible absence of sound led Cage to believe that there could never be such a thing as silence, as there is always something which produces a noise.[37]

This changed his perspective on silence, "after convincing oneself ignorantly that sound has, as its clearly defined opposite, silence," his anechoic chamber experience challenged this idea.[38] Cage writes that this experience, and his experience of Rauschenberg's white paintings, led to him composing 4'33".[39] If this is what silence is, an absence of sound, the search for silence

---

34. Larson, *Where the Heart Beats*, xiii.
35. Cage, *Silence*, 51.
36. Cage, "John Cage," para. 17.
37. Cage, *Silence*, 191.
38. Ibid., 13.
39. Cage, "John Cage," para. 24.

would have to lead to disembodiment, or death.[40] Cage notes pertinently that there are always sounds which one can listen to "if one is alive to hear them."[41] In other words, "Until I die there will be sounds."[42] Embodied human life is noisy, and yet, the perception of silence is possible, perhaps more habitually through music than any other process.

The anechoic chamber allowed Cage to re-evaluate his concept of silence, and led to experimentation with sounds and lack of sounds. In his writings, he attempts to portray silence through the empty spaces he leaves. Cage writes, "What we require is silence; but what silence requires is that I go on talking."[43] In other words, it is only because there is speech surrounding them that the silence is recognized as silence. In other words, experience of silence is context-based. The implications of this for music are perhaps that musical silence requires musical sound, which may explain why it is difficult to experience the silence in 4'33".

Resisting Human Nothingness

As a framework for a negative reading of musical silence, I turn to Pickstock, who notes that Augustine grants that humans can ultimately create "something new"[44]—rather than merely replicating the perfect form. Indeed, it is the fact that a new composition can seemingly come out of nothing that reinforces Augustine's view that creation itself was out of nothing: Pickstock says "The fact that things are continuously *coming to be*, and continuously emerging from points which are nothing, implies for Augustine that it is most rational to see finite reality as having emerged in its entirety from nothing."[45] Whilst humans have a role in creating something new out of creation, it is important to Pickstock that they recognize the nature of their own created being first.

For Pickstock it is important that humans recognize the nothingness out of which creation arises: "Indeed, it is when human creatures fail to confess this nothingness, when their lives in time are without pauses, that this

---

40. Crispin believes that Cage's use of the prepared piano to alter the sounds it produced is also linked to his understanding of silence, in that he "silence[d] an instrument in its normal function, and then [had] it sound in different way" (Losseff and Doctor, *Silence, Music, Silent Music*, 127–35, 137).

41. Cage, *Silence*, 152.

42. Ibid., 8.

43. Ibid., 109.

44. Milbank et al., *Radical Orthodoxy*, 248.

45. Ibid., 248.

order is denied and a greater nothingness of dishonesty ensues."⁴⁶ In other words, human creation that does not acknowledge nothingness is by necessity limited. Pickstock highlights Augustine's discussion that allows humans to also play a role in creation, in making new creations, which stem from "nothing" but must also embrace this "nothingness" in order to flourish. She writes "for Augustine, creation exhibits a *perfect* order or beauty, albeit in its own restricted degree, and the nothingness intrinsic to creation on its own is a necessary part of this order."⁴⁷ This "nothing" is a depth from which creativity stems, and from which both sounds and silences can be drawn.

In musical terms, then, composition must include both sounds and silences to reflect the essence of creation in its fullness and nothingness. Pickstock writes, the "alternation of sound and silence in music is seen by Augustine as a manifestation of the coming into being and the passing into non-being which must characterise a universe created out of nothing."⁴⁸ In other words, the sounds and silences represent the transient nature of creation: they reflect the fullness and nothing of creation. In music, if a composer does not interweave sounds and silence, they misrepresent creation. The alternation of the sounds and the silences in music, the fact that they have a defined start and end, expresses the finitude of creation and all created beings. It is an expression of the theological conception of creation *ex nihilo*, that nothing endures indefinitely, and nothing can exist except out of nothingness.

Following this understanding, to have an entirely silent work without this alternation between sound and silence, as in Cage's 4'33", is to misunderstand creation. Cage's work places the corporeal experience of silence in contrast with the realm of creation. He fails to characterize the universe created *ex nihilo* by attempting to make silence endure exclusively—in terms of the work, in its entirety. Indeed, he makes the prolonged silence more indefinite in his sequel o'oo", the length of which is left to the performer's discretion. Following the negative approach outlined here, this is an even greater failure than 4'33". Not only does it not acknowledge the nothingness in creation, but in having no definite ending, it also refutes the finitude of creation.

---

46. Ibid., 247.
47. Ibid., 247.
48. Ibid., 247.

Denying Material Finitude

Following the negative reading, silence treats music as a limitation. Aspiring to overcome the limitations of creation through silence means denying real material finitude. For Pickstock, "Augustine regards only infinity, which is without measure, as the one true equal measure."[49] In terms of music, silent music aspires to be the measure itself, in aspiring to surpass the usual musical measures. If the form of music must therefore be measured against the form of the immeasurable infinite, this may be best represented by an indefinite, silent form, such as Cage's *o'oo"*.

Music is not only something to *be* measured, however, but Pickstock notes that for Augustine it is also a measure: "music is at once a thing measured and the measure itself; it is for us supremely the measure of the psychic-corporeal relationship."[50] Music's form must therefore be analysed in two ways: against infinity and against itself as a part of the created world. According to this outlook, silent music always falls short against itself, as it does not reflect the true source of creativity, though it may stand up to a measure against infinity.

Pickstock emphasizes Augustine's discussion of salvation through the corporeal in relation to Christ as the incarnation of the divine: "Christ can accomplish our salvation, can influence us, only through corporeal means."[51] The body is not only important to our human lives, but is crucial beyond that. Cage's *4'33"* is in tension with this need to acknowledge the limits of creation, given Cage's discovery that there is no absolute lack of sound in music, even when there is an absence of intentional sound. Cage's own writing may be interpreted as supporting this account. He writes "sounds (which are called silence only because they do not form part of a musical intention) may be depended upon to exist."[52] Although there will always be some unintentional sound during the performance, Cage strives to create an experience of silence for listeners. Rather than denying the limits of the human body, Cage affirms them in an attempt to immerse the human body in experience of silence, through the performance of his work.

---

49. Ibid., 248.
50. Ibid., 255.
51. Ibid., 264.
52. Cage, *Silence*, 22–23.

Celebration of Limits of Embodiment

I propose that the relationship between embodied experience and the striving toward musical form of silence in *4'33"* (however misguided some think the attempt is) encourages a positive theological reading of embodiment, celebrating the physical and temporal limits of the human body, and allowing humans to participate in the mystery of God. Cage's use of silence affirms embodied human life. Crispin writes that "Like others of his later generation, but more completely than most, Cage was more relaxed in his contemplation of the void and content to inhabit it, examining the possibilities of the space itself."[53] In other words, Cage was comfortable to explore the nothingness of silence. He has created a musical work in which those who experience is can also contemplate the void and be immersed in it. Exploring the void allows the human to enter into and retreat from it, to stand against it, affirming the "something" rather than "nothing" of creation. Moreover, this celebrates the body's limits: it acknowledges and affirms the complexity of the "in-the-moment" human experience.

4'33" is best experienced as a live performance as the performer captures the audience and holds their attention for the four and a half minutes of perceived silence. For Cage, this ability to experience an all-consuming silence is part of the embodied experience. The work does not create silence by passing through intentional sounds, as when he suggested that silence requires him to go on talking. For Cage, music is not measured by the passing of sounds and silences. Rather, *4'33"* immerses humans in their embodied experience of the void, and in doing so affirms the physical and temporal limitations of what it means to be human in relation to the mystery of God and God's creation.

Zen Silence

Cage's striving for silence stemmed partly from his interest in Zen Buddhism. I will draw on Gawronski's reading of Balthasar's discussion of Zen to understand Cage's *4'33"*. Gawronski interprets Balthasar as saying all religions aspire toward silence.[54] If there is something spiritual about the silence, this particular quality of music may help humanity to celebrate the limits of the corporeal by being immersed in them. However, Gawronski understands this silence as nothingness, which is not necessarily the case in Cage's use of Zen, where perhaps there was a fullness in silence for Cage

---

53. Losseff and Doctor, *Silence, Music, Silent Music*, 128.
54. Gawronski, *Word and Silence*, 1.

rather than a nothingness. I will draw Balthasar's idea that Zen art is not an end in itself, and I propose that Zen silence points beyond itself to something greater, God: the notion that silence expresses the mystery of God leads to a conclusion that revelation must never be lost sight of, even in darkness and silence. Embodied experience of silence, therefore, is participation in the mystery of God.

Gawronski gives a strong reading of Balthasar, writing that, according to Balthasar, "the *via negativa* must ultimately destroy all that is other than the One, as the "other" is either illusion or inferior being. Zen, of course, destroys the One as well."[55] On this reading, zen (musical) silence could be a negative path that reduces God to an illusion or to a lesser being than God.

Gawronski highlights that Balthasar understands Zen's quest for silence as a denial of the body in its quest for absolute nothingness and its abstraction from the fullness of the person.[56] Zen negates personhood in its quest for the Absolute form of silence. This makes experience of the world an illusion.[57] The work of art can "serve as an immediate referent to the mystery of emptiness."[58] For Gawronski, silence is not about human control, but is to do with the mystery of God—as with all legitimate experience of God outside of the Bible, "it will be permeated with the sense of God's incomprehensibility."[59]

Zen silence, or nothingness, is the ground out of which everything springs, not entirely unlike Pickstock's creation *ex nihilo*, explored above. Cage strove to create an experience of Zen silence in his work.[60] Unlike Gawronski's understanding of Zen silence, Cage's work does not deny the bodily. Rather, it affirms it through experimenting with the embodied experience of musical silence that allows the body to continue noisily on. Cage writes that "no silence exists that is not pregnant with sound."[61] Silence is thus filled with potential: sound is always breaking out of silence, and yet silence continues to be perceived. The mystery by which this is possible is an evocation of the greater mystery in the relation of the human being to the silent divine Other. They mystery of God might thus be expressed through

---

55. Ibid., 73.
56. Ibid., 46.
57. Ibid., 46.
58. Ibid., 46.
59. Ibid., 53.
60. Larson explores the influence of Zen Buddhism on Cage's creative work in *Where the Heart Beats*.
61. Cage, *Silence*, 135.

entering into silence, immersed in the mystery of the experience, better than through any sound.

Cage's silent work is not bleak: "the employment of silence as a spur to awareness, the perception of sound, or silence, for its own sake, is affirmative of life in general, and of new directions in music in particular."[62] In other words, the lack of literal silence and the existence of an experience of silence against the backdrop of sound affirm both the limitations and possibilities of embodied human life. Cage's work does not suggest that silence is only possible through disembodiment, as his early understanding of silence would suggest. Moreover, the performance does not come out of nothingness, but, rather, out of the relation of at least one performer to a community of listeners. The experience of the listener is not an illusion, but affirms their personhood in relation to others, and ultimately, in relation to the transcendent.

Participation in the Mystery of God

Cage's work uses Zen's quest for silence to go beyond everyday experience. Gawronski suggests that Zen art is not an end in itself: it points beyond itself to something greater. Gawronski writes: "In the words of the Zen saying, art can serve as a finger pointing to the moon. One would be foolish indeed to focus one's attention on the finger."[63] In other words, for Gawronski, the experience of silence is not an end in itself, but it points toward something greater: it is the Absolute, or God, that it attempts to direct the perceiver toward.

Silence is not about human control, but is to do with the mystery of God. As with all legitimate experience of God outside of the Bible, Gawronski writes, "it will be permeated with the sense of God's incomprehensibility."[64] This is not a pessimistic outlook on the relationship between humans and God: it is negative only in the sense of mystery, not in expressing limitations of humanity. Gawronski notes that it is "negative theology *not* out of resignation to human inability to know more, but rather because of the positive elements in that 'dark knowledge.'"[65] In other words, it is human participation in the mystery of God. Revelation is present, even in darkness and silence. The negative paths do not reflect the limited ability of the

---

62. Losseff and Doctor, *Silence, Music, Silent Music*, 139.
63. Ibid., 46.
64. Ibid., 53.
65. Ibid., 53.

human to know about God, but rather reflect human participation in the mystery of God.

Silence is not part of a negative path that reduces God to an illusion or to a lesser being than God. I hold, with Balthasar, that silence does not reflect the limited ability of the human to know about God, but rather reflects human participation in the mystery of God. The musical silence of Cage's work upholds the relation of the human to the divine Other, shrouded though it is in mystery, rather than negating it. Therefore, I have argued that Cage's work is not focused on emptiness, however, but rather on the fullness of the person, in relation to God. It affirms the living relationship of the person with reality beyond the embodied human and the musical form.

Cage's work affirms a sense of mystery: in particular in the physically impossible, yet musically given, experience of silence. It takes the human community to a new place in the silence and embraces the mystery of human relation to God thus disclosed. In affirming human silence in the face of this mystery, it also affirms the human relationship with the divine. The celebration of the limits of the corporeal in the experience of silence in 4'33" is a means of entering into this deeper mystery with God, which goes some way to breaking barriers between the invisible divine and human experience in this world.

Summary

Analysis of Cage's 4'33" has highlighted the celebration of the temporal, or "in-the-moment," nature of the embodied experience of musical silence. In its use of silence, rather than negating or denying the limits of embodied human life, the experience of musical silence immerses the listener in them. The silent musical form exists only in relation to a listener: there is no real need for it to be written. This reflects the shifting emphasis from the written score to the experienced score, from the Classical era to the Modern, as demonstrated in the second part of this book.

The positive understanding of musical silence as celebrating bodily limits has avoided the possible negative reading drawn from Pickstock's theology of creation *ex nihilo*. Human musical experience is more complex than "sound on, sound off," and the experience "in-the-moment" of Cage's 4'33" points beyond itself to something greater. In this way, Cage's 4'33" allows for experience of horizontal transcendence. Drawing a more positive reading of silence from Gawronski's reading of Balthasar, experience of silence allows humans to participate bodily in the mystery of God. The encounter with musical silence takes the embodied participant to a new place of mystery in relation to God.

Silence and the *Requiem for String Orchestra*

Toru Takemitsu (1930–1996) was a Japanese composer who grew up in Tokyo with its Western musical influence. Takemitsu was greatly influenced by Cage, writing that "John Cage shook the foundations of Western music and, with almost naïve clarity; he evoked silence as the mother of sound. Through John Cage, sound gained its freedom."[66] Takemitsu thus viewed Cage's use of musical silence as a liberation from existing musical forms.

The trajectory of requiems, from the Classical to the Modern eras, has highlighted the trend toward individualization of religious forms. It has been seen that the requiem, as a liminal form, provides interesting theological reflections on the boundary between life and death. Takemitsu's *Requiem for String Orchestra* moves further away from the sacred form of the church, dispensing with text entirely, being composed for string orchestra. The associations with the liminal form remain, however, through its title, and through the use of silence. Musical silence is the ultimate liminal musical tool, and therefore it is well-suited to the liminal form of the requiem. For Takemitsu, life is a sound that confronts the silence, but in this work he deliberately obfuscates the distinction between sound and silence. In doing so, this *Requiem* has much to say about the boundary between life and death.

Some differences in compositional thought exist between Cage and Takemitsu, however, as Burt underlines: Takemitsu "compares composition explicitly to a natural spontaneous emotional self-expression . . . diametrically opposed to Cage's philosophy of non-intentionality, to his belief that tones should simply be themselves, not vehicles for personal theories or human emotions."[67] Moreover, Takemitsu's music is intensely personal: his *Requiem* is an expression of his own feelings on life and death. There are similarities between the context of Takemitsu's *Requiem* and Mozart's, in that Takemitsu was confined to his bed through illness during its composition.[68] As with Mozart's, this *Requiem* was a commission which came to be associated with his own death. Whilst Takemitsu originally had someone in mind to pay tribute with the requiem, he came to consider the possibility

---

66. Takemitsu, *Confronting Silence*, 137.
67. Burt, *Music of Toru Takemitsu*, 97.
68. Ibid., 50.

that he was writing his own requiem, as he commented following his recovery from illness.[69]

Ma

Takemitsu sought to make use of the boundary between sound and silence in his musical work before he met Cage or came to know his works in the early 1960s.[70] This is evident in his film scores, but is used to utmost effect in his 1957 *Requiem for String Orchestra*. This work, being written for a string orchestra, is not a requiem in the traditional sense, but Takemitsu conveys the emotions of a requiem through musical techniques. The most notable feature of the music is the sustained notes which emerge at an indistinct moment, blurring the boundary between silence and sound.

In the *Requiem* Takemitsu's sounds slowly crescendo from the silence in a way that blurs the boundary between silence and sound. The *Requiem* is liminal in its concern with the boundary between life and death, and the music reflects this, crossing the threshold between sound and silence in such a way that the listener is not certain which is which. His desire to communicate something of a bare essence of the sound is evident in listening to his music, and this compositional process pervades much of his work. As Doctor writes, "for Takemitsu sound reduction was a concentration, a way of finding essential meaning within the complex sound continua underlying his compositional sphere."[71] Indeed, the chords Takemitsu uses in his *Requiem* represent a concentration of the emotion he intended to convey. There does not seem to be an unnecessary or superfluous note in the music. Indeed, there is much economy in the double- or triple-stopping.[72] This is not an unusual technique for compositions for strings, but is used here to give the sounds a particularly intense precision.

Takemitsu was originally trained in Western music, but as his compositional style developed he began to search for meaning in the Eastern traditions of his home country. In particular, the Japanese concept of *ma* came to influence Takemitsu's musical work. For Takemitsu, *ma* is the moment of intense silence just before the sound breaks, before the moment when

---

69. Ibid., 50.

70. Siddons writes that Takemitsu met Cage at the electronic music festival in the San Francisco Tape Music Centre in 1964 (Siddons, *Toru Takemitsu*, 9).

71. Losseff and Doctor, *Silence, Music, Silent Music*, 32.

72. Double-stopping and triple-stopping occur when a string instrument plays two or three (respectively) notes simultaneously.

THE SELF-REFLECTIVE SELF

"sound and silence confront each other."[73] In other words, it is the point of threshold between silence and sound.For him, it is the *ma* which "gives life to the sound and removes it from its position of primacy."[74] It implies action, not inaction; it makes silence integral to the movement of the piece, the opposite of the way some use silence to halt motion.

Takemitsu writes that in his music he wants to "carve away the excess to expose the single real existence."[75] Each phrase in the *Requiem* seems to emerge out of silence, crescendos to a climax, and then diminuendos back into silence. In particular, it is the melodic line that is "clearly segmented into a number of phrases, articulated here by means of silences," as Burt notes.[76] This is how Takemitsu uses *ma*: these "different sound events are related by silences that aim at creating a harmony of events."[77] In the *Requiem*, sounds are drawn from the silence, since they emerge slowly and quietly out of the silence such that it is very difficult to discern when the silence stops and the sound begins.

For Takemitsu, the powerful silence of *ma* removes sound "from its position of primacy."[78] Sound is no longer the dominant feature of the work, nor is it all-encompassing. Silence is given a place in the listener's experience of music: as Doctor notes, "for Takemitsu, silence did not serve merely as mediator, articulating structures of sound; instead, there was an essential merging of the two polarities."[79] Takemitsu aims to immerse a Western listener in an experience that his Japanese listeners may take for granted, to listen to the silence, and to understand its deep relationship with the sounds in "confronting" it. For the Japanese listener, *ma* has a spiritual dimension that Takemitsu aims to bring to the Western world of composition.

As Doctor explains, it is "spiritual motion that is the aspiration behind performance spaces within Japanese sound events, and this is of fundamental significance to *ma*."[80] It is interesting choice of the word "space," which is reminiscent of Ward's understanding of breathing space in silence, suggesting that *ma* allows a moment of—conceptual if not physical—silent space. This is caused by the fact that body is totally involved in the perception of silence: the experience of *ma* is a moment of *ekstasis* in which the body

73. Takemitsu, *Confronting Silence*, 51.
74. Ibid., 51.
75. Ibid., 16.
76. Burt, *Music of Toru Takemitsu*, 51.
77. Takemitsu, *Confronting Silence*, 84.
78. Ibid., 51
79. Losseff and Doctor, *Silence, Music, Silent Music*, 32.
80. Ibid., 32.

is totally committed. The transitory nature of this silent space makes for a pre-reflective experience. *Ma* therefore allows for a liminal experience, in which sound and silence come together in a fleeting moment of tension, and, following the understanding of the sublime moment of *ekstasis* outlined in chapter 2 in relation to Schleiermacher and Stone-Davis, allows the boundary between the human subject and divine object to be temporarily suspended.

If, as is assumed here, music can be properly called revelatory, the music of this *Requiem* would be a prime example. This work is particularly liminal in its use of silence and sound, and this reflects the understanding of the way in which music suspends the boundary between human subject and divine object in the understanding of revelation outlined in chapter 2.

Life and Death

The sounds and silence in Takemitsu's *Requiem* directly correlate with his understanding of life and death. He speaks of choosing sound over silence: "As long as I shall live I shall choose sound as something to confront a silence."[81] For Takemitsu, living means choosing sound over silence, but the sounds he chooses are bold and simple. He writes that the sound that confronts silence should be "a single, strong sound,"[82] and that the sound he chooses is given meaning "by returning it to its original state as a naked being."[83] This idea of the single strong sound that confronts silence gives rise to one of the characteristic features in Takemitsu's music: Burt calls this "single, unaccompanied sustained pitch which . . . reveals itself as the first note of a melodic phrase" a "characteristic Takemitsu gesture."[84] This is also a feature of the *Requiem*, with the first violins emerging out of silence on a note that becomes the melody once the other strings join it in an ominous harmony. This single note is a simple representation of life.

Takemitsu, as Burt highlights, "invokes a favourite metaphor of his: that of the "stream of sound" running through humanity and the world, of which the composer has simply extracted a segment."[85] Takemitsu's music seems to come out of nothing, and fades back into nothing, suggesting it is part of a continuous stream that continues even when the music is not heard. In its use of sounds and silence, it reflects the first reading of sound

---

81. Takemitsu, *Confronting Silence*, 5.
82. Ibid., 5.
83. Ibid., 16.
84. Burt, *Music of Toru Takemitsu*, 30.
85. Burt, *Music of Toru Takemitsu*, 53.

and silence here, in that human creations must acknowledge both the plenitude and the nothingness of creation. However, Takemitsu does not set up a dichotomy between sound and silence.

For Takemitsu, musical sound is something with which he can confront the silence, but this sound is used in as simple a manner as possible, drawing on its "real existence" in contrast to the silence. Burt writes that this "suggests a conception of music as contiguous with, rather than separate from, the silence surrounding it."[86] In other words, the music itself is liminal: it traverses the boundary between sound as silence. For Takemitsu, this sound is affirmative of life: "The fear of silence is nothing new. Silence surrounds the dark world of death. Sometimes the silence of the vast universe hovers over us, enveloping us."[87] Silence may thus be something to be resisted, even if it is a fundamental aspect of both music and life. As Doctor notes, "for Takemitsu the act of composition was a confrontation with silence, which was itself a kind of death."[88] The *Requiem* thus affirms the liminal nature of human life, through the use of *ma*, holding in tension sound and silence, life and death, and liminally overcoming the boundary between the two.

Summary

Takemitsu's *Requiem* reflects the trend toward an emphasis on experience of the musical form, rather than interpreting it in its written form. In dispensing with words, it becomes a more accessible—some might say universal—requiem. It theological impact is not dependent upon language. It continues the trend away from the traditional religious form of the requiem toward an individualised conception of the form. It is at once personal, bound up in Takemitsu's individual circumstances at the time of its composition, and general, being accessible to all, more so because of its lack of words and therefore determinate meaning. The lack of words in this *Requiem* means that it conveys all its meaning through the title and, most importantly, the music. The context of the work is important, but this also requires those who experience the music to make more input in order to derive meaning from the music.

The silence which surrounds the *Requiem* is easily interpreted as a silence representing death. The *Requiem* begins in a silence that endures to an indefinite point where the strings take over with a simple chord, played

---

86. Ibid., 30.
87. Takemitsu, *Confronting Silence*, 17.
88. Losseff and Doctor, *Silence, Music, Silent Music*, 7.

pianissimo, such that the listener cannot exactly determine where the sound begins. At the end, the chord diminuendos to ppp, again with the sound ending at a point that is indistinguishable from the silence that follows. Takemitsu's *Requiem* subverts Picard's thought that links silence to creation in an ontological manner, which is not strongly tied to duration of sounds or form: "There is no beginning to silence and no end: it seems to have its origins in the time when everything was still pure Being. It is like uncreated, everlasting Being."[89] For Takemitsu, there is also no beginning and end to sound. Takemitsu plays with the boundary between life and death. This also reflects something of the simple facts of human existence: we cannot remember our birth, and cannot know when our death will occur.

The merging of sound and silence in this *Requiem* is both an affirmation of life and acknowledgement of death. Created sounds emerge from the silence against the backdrop of the underlying continuum of a "stream of sound," or in other words, they take their place against a bigger picture. This musical time—or perhaps even the silence of eternity—is the backdrop to both the music, and the human life. The blurred boundary between the sound and silence blurs the boundary between life and death. The *Requiem* is the most liminal through its evocation of *ma* through silence: it is on the threshold of sound and silence, signifying the threshold of life and death. By blurring the distinction between sound and silence, it represents the liminality of life and death.

Conclusion

Whilst Modern music branched off into many directions in a quest for new forms, silence is one element that became integral to the certain musical works and composers of music of the Modern era. It is an important compositional tool, and is utilized in some of the key revolutionary works of the twentieth century, which had a lasting impact on much of the composition that followed. Silence has played a key role in the music of many modern composers, but has also been an issue discussed in the writing of prominent figures John Cage and Toru Takemitsu.

Silence is a bodily form of communication. Silence has been equated in some cases with death, either literally in Cage's thought from his experiences in an anechoic chamber, or metaphorically in the reflection of Takemitsu, as a textural part of an ongoing "stream of sound."

Musical meaning is indeterminate, and is created in the relation of the embodied experiencing human subject and the musical form. Silence is yet

---

89. Picard, *World of Silence*, 17.

more indeterminate, having little graspable content with which to associate. In a musical work which is entirely silent, meaning can be imparted by its title or other associated text, as in the examples of Allais's prelude, and Denver and Lennon's song titles. However, Cage revealed little in the titles of his silent works: *4'33"* and *0'0"*. The embodied experience is therefore more important in determining the meaning of such works. Musical silence is the most embodied musical form, as without the embodied listener, the work does not exist. Therefore, I have argued that a study of Cage's *4'33"* affirms the embodied nature of human being, celebrating the body's limits. The experience of *4'33"* goes deeper than the in-the-moment experience of music, and allows humans to participate in the mystery of relation with God.

Takemitsu's *Requiem* has shown that silence is the ultimate liminal form, which best epitomises the liminal form of the requiem. The Japanese understanding of *ma* has contributed to the theological understanding of the role of silence, in the expectation that there is more to come than the silence. Takemitsu's *Requiem* has continued the trajectory of moving from the traditional religious forms of the church toward more individualised forms. The requiem form has become a personal expression of the meaning of life and death. Takemitsu's *Requiem* is also ultimately accessible: life and death are, after all, universal phenomena, but always also personal. Each person is ultimately on their own in their death: it is theirs alone.

Musical silence both affirms life and points beyond the immanent. The merging of sound and silence in music is not an attempt to negate the body, but a celebration of the body's limits and potential: even in a noisy human body, through music, silence can be experienced. Moreover, this silence reflects a certainty of human existence, death. In an experience of musical silence, and in understanding it in relation to embodied human life, we contemplate the mystery of death.

The experience of musical silence is an encounter with the mystery of God: absolute revelation in the utmost concealment, just as Balthasar considers the revelation of Christ to be. Musical silence needs relation to create meaning, relation between performers and listeners, and ultimately relation between the embodied human and the mystery we name God.

"In the beginning, there were answers
Then they came along and changed
All these questions and their answers seemed to change."

—Idlewild, "In Remote Part/Scottish Fiction"

6

Conclusion

This book set out to outline an understanding of music as an embodied encounter with God, and in this way understands music *as* theology. Music is a non-linguistic experience of revelation, always in relation to the embodied human, in sacramentally encountering the mystery that is named God.

Music is distinctive amongst the arts, though not exclusively so, but its temporality, non-linguistic nature, and impact on embodied experience make it unique. Like any human creation, music is varied, and yet all music, indeed all of creation, may be sacramental. The meaning of music is necessarily indeterminate, which poses a challenge to theology, which is more comfortable in the realm of words. Music, as with all theology, exists within a social and cultural context, which adds layers of meaning. This approach acknowledges the individual nature of experience as well as the social aspect of the experiential.

The relationship between existing theologies of music and different musical eras have been explored, showing that different theological emphases arise from different musical eras, in particular from the relationship between the musical form and the account of embodiment. In exploring the possible methods of approach to music from theology, existing theologies of music have been investigated, along with the tools and concepts they use to understand music theologically, which have at times focused on a particular era or style of music.

An approach to music as theology has been outlined that can be applied to all musical eras and genres, taking into account the context, and allowing for diverse outcomes. This book addresses questions that might be raised by different musical eras.

Book Summary

Two approaches to music in modern theology were outlined in chapter 1: firstly, from the stance of human experience as revelatory, exploring the idea that theologies which allow music to be revelatory can challenge existing theological thought; secondly, exploring a different and perhaps complementary approach, based on the thought that music can expound given theological truths, helping to understand existing theology.

Following the theology of Schleiermacher, Brown and Stone-Davis outlined in chapter 1, music is described as revelatory, it must be in relation to a human subject. For theology to understand music, it must first address how the music is experienced, before exploring it in its written form. Theologies of popular culture allowed the development of an account of music's created nature, as well as its social and contextual aspects. Music does not exist in a cultural vacuum and should not be treated as such. The social and cultural aspects of the context of both the creation of the music and the later experience of it are influencing factors in the meaning of the music.

It has been profitable to integrate theological thought on music with musicology, and this has brought theology together with the cultural context of the musical works studied. Given the positive assessment of human creativity that stems from theologies of culture, there is potential for a re-enchantment with the world as a mediator of truth and meaning. Theology is the process of seeking meaningful answers to ultimate questions, taking into account the particular social and cultural context. Gorringe's theology has been the basis of the understanding that music is one part of culture through which we develop humanity. The liminal experience is key to the human encounter with the divine other.

Having begun by surveying existing approaches to music from within theology, chapter 2 explored the concepts on which these theologies are based. That music is inherently linguistically indeterminate is both a gift and a challenge to theology: gift in allowing freedom from assumptions and presuppositions; challenge in defying the possibility of saying anything meaningful about the musical experience theologically. Therefore an exploration of how music might act as theology without words was explored through the concepts of embodiment, sacramentality, revelation, transcendence and liminality. The bodily nature of music was explored in relation to incarnational theology. The encounter between human and divine in the musical experience was through the interaction of the musical form on the human body. This chapter highlights the necessity to resist the temptation to compartmentalize religious aspects of life from whatever remains. An understanding of music as theology, of all music as sacramental, approaches human life in a holistic way, which allows for understanding of God through all aspects of life.

Chapters three, four and five, represent an attempt to apply this understanding of music as theology to particular works in particular musical eras of Western classical music. These studies do not only take into account traditionally religious music, but all forms of music. In this part of the book, specific musical examples from three musical periods were analysed. In examining their theological value, musicology was integrated with theology, also considering composers' own writing in relation to their music.

The requiem form has been a theme throughout the second part of the book, and its progress through three eras of classical music has been followed. Whilst all music may be sacramental without giving precedence to the forms of sacred music, it is important that traditional religious forms are not therefore neglected. The form of the requiem was analysed based on its unique status as a liminal form, on the boundary of life and death. It is both the most personal and the most universal form, in that it relates to death, a universal feature of human life, but also the most personal feature of any one life, in that it is the one part of life which is truly individual: you can only die your own death. The requiem form has been seen to reflect the cultural context of its time, from the standard religious form in the Classical era, to the personal yet open-ended form without text in the Modern era.

In chapter 3, Classical Music was explored through the theological aesthetics of Hans Urs von Balthasar. Balthasar's understanding of beauty as form and splendour, when applied to music, leads to a consideration of the abstract form of music. This is particularly relevant to the Classical era, in which forms were used more in the abstract. However, this does not account for the embodiment of form still present in the musical experience, even in the era when form is used at its most abstract. An account of music based only on the form discernible in the music as it is written therefore overlooks the layers of meaning found in the human experience of the music.

In chapter 4, the development of Romantic thought brought with it more focus on the individual self. In music it brought more emphasis on the way in which the music is experienced by the listener. In this era composers take more account of the feelings of the listener in their construction of musical form. This emphasis on feeling is also found in the theology of Schleiermacher, and is key to theological understandings of music. Musical analysis has begun to appreciate this, as evident in Scott Burnham's interpretation of the heroic form in Beethoven, but it does not go far enough in accounting for the form as experienced. Form in this era is closely related to feeling, and therefore embodiment is an essential dimension of any understanding of form.

The twentieth century saw the development of music in many different directions, as composers strove to create new music, and therefore in chapter 5 silence was chosen as a key feature of one of the ways in which music developed. The different possible theological interpretations of silence were explored. Silence, as a means of communication, was seen to require active bodily participation. Music, which itself communicates indeterminately, allows communicates through silence, which leaves open spaces for and of breathing, and creates space for listening. Musical silence might allow further freedom from the desire to explain the mystery of God in words. Experience of silence is a moment of presence, individual and collective.

Silence as a musical experience affirms and celebrates the limits of human embodiment. It is not a physical state in which sound does not exist, but an experience of a moment. Paradoxically, then, silence is always experienced against a backdrop of sound. The human body itself is the source of many of the ongoing sounds, and thus the experience of silence is, like the incarnation, an embodied paradox.

Music as Theology

This book has contended that theology should not treat music only in its written form. Music is not an object to be measured by theological tools. It is always an embodied human experience, and is therefore always in relation to an individual subject. Musical form is therefore reconstructed with every musical experience, and its meaning is determined only in relation to an individual experiencing it bodily.

The meaning of music is determined in the relationship between musical form and the embodied experience thereof. This relationship was seen to change between the Classical, Romantic and Modern eras. Musical form in the Classical era conformed largely to expected and established forms. Understanding these forms in relation to embodied experience added new layers of meaning to the work. Composers of the Romantic era took more account of the individual's experience, and forms were developed to take into consideration the experience of the music, in particular the feelings it evokes. The Modern era saw the most integration between musical form and embodied experience. Composers often wrote their music for the sake of the experience of it. The self-reflective use of silence in some music of the

Modern era also challenged understandings of human embodiment. New levels of theological meaning are therefore offered by considering a human subject in relation to a musical form.

A theological approach that concerns itself only with music in its written form does not allow for investigation of its true bodily nature. Music is never merely dots on a page, but exists only in embodied form, as music is always known through bodily experience. Indeed, it is only once it has been embodied that it becomes known to an individual as music, and therefore it only exists in the passing of time, in relation to embodied performers and listeners. Music gives theology insight into the nature of embodiment, without smoothing over the issues raised by embodiment, but presenting the transient and temporal nature as an inescapable part of the musical experience. Music is seen to be as fragile as the human body: it only lasts as long as the final chord.

This construal of music as theology is influence by theologies of popular culture in accounting for the embodied, social and contextual nature of music, and applying these insights to classical music. The focus has shifted from the emphasis of these theologies of popular on the written text, to the experience of music. Drawing on theology of popular culture, an analysis of music that does not divide it into sacred and secular allows music to act sacramentally and allows liminal experience of transcendence to come to the fore. Music can be used to strive for conditions that are ultimately beyond the realm of human experience, and, whilst it may give glimpses of revelation, it always returns to the present. Music is particularly good at suspending boundaries, and that it is therefore an important vehicle of revelation. The musical experience allows progress, and can develop theological understanding.

Music must be understood as a relation between form and embodiment, and a preference for any one particular era drives theology toward one particular method of understanding embodiment, and therefore music. Different musical eras relate these form and embodiment in different ways, and therefore the context is particularly important. As the musical eras progress, embodiment becomes more important to musical form, as form develops in relation to the musical experience. It is therefore important that theology engages with music in particular rather than in general: different musical examples offer different theological insights, as different musical eras do. Music is always particular as well as embodied.

Further Research

Although insights from theologies of popular culture have been deliberately applied to music that might not be thought of as popular, Western classical music, in the interests of challenging existing assumptions within the theology of music, the arguments advanced here would be further developed by applying these ideas to popular music. The form of popular music is often more condensed than classical music, and it is performed and received differently to classical music as a rule, and therefore the personal and social implications of such a study are likely to add a new dimension to a theology of music.

The manner of listening to classical music often differs from popular music, particularly in the context of performances. In classical music the listeners often intentionally experience the music and consciously listen to it. They are usually seated and remain still for the duration of the performance. Popular music encourages more bodily participation, more energetically, by singing or dancing. In particular, popular culture may be helpful to theology in understanding human identity, as popular music is one important way in which people construct their individual and social identity.

This account of music as theology suggests that the embodied experience of music is important in relation to the musical form. However, the scope did not allow for qualitative research into embodied experiences of musical forms. This further stage of research would give allow those experiencing the music to give voice to their individual, subjective interpretations of musical meaning. This could be analysed alongside the theological claims made in this book, such as whether music assists in self-reflection, in particular with regard to relationships to other humans, the world, and God.

This research has highlighted the importance of context in theologically understanding the musical work. It has been deliberately limited to Western classical music, and has made no attempt to study music from different cultures. A comparative study with music from a different cultural context using the same framework outlined would develop understanding of the different ways in which musical form might relate to embodied experience. Further research of non-Western musical contexts might also bring different issues to the fore, perhaps related to the different instruments, or the different cultural and social associations with music.

This book has stressed the importance of the relationship between musical form and the embodied experience of music. However, there has been no account of the way in which prior musical experiences play a role in interpretation of music, other than as regards general musical expectations within a particular era. A qualitative study of anamnesis would therefore develop understanding of how prior musical experience affects how individuals interpret music. Out of this would develop an interesting theological correlation between musical memory and theological understanding of memory, in particular in relation to the Eucharist. In exploring music as an embodied experience, prior musical experiences impact on the meaning they find in the music. Their musical memory therefore plays a role in the impact the music has on them. Performances are often re-enactments of previously performed works.

Coda

This book has outlined an account of music as theology, highlighting the importance of the embodied, social and contextual nature of music, and applying this to classical music. It has further developed an understanding of embodiment in relation to musical form, thereby refocusing the emphasis in theology of popular culture and theology of music from the musical score and accompanying text to the embodied experience of music. It has shown that musical form and human embodiment are inextricably linked, though enacted in different ways in different musical eras, and this impacts on the theological meaning derived from the music. It has therefore shown that, whilst it is possible to discuss music in general, in particular in relation to particular genres, styles, or eras, further layers of meaning on found in discussing music in particular, and in understanding the way in which the form of each musical work impacts on the embodied experience of the music. Above all, the claim is made that music, as a sacramental experience, allows an embodied encounter with the mystery of God. Therefore, music is a way of doing theology.

> "Think about meaning more as an after word
> As in afterward."
>
> —Idlewild, "Live in a Hiding Place"

Afterword

As an afterword, I direct you to www.danielleannelynch.com to listen to some of my music. I hope that some of that which I left unsaid in the words I wrote in this book can sound meaning in the music I leave as an afterword. The link between the words of the book and the music is that they both speak to "music as theology." Both are expressions of what makes meaning in my life, from the depths of who I am as an embodied human being in relation to the infinite mystery I name God.

"Can't stop the spirits when they need you
This life is more than just a read through."

—Red Hot Chili Peppers, "Can't Stop"

Bibliography

Abrams, M. H. *A Glossary of Literary Terms*. 6th ed. San Diego, CA: Harcourt College, 1992.
Augustine. *Confessions*. Translated by R. S. Pine-Coffin. London: Penguin, 1961.
Balthasar, Hans Urs von. *The Development of the Idea of Music: The Search for a Synthesis on Music*. Reprint edition. Freiburg, Germany: Verlag, 1998.
———. *Glory of the Lord: A Theological Aesthetics, Volume I: Seeing the Form*. San Francisco: Ignatius, 1982.
———. *Truth is Symphonic*. Translated by Graham Harrison. San Francisco: Ignatius, 1987.
Barth, Karl. *Church Dogmatics*. 14 vols. London: T. & T. Clark, 1958–1988.
———. *Dogmatics in Outline*. New York: Harper & Row, 1959.
———. *The Epistle to the Romans*. Oxford: Oxford University Press, 1933.
———. *Theology and Church, Shorter Writings 1920–1928*. Translated by Louis Pettibone Smith. London: SCM, 1962.
———. *The Theology of Schleiermacher: Lectures at Göttingen, Winter Semester of 1923/24*. Edinburgh: T. & T. Clark, 1982.
———. *Wolfgang Amadeus Mozart*. Translated by Clarence K. Pott. Eugene, OR: Wipf & Stock, 1986.
Barton, Stephen C. *Holiness: Past and Present*. London: T. & T. Clark, 2003.
Beaudoin, Tom. *Virtual Faith: The Irreverent Spiritual Quest of Generation X*. San Francisco: Jossey-Bass, 1998.
Beaudoin, Tom, ed. *Secular Music and Sacred Theology*. Collegeville, MN: Liturgical, 2013.
Begbie, Jeremy. *Resounding Truth (Engaging Culture): Christian Wisdom in the World of Music*. Grand Rapids: Baker Academic, 2007.
———. *Theology, Music and Time*. Cambridge: Cambridge University Press, 2000.
Begbie, Jeremy, and Steven Guthrie, eds. *Resonant Witness: Conversations between Music and Theology*. Cambridge: Eerdmans, 2011.
Blackwell, Albert L. *The Sacred in Music*. Cambridge: Lutterworth, 1999.
Boff, Leonardo. *Faith on the Edge: Religion and Marginalized Existence*. New York: Harper & Row, 1990.
Bokyan, Martin. *Silence and Slow Time: Studies in Musical Narrative*. Oxford: Scarecrow, 2004.
Bonhoeffer, Dietrich. *Letters and Papers from Prison*. New York: Macmillan, 1972.

Brant, Jonathan. *Paul Tillich and the Possibility of Revelation through Film*. Oxford: Oxford University Press, 2012.
Brown, David. *Discipleship and Imagination: Christian Tradition and Truth*. Oxford: Oxford University Press, 2000.
———. *God and Enchantment of Place: Reclaiming Human Experience*. Oxford: Oxford University Press, 2006.
———. *God and Grace of Body: Sacrament in Ordinary*. Oxford: Oxford University Press, 2007.
———. *God and Mystery in Words: Experience through Metaphor and Drama*. Oxford: Oxford University Press, 2011.
———. *Tradition and Imagination: Revelation and Change*. Oxford: Oxford University Press, 1999.
Brown, Frank Burch. *Good Taste, Bad Taste, and Christian Taste*. Oxford: Oxford University Press, 2000.
Browning, Don. *A Fundamental Practical Theology*. Minneapolis: Fortress, 1991.
Burke, Edmund. *A Philosophical Enquiry into the Origin of Our Ideas of the Sublime and Beautiful*. Oxford: Oxford University Press, 2008.
Burnham, Scott. *Beethoven Hero*. Princeton: Princeton University Press, 1995.
Burt, Peter. *The Music of Toru Takemitsu*. Cambridge: Cambridge University Press, 2011.
Butler, Judith. *Bodies That Matter*. London: Routledge, 1993.
Cage, John. "John Cage: An Autobiographical Statement." http://johncage.org/autobiographical_statement.html.
———. *Silence: Lectures and Writings*. London: Boyars, 1994.
Callaway, Kutter. *Scoring Transcendence: Contemporary Film Music as Religious Experience*. Waco, TX: Baylor University Press, 2013.
Caplin, William E. *Classical Form: A Theory of Formal Functions for the Instrumental Music of Haydn, Mozart and Beethoven*. Oxford: Oxford University Press, 1998.
Caplin, William E., et al. *Musical Form, Forms & Formenlehre: Three Methodological Reflections*. 2nd ed. Leuven, Belgium: Leuven University Press, 2010.
Carey, John. *What Good are the Arts?* London: Faber & Faber, 2005.
Chapman, Geoffrey. *Catechism of the Catholic Church*. London: Cassell, 1992.
Chua, Daniel. *Absolute Music and the Construction of Meaning*. Cambridge: Cambridge University Press, 1999.
Clark, Caryl, ed. *The Cambridge Companion to Haydn*. Cambridge: Cambridge University Press, 2005.
Clarke, Martin V., ed. *Music and Theology in Nineteenth-Century Britain*. Farnham, UK: Ashgate, 2012.
Clements, Keith. *Friedrich Schleiermacher: Pioneer of Modern Theology*. London: Collins, 1987.
Cobb, Kelton. *The Blackwell Guide to Theology of Popular Culture*. Oxford: Blackwell, 2005.
Cobussen, Marcel. *Thresholds: Rethinking Spirituality through Music*. Aldershot, UK: Ashgate, 2008.
Cook, Nicholas, and Anthony Pople, eds. *The Cambridge History of Twentieth Century Music*. Cambridge: Cambridge University Press, 2004.
Corness, Greg. "The Musical Experience through the Lens of Embodiment." *Leonardo Music Journal* 18 (2008) 21–24.

Costelloe, Timothy. *The Sublime: From Antiquity to the Present*. Cambridge: Cambridge University Press, 2012.
Cox, Arnie. "Embodying Music: Principles of the Mimetic Hypothesis." *Music Theory Online* 17.2 (2011).
Crockett, Clayton. *Theology of the Sublime*. London: Routledge, 2001.
Crowther, Paul. *The Kantian Sublime: From Morality to Art*. Oxford: Oxford University Press, 1991.
Dauenhauer, Bernhard. *Silence: The Phenomenon and its Ontological Significance*. Bloomington: Indiana University Press, 1980.
Davies, Oliver, and Denys Turner, eds. *Silence and the Word: Negative Theology and Incarnation*. Cambridge: Cambridge University Press, 2002.
Deacy, Christopher, and Gaye Williams Ortiz. *Theology and Film: Challenging the Sacred/Secular Divide*. Oxford: Blackwell, 2008.
DeCou, Jessica. *Playful, Glad, and Free: Karl Barth and a Theology of Popular Culture*. Minneapolis: Fortress, 2013.
de Nora, Tia. *Music in Everyday Life*. Cambridge: Cambridge University Press, 2000.
Dumbreck, Geoff. *Schleiermacher and Religious Feeling*. Leuven, Belgium: Peeters, 2012.
Epstein, Heidi. *Melting the Venusberg: A Feminist Theology of Music*. New York: Continuum, 2004.
Ford, Charles. *Music, Sexuality and the Enlightenment in Mozart's Figaro, Don Giovanni and Cosi Fan Tutte*. Farnham, UK: Ashgate, 2012.
Ford, David, and Rachel Muers, eds. *The Modern Theologians*. Oxford: Blackwell, 2005.
Forte, Bruno. *The Portal of Beauty: Towards a Theology of Aesthetics*. Grand Rapids: Eerdmans, 2009.
Gadamer, Hans-Georg. *Truth and Method*. London: Sheed & Ward, 1989.
Gawronski, Raymond. *Word and Silence: Hans Urs von Balthasar and the Spiritual Encounter between East and West*. Grand Rapids: Eerdmans, 1995.
Geest, Paul van, et al., eds. *Aquinas as Authority*. Utrecht, Netherlands: Peeters-Leuven, 2002.
Gennep, Arnold van. *Rites of Passage*. Chicago: University of Chicago Press, 2011.
Gerrish, Brian A. *Prince of the Church: Schleiermacher and the Beginnings of Modern Theology*. Eugene, OR: Wipf & Stock, 2001.
Gibbs, Christopher, ed. *The Cambridge Companion to Schubert*. Cambridge: Cambridge University Press, 1997.
Goris, Wouter, and Jan Aertsen. "Medieval Theories of Transcendentals." https://plato.stanford.edu/archives/win2016/entries/transcendentals-medieval/.
Gorringe, T. J. *The Common Good and the Global Emergency: God and the Built Environment*. Cambridge: Cambridge University Press, 2011.
———. *Earthly Visions: Theology and the Challenges of Art*. New Haven: Yale University Press, 2011.
———. *The Education of Desire: Towards a Theology of the Senses*. London: SCM, 2001.
———. *Furthering Humanity: A Theology of Culture*. Farnham, UK: Ashgate, 2004.
———. *God's Theatre: A Theology of Providence*. London: SCM, 1992.
———. *A Theology of the Built Environment: Justice, Empowerment, Redemption*. Cambridge: Cambridge University Press, 2002.
Hannaford, Robert, and J'annine Jobling, eds. *Theology and the Body: Gender, Text and Ideology*. Leominster: Gracewing, 1999.

Hannay, Alastair, and Gordon Daniel Marino, eds. *The Cambridge Companion to Kierkegaard*. Cambridge: Cambridge University Press, 1997.
Hanslick, Eduard. *On the Musically Beautiful*. Cambridge: Hackett, 1986.
Harries, Richard. *Art and the Beauty of God: A Christian Understanding*. London: Mowbray, 1993.
Harrison, Victoria. *The Apologetic Value of Human Holiness: von Balthasar's Christocentric Philosophical Anthropology*. Dordrecht, Netherlands: Kluwer, 2000.
Hart, David Bentley. *The Beauty of the Infinite: The Aesthetics of Christian Truth*. Grand Rapids: Eerdmans, 2003.
Heaney, Maeve Louise. "Mercy, Music and the Prophetic Voice of Theology." In *Music, Theology and Justice*, edited by Michael O'Connor et al., 43–62. Lanham, MD: Lexington, 2017.
———. *Music as Theology: What Music Says About the Word*. Eugene, OR: Pickwick, 2012.
Heartz, Daniel, and Bruce Alan Brown. "Classical." https://doi.org/10.1093/gmo/9781561592630.article.05889.
Holmes, Christopher R. J. *Revisiting the Doctrine of Divine Attributes: In Dialogue with Karl Barth, Eberhard Jungel, and Wolf Krotke*. New York: Peter Lang, 2007.
James, William. *The Varieties of Religious Experience*. New York: Barnes & Noble, 2004.
Jankelevitch, Vladimir. *Music and the Ineffable*. Princeton: Princeton University Press, 2003.
Johnson, William. *Silent Music: The Science of Meditation*. New York: Fordham University Press, 1997.
Kahn, Charles H. *Pythagoras and the Pythagoreans: A Brief History*. Indianapolis: Hackett, 2001.
Kant, Immanuel. *Critique of Judgement*. Translated by J. H. Bernard. Mineola, NY: Dover, 2005.
———. *Observations on the Feeling of the Beautiful and Sublime*. Translated by John T. Goldthwait. Berkeley, CA: University of California Press, 1960.
Keefe, Simon P., ed. *The Cambridge Companion to Mozart*. Cambridge: Cambridge University Press, 2003.
———. *Mozart's Requiem: Reception, Work, Completion*. Cambridge: Cambridge University Press, 2012.
Kennedy, Michael, and Joyce Kennedy, eds. *The Concise Oxford Dictionary of Music*. 5th ed. Oxford: Oxford University Press, 2007.
Keuss, Jeffrey F. *Your Neighbor's Hymnal: What Popular Music Teaches Us about Faith, Hope, and Love*. Eugene, OR: Wipf & Stock, 2011.
Kierkegaard, Søren. *Either/Or: A Fragment of Life*. Translated by Alastair Hannay. London: Penguin, 1992.
Kreuzer, Gundula. *Verdi and the Germans: From Unification to the Third Reich*. Cambridge: Cambridge University Press, 2010.
Küng, Hans. *Mozart: Traces of Transcendence*. Grand Rapids: Eerdmans, 1996.
Larson, Kay. *Where the Heart Beats: John Cage, Zen Buddhism, and the Inner Life of Artists*. London: Penguin, 2012.
Lash, Nicholas. *Easter in Ordinary*. London: SCM, 1988.
Leeuw, Ton de. *Music of the Twentieth Century: A Study of its Elements and Structure*. Amsterdam: Amsterdam University Press, 2005.

Leman, Marc. *Embodied Music: Cognition and Mediation Technology.* Cambridge: MIT Press, 2007.

Leppert, Richard. *The Sight of Sound: Music, Representation, and the History of the Body.* Berkeley, CA: University of California Press, 1995.

Levine, Flora R. *Greek Reflections on the Nature of Music.* Cambridge: Cambridge University Press, 2014.

Lippitt, John, and George Pattison, eds. *The Oxford Handbook of Kierkegaard.* Oxford: Oxford University Press, 2013.

Lochhead, Judy. "The Sublime, the Ineffable, and Other Dangerous Aesthetics." *Women & Music: A Journal of Gender and Culture* 12 (2008) 63–74.

Losseff, Nicky, and Jenny Doctor, eds. *Silence, Music, Silent Music.* Aldershot, UK: Ashgate, 2007.

Lynch, Gordon, ed. *Between Sacred and Profane: Researching Religion and Popular Culture.* London: Tauris, 2007.

———. *The New Spirituality: An Introduction to Progressive Belief in the Twenty-First Century.* London: Tauris, 2007.

———. *On the Sacred.* London: Routledge, 2012.

———. *The Sacred in the Modern World: A Cultural Sociological Approach.* Oxford: Oxford University Press, 2012.

———. *Understanding Theology and Popular Culture.* Oxford: Blackwell, 2005.

Lynch, Gordon, et al., eds. *Religion, Media and Culture: A Reader.* Oxford: Routledge, 2012.

MacSwain, Robert, and Taylor Worley, eds. *Theology, Aesthetics and Culture: Responses to the Work of David Brown.* Oxford: Oxford University Press, 2012.

Maes, Francis. *A History of Russian Music: From Karaminskaya to Babi Yar.* Berkeley, CA: University of California Press, 2002.

Marina, Jacqueline, ed. *The Cambridge Companion to Friedrich Schleiermacher.* Cambridge: Cambridge University Press, 2005.

Marsh, Clive, and Vaughan S. Roberts. *Personal Jesus: How Popular Music Shapes Our Souls.* Grand Rapids: Baker, 2013.

McBrien, Richard P. *Catholicism.* Minneapolis: Winston, 1980.

McClary, Susan. *Conventional Wisdom: The Content of Musical Form.* Berkeley, CA: University of California Press, 2000.

McCosker, Philip. "Blessed Tension: Barth and von Balthasar on the Music of Mozart." *The Way* 44.4 (2005) 81–95.

McDermott, Gerald R. *Jonathan Edwards Confronts the Gods: Christian Theology, Enlightenment Religion, and non-Christian Faiths.* Oxford: Oxford University Press, 2000.

McElwain, Hugh T. *Theology of Limits and the Limits of Theology: Reflections on Language, Environment, and Death.* Lanham, MD: University Press of America, 1983.

McGregor, Bede, and Thomas Norris, eds. *The Beauty of Christ: An Introduction to the Theology of Hans Urs von Balthasar.* Edinburgh: T. & T. Clark, 1994.

Messiaen, Olivier. *Quatuor pour la fin du temps.* Paris: Durand, 1942.

Meyer, Leonard B. *Emotion and Meaning in Music.* Chicago: University of Chicago Press, 1956.

Miell, Dorothy, et al., eds. *Musical Communication.* Oxford: Oxford University Press, 2005.

Milbank, John, et al. *Theological Perspectives on God and Beauty*. London: Trinity, 2003.
Milbank, John, et al., eds. *Radical Orthodoxy: A New Theology*. London: Routledge, 1999.
Muers, Rachel. *Keeping God's Silence*. Oxford: Blackwell, 2004.
Murphy, Francesca Aran. *The Beauty of God's House*. Eugene, OR: Cascade, 2014.
Musgrave, Michael, ed. *The Cambridge Companion to Brahms*. Cambridge: Cambridge University Press, 1999.
Navone, John. *Toward a Theology of Beauty*. Collegeville, MN: Liturgical, 1996.
Nicholls, David. *The Cambridge Companion to John Cage*. Cambridge: Cambridge University Press, 2002.
O'Daly, Gerard J. P. *Augustine's Philosophy of Mind*. Berkeley, CA: University of California Press, 1987.
Osborne, Richard. "The Sounds of Silence: A Very, Very Quiet Top Ten." *New Statesman* (blog), August 21, 2012. https://www.newstatesman.com/blogs/cultural-capital/2012/08/sounds-silence.
Otto, Rudolf. *The Idea of the Holy*. Oxford: Oxford University Press, 1958.
Palma, Robert J. *Karl Barth's Theology of Culture: The Freedom of Culture for the Praise of God*. Eugene, OR: Pickwick, 1983.
Partridge, Christopher. *The Lyre of Orpheus: Popular Music, the Sacred and the Profane*. Oxford: Oxford University Press, 2013.
Pate, C. Marvin. *From Plato to Jesus: What Does Philosophy Have to Do with Theology?* Grand Rapids: Kregel, 2011.
Peacocke, Arthur, and Ann Pederson. *The Music of Creation*. Minneapolis: Fortress, 2006.
Picard, Max. *The World of Silence*. London: Harvill, 1948.
Pople, Anthony. *Messiaen: Quatuor pour la Fin du Temps*. Cambridge: Cambridge University Press, 1998.
Putnam, Ruth Anna. *The Cambridge Companion to William James*. Cambridge: Cambridge University Press, 1997.
Radcliffe, Timothy. *Why Go to Church? The Drama of the Eucharist*. London: Continuum, 2008.
Randel, Don Michael, ed. *The Harvard Dictionary of Music*. Cambridge: Belknap, 2003.
Ratzinger, Joseph. *Salt of the Earth*. Translated by by Adrian Walker. San Francisco: Ignatius, 1997.
Reay, Barry. *Popular Cultures in England 1550–1750*. London: Routledge, 1998.
Re Manning, Russell. *Theology at the End of Culture: Paul Tillich's Theology of Culture and Art*. Leuven, Belgium: Peeters, 2006.
Rischin, Rebecca. *For the End of Time: the Story of the Messaien Quartet*. New York: Cornell University Press, 2003.
Rosen, Charles. *The Classical Style: Haydn, Mozart, Beethoven*. London: Faber & Faber, 1997.
———. *The Romantic Generation*. Massachusetts: Harvard University Press, 1995.
Rust, Eric C. *Religion, Revelation and Reason*. Macon: Mercer University Press, 1981.
Sabin, Roger, ed. *Punk Rock: So What? The Cultural Legacy of Punk*. London: Routledge, 1999.
Schindler, David L., ed. *Hans Urs von Balthasar: His Life and Work*. San Francisco: Ignatius, 1991.

Schleiermacher, Friedrich. *The Christian Faith*. Edited by H. R. Mackintosh and J. S. Stewart. 2nd ed. Berkeley, CA: Apocryphile, 2011.

———. *Christmas Eve Celebration: A Dialogue*. Translated by Terrence N. Tice. Eugene, OR: Cascade, 2010.

———. *On Religion: Speeches to Its Cultural Despisers*. Translated by Richard Crouter. Cambridge: Cambridge University Press, 1996.

Schwartz, Regina, ed. *Transcendence: Philosophy Literature and Theology Approach the Beyond*. London: Routledge, 2004.

Scott, Peter M., and Michael S. Northcott, eds. *Systematic Theology and Climate Change: Ecumenical Perspectives*. London: Routledge, 2014.

Scruton, Roger. *Beauty*. Oxford: Oxford University Press, 2009.

Siddons, James. *Toru Takemitsu: A Bio-Bibliography*. Westport, CT: Greenwood, 2001.

Sisman, Elaine, ed. *Haydn and His World*. Princeton: Princeton University Press, 1997.

Smith, Sid. "Good Ol' Boy? John Denver Can Be A Merchant Of Venom When He's Riled." *Chicago Tribune*, August 17, 1986. http://articles.chicagotribune.com/1986-08-17/entertainment/8603010583_1_singer-john-denver-rocky-mountain-highs-venom.

Spitzer, Michael. *Music as Philosophy: Adorno and Beethoven's Late Style*. Bloomington, IN: Indiana University Press, 2006.

Stapert, Calvin R. *A New Song for an Old World: Musical Thought in the Early Church*. Grand Rapids: Eerdmans, 2007.

Steinberg, Michael. *Choral Masterworks: A Listener's Guide*. Oxford: Oxford University Press, 2005.

Stone-Davis, Férdia, ed. *Music and Transcendence*. Farnham, UK: Ashgate, 2015.

———. *Musical Beauty: Negotiating the Boundary between Subject and Object*. Eugene, OR: Cascade, 2011.

Suurpää, Lauri. *Death in Winterreise: Musico-Poetic Associations in Schubert's Song Cycle*. Bloomington, IN: Indiana University Press, 2014.

Sykes, Stephen. *Friedrich Schleiermacher*. Woking, UK: Lutterworth, 1971.

Takemitsu, Toru. *Confronting Silence: Selected Writings*. Translated by Yoshinko Kakudo and Glenn Glasgow. Berkeley, CA: Fallen Leaf, 1995.

Taylor, Charles. *A Secular Age*. Cambridge: Harvard University Press, 2007.

Taylor, Mark Lewis. *New and Enlarged Handbook of Christian Theology*. Nashville: Abingdon, 2003.

Temperley, Nicholas. *Haydn: The Creation*. Cambridge: Cambridge University Press, 1991.

Thomas, John Heywood. *Tillich*. London: Continuum, 2000.

Thomassen, Bjorn. *Liminality and the Modern: Living Through the In-Between*. Farnham, UK: Ashgate, 2014.

Tillich, Paul. *Dynamics of Faith*. New York: Perennial, 2001.

———. *Systematic Theology I: Reason and Revelation*. Chicago: Chicago University Press, 1973.

———. *Systematic Theology II: Existence and the Christ*. Chicago: Chicago University Press, 1975.

———. *Systematic Theology III: Life and the Spirit; History and the Kingdom of God*. Chicago: Chicago University Press, 1976.

———. *Theology of Culture*. Oxford: Oxford University Press, 1964.

Ting-Toomey, Stella. *Communicating Across Cultures*. New York: Guilford, 1999.

Treier, Daniel, et al., eds. *The Beauty of God: Theology and the Arts*. Downer's Grove: InterVarsity, 2007.
Turner, Victor. *The Forest of Symbols*. Ithaca, NY: Cornell University Press, 1967.
———. *Process, Performance, and Pilgrimage: A Study in Comparative Symbology*. New Dehli: Concept, 1979.
Varon, Jeremy. *Bringing the War Home: The Weather Underground, the Red Army Faction, and Revolutionary Violence in the Sixties and Seventies*. Berkeley, CA: University of California Press, 2004.
Viladesau, Richard. *The Beauty of the Cross: The Passion of Christ in Theology and the Arts, from the Catacombs to the Eve of the Renaissance*. Oxford: Oxford University Press, 2005.
———. *The Pathos of the Cross: The Passion of Christ in Theology and the Arts—The Baroque Era*. Oxford: Oxford University Press, 2014.
———. *Theological Aesthetics: God in Imagination, Beauty and Art*. Oxford: Oxford University Press, 1999.
———. *Theology and the Arts: Encountering God Through Music, Art and Rhetoric*. Mahwah, NJ: Paulist, 2000.
———. *The Triumph of the Cross: The Passion of Christ in Theology and the Arts from the Renaissance to the Counter-Reformation*. Oxford: Oxford University Press, 2008.
Wallhauser, John. *Schleiermacher: Life and Thought*. Philadelphia: Fortress, 1973.
Walton, Heather, ed. *Literature and Theology: New Interdisciplinary Spaces*. Farnham, UK: Ashgate, 2011.
Watson, Francis. "Theology and Music." *Scottish Journal of Theology* 51.4 (1998) 435–63.
Webster, John, ed. *The Cambridge Companion to Karl Barth*. Cambridge: Cambridge University Press, 2000.
Whiting, Steven Moore. *Satie the Bohemian: From Cabaret to Concert Hall*. Oxford: Oxford University Press, 1999.
Yoder, John Howard. *Non-Violence: A Brief History*. Waco, TX: Baylor University Press, 2013.
———. *Revolutionary Christianity*. Eugene, OR: Wipf & Stock, 2011.
Zager, Daniel, ed. *Music and Theology: Essays in Honour of Robin A. Leaver*. Lanham, MD: Scarecrow, 2006.
Zahl, Paul F. M. *A Short Systematic Theology*. Cambridge: Eerdmans, 2000.

Subject Index

beauty, 18–21, 23, 24, 35, 37, 47, 50, 54, 55, 58, 59, 61, 71, 77, 83, 84, 92, 99–109, 113, 124, 126, 127, 128, 134, 138, 142, 173, 189

creation, 23–25, 27, 29–30, 32–35, 48–51, 53, 57–58, 65, 71–73, 76–77, 79–81, 94, 98–100, 102, 105, 107, 109–15, 120–21, 124–29, 132, 134, 141, 143–44, 162, 170, 172–76, 178, 183–84, 187–88

culture, 1–3, 5, 7, 13–15, 17, 21, 24, 25, 26, 30–43, 45, 48–49, 51, 53, 59–60, 66–67, 69–70, 72–74, 76, 79–80, 83, 84, 85, 87, 88, 92, 94, 149, 160, 188, 191, 192, 193

death, 27, 29, 30, 42, 99, 117, 122–26, 128–29, 133, 134, 140–41, 151–57, 1/2, 179–80, 182–85, 189

embodiment, 2, 6–7, 10–11, 13, 15, 21–22, 25, 30–31, 39, 41, 42, 47–48, 50, 51, 53–57, 59–65, 67, 69, 90, 94, 97–100, 103–10, 113–22, 124, 127–29, 134–35, 139, 142, 144–45, 147–51, 156–57, 159–61, 167–68, 170, 172, 175–79, 184–85, 187–93, 195

imagination, 15, 19–20, 133, 135–36, 143, 156

incarnation, 32–33, 35, 54, 57, 60, 63–64, 69–72, 94, 100, 103, 108–9, 116, 120, 127, 135, 167–68, 174, 188, 190

individuality, 1–2, 4–8, 13, 20, 38, 40, 46, 50, 51, 57–60, 62, 69, 71, 73, 82–85, 87–88, 90–91, 93, 105–6, 108, 114–15, 121, 124–29, 132–52, 156–57, 169, 171, 179, 183, 185, 187, 189–93

knowledge, 2, 3, 9, 16, 17, 18–25, 27, 30, 42, 48–50, 53–54, 58–60, 64, 70, 73–78, 82, 84, 86, 90–91, 93–94, 106, 109, 115, 120, 124, 128, 136, 140, 148, 154, 169, 177

liminality, 53, 62, 64–65, 88–94, 126, 128, 133, 140, 144, 156, 160, 179–80, 182–85, 188–89, 191

nothingness, 57–58, 170, 172–73, 175–77, 183
numinous, 8–13, 22, 38–39, 85

requiem, 65, 99, 122–26, 128–29, 132–33, 135, 151–57, 160–61, 163–64, 179–85, 189
revelation, 2, 3, 6–8, 12, 15, 17–18, 22, 28–30, 34, 43, 44, 47, 48, 50–51, 53, 54, 58, 63, 64, 66–76, 79–82, 88, 94, 97, 100–103, 105–9, 120, 127, 135, 137, 138, 163, 176, 177, 182, 185, 187, 188, 191

sacramentality, 15–18, 29, 49, 51, 53, 57, 60, 63, 65, 67, 68–70, 78, 88, 93–94, 97, 127, 142, 157, 187, 188–89, 191, 193
silence, 12, 34, 47, 57–58, 159–85, 190
spiritual, 32, 57, 61, 77, 82–84, 88, 91, 163, 175, 181
sublime, 6, 99, 109, 112–15, 122, 124–26, 128–29, 130, 131–33, 134–35, 137, 143–44, 182

transcendence, 6, 13, 18, 34–35, 37, 38–39, 46, 47, 48, 53, 57, 59–64, 71–72, 76–94, 101, 131–32, 134, 135, 137, 140, 141, 143, 151, 162, 169, 170, 177, 178, 188, 191
Transcendentals, 18, 71, 101–2, 105, 108
truth, 1, 3, 6, 14, 22–23, 25, 26–31, 34–35, 37–38, 40–46, 48, 50, 51, 54, 57, 66–67, 69–76, 78, 81, 83–84, 86–87, 88, 91, 102, 109, 110, 136, 142, 170, 188

Name Index

Augustine, Saint, 16, 54–59, 102, 172–74

Balthasar, Hans Urs von, 1, 22–25, 26, 29, 32, 50, 58, 71–72, 74, 76–77, 80–81, 87–88, 98–105, 107–9, 113, 120, 127, 135, 162–63, 170, 175–76, 178, 185, 189
Barth, Karl, 6, 24–25, 26, 33–34, 50, 72–73, 76–77, 79–81, 86, 87–88, 98, 101, 120–21, 125
Beaudoin, Tom, 68–70
Begbie, Jeremy, 16, 25, 26–29, 30, 51, 65, 93
Blackwell, Albert L., 68–69
Brown, David, 15–18, 29, 37, 63–64, 68, 69, 75–76, 97, 113, 116, 125, 135, 140, 141–42
Brown, Frank Burch, 78, 82
Burke, Edmund, 134, 143
Burnham, Scott, 132, 144–50, 156–57

Cage, John, 160–62, 165, 167, 170–180, 184–85
Cobb, Kelton, 13, 31, 39–42, 92

Dauenhauer, Bernhard, 161–61
Doctor, Jenny, 180, 181, 183

Epstein, Heidi, 54, 55, 57, 59, 97, 108, 118, 128

Gadamer, Hans-Georg, 113–14
Gawronski, Raymond, 162–63, 170, 175–78

Gennep, Arnold van, 89, 92
Gorringe, T. J., 31, 32–35, 41, 87, 187, 188

Iafrate, Michael, 31, 43–44, 51

Kant, Immanuel, 18–20
Keefe, Simon P. 123–24, 126
Keuss, Jeffrey F., 47–48
Kierkegaard, Søren, 116–18, 120, 128, 150

Lynch, Gordon 35–39, 40, 41, 42, 44, 66–67, 77, 83–88, 132, 169

Marsh, Clive, 54, 59–61, 69, 77, 82–84, 88
McCosker, Philip, 101, 104
Messiaen, Olivier, 166–68
Messina-Dysert, Gina, 31, 45–47, 51
Meyer, Leonard B., 106
Muers, Rachel, 161–62

Otto, Rudolf, 8–13, 17, 22, 38, 125

Partridge, Christopher, 89–91, 93
Picard, Max, 163, 184

Roberts, Vaughan S., 54, 59–61, 69, 77, 82–84, 88
Rosen, Charles, 38, 111, 112, 114, 135, 136, 139, 156

Schleiermacher, Friedrich 3–8, 9, 10, 14, 18, 20, 21, 32, 50, 61–62, 73,

Schleiermacher, Friedrich (*cont.*)
   76, 91, 93, 133–34, 136–38,
   145, 146, 148, 149, 150–51, 153,
   156–57, 182, 188, 189
Schwartz, Regina, 77–78
Scruton, Roger, 19, 102
Stone-Davis, Férdia, 18–21, 50, 54, 59,
   61–62, 76, 91–93, 182, 188

Takemitsu, Toru, 160–61, 179–85

Taylor, Charles, 78, 82
Temperley, Nicholas, 110, 111, 114
Tillich, Paul, 13–15, 21, 32, 35, 39–40,
   68, 73–74, 76, 84, 101, 107
Turner, Victor, 89, 92

Viladesau, Richard, 22, 102

Werntz, Myles, 31, 44–45, 51